Human Rights and Corporate Wrongs

CORPORATIONS, GLOBALISATION AND THE LAW

Series Editor: Janet Dine, *Director, Centre for Commercial Law Studies, Queen Mary, University of London, UK*

This uniquely positioned monograph series aims to draw together high quality research work from established and younger scholars on what is an intriguing and under-researched area of the law. The books will offer insights into a variety of legal issues that concern corporations operating on the global stage, including interaction with the World Trade Organization (WTO), international financial institutions and nation states, in both developing and developed countries. While the underlying foundation of the series will be that of company law, broadly-defined, authors are encouraged to take an approach that draws on the work of other social sciences, such as politics, economics and development studies and to offer an international or comparative perspective where appropriate. Specific topics to be considered will include corporate governance, corporate responsibility, taxation and criminal liability, amongst others. The series will undoubtedly offer an important contribution to legal thinking and to the wider globalisation debate.

Human Rights and Corporate Wrongs

Closing the Governance Gap

Simon Baughen

Institute of International Shipping and Trade Law, College of Law and Criminology, Swansea University, UK

CORPORATIONS, GLOBALISATION AND THE LAW

 Edward Elgar
PUBLISHING

Cheltenham, UK • Northampton, MA, USA

Published by
Edward Elgar Publishing Limited
The Lypiatts
15 Lansdown Road
Cheltenham
Glos GL50 2JA
UK

Edward Elgar Publishing, Inc.
William Pratt House
9 Dewey Court
Northampton
Massachusetts 01060
USA

A catalogue record for this book
is available from the British Library

Library of Congress Control Number: 2015945549

This book is available electronically in the **Elgar**online
Law subject collection
DOI 10.4337/9780857934765

ISBN 978 0 85793 475 8 (cased)
ISBN 978 0 85793 476 5 (eBook)

Typeset by Columns Design XML Ltd, Reading
Printed and bound in Great Britain by TJ International Ltd, Padstow

Contents

Preliminary table of authorities

NATIONAL CASES

United States of America

INTERNATIONAL CASES

African Commission

CAFCA Arbitration

Court of Justice of the Economic Community of West African States (ECOWAS)

European Court of Justice

European Court of Human Rights

NATIONAL LEGISLATION

EU LEGISLATION

TREATIES AND INTERNATIONAL INSTRUMENTS

VOLUNTARY CODES

Introduction

The spread of globalisation towards the end of the twentieth century has led to the rise of the transnational corporation (TNC). In 2002 the United Nations Conference on Trade and Development (UNCTA) estimated that 29 of the world's 100 largest economies are companies. Using the metric of value added, in 2000 the world's largest TNC was ExxonMobil, with a value added of $63 billion, exceeding the GDP of countries such as Pakistan, New Zealand, Hungary, and Vietnam. Using the same metric the 100 largest corporations account for 4.3 per cent of world GDP. The spread of globalisation has seen a rapid increase in investment in the developing world by TNCs. Too often this has become a focus for human rights abuses by States. Three notorious examples from the mid-1990s are the abuses committed by the Burmese military while providing security for the Yadana pipeline, the suppression of the protests against Shell's activities in Ogoniland culminating in the execution of Ken Saro-Wiwa, and the environmental pollution caused by mining operations in Bougainville which led to a civil war which led to a blockade of the island during which it was claimed that an official of Rio Tinto urged the Papua New Guinea Defence Forces to '[s]tarve the bastards out, some more, and they [will] come round.'[1]

In July 2005 the UN appointed Professor John Ruggie as its Special Representative on the issue of human rights and transnational corporations and other business enterprises. In 2008 in presenting his 'Protect, Respect, Remedy' framework for business and human rights to the UN, Ruggie concluded that:

> The root cause of the business and human rights predicament today lies in the governance gaps created by globalization – between the scope and impact of economic forces and actors, and the capacity of societies to manage their adverse consequences. These governance gaps provide the permissive environment for wrongful acts by companies of all kinds without adequate sanctioning or reparation.[2]

---

[1]   *Sarei v. Rio Tinto plc*, 221 F Supp 2d 1116, 1126 (CD Cal 2002).
[2]   A/HRC/8/50 7 April 2008.

The governance gap is particularly acute in the activities of extractive industries in conflict areas, such as Bougainville, Colombia, Sudan, Burma, and with a depressing number of international crimes emerging from the Democratic Republic of Congo. In 2011 Ruggie completed his mandate and the UN adopted his Guiding Principles on Business and Human Rights.

The 'governance gap' involves three participants. Host States where the wrongful acts occur; home States where the corporations participating in the wrongful acts are based; and corporations participating in the wrongful acts. This book will consider three ways in which this governance gap might be closed. Chapter 1 will consider the position of corporations under international law. Are corporations subject to any obligations under international law? If so, how do those obligations translate into criminal and civil liabilities? What are the responsibilities of States in respect of the actions of corporations within their territory and jurisdiction? In doing so, we shall consider the effects of bilateral investment treaties (BITs) in constraining the host State's regulatory powers over corporations. What are the responsibilities of States in respect of the actions of corporations outside their territory and jurisdiction?

We shall then move on to consider extraterritorial home State civil actions that have taken place in the US and in other common law jurisdictions, such as the UK and Canada. First, however, it is important to establish why claimants in these cases choose to proceed in the jurisdiction in which the parent company is located rather than having recourse to the courts of the jurisdiction in which the harm occurred. The obvious advantages of what is sometimes referred to as 'forum shopping' are the obtaining of a more favourable legal environment as regards key procedural matters such as discovery and the likelihood of obtaining a higher award of damages (particularly if the case comes before a US jury) than would be the case where the claim to be heard in the courts of the claimant's home jurisdiction.

However, the perjorative epiphet of 'forum shopping' overlooks one reason why it is imperative that such claims be brought in the foreign forum if the claimant is to make *any* recovery at all. Usually the foreign subsidiary will have insufficient assets to meet any eventual judgment in full. Thus, in the Bhopal case, the assets of the subsidiary, UCIL, at the time of the litigation were estimated to be no more than $39 million which would clearly be inadequate for the purpose of meeting any judgment against it given the likely size of any ultimate award of damages.[3] In contrast the parent, Union Carbide, was estimated to hold some $200 million of liability cover[4] and assets of $500 million realised from its recent restructuring.[5] The claimant must therefore direct its fire at the parent company who in most cases will have sufficiently deep pockets to satisfy any judgment in full. Proceeding against the parent company in the foreign jurisdiction, though, entails the very real risk that such a judgment would be ultimately unenforceable. Under the general principles of private international law, for such a judgment to be enforceable, the defendant would have had to have submitted to the jurisdiction of the foreign court. Alternatively, it would have had to have been 'present' in the jurisdiction at the time the proceedings were started. Unless and until the parent corporation agrees to submit to the jurisdiction of the claimant's home jurisdiction, the claimant has no alternative but to commence proceedings before the courts of the parent's jurisdiction. Furthermore, the courts of the host State may be unwilling or unable to take on the litigation,[6] and in cases involving human rights abuses the plaintiffs may be wary of litigating in the host State for fear of reprisals.[7]

Since the Bhopal gas explosion of 4/5 December 1984 there has been a series of environmental tort claims brought against TNCs in their home

---

[3] The Guardian, May 14 1986. 'India to speed up Bhopal claim.'

[4] Financial Times. March 24 1986. 'Union Carbide agrees tentative Bhopal deal.'

[5] The Times. January 22 1986, p17.

[6] For instance in *Lubbe v. Cape plc*, [2000] 1 WLR 1545 (HL) asbestosis claims by South African miners were brought in the UK against the employer's UK parent company. There was a strong probability that the claimants would be unable to obtain both the legal representation and the expert evidence required to substantiate their claims in South Africa, and there was also a lack of any established procedures to deal with multiparty actions in South Africa. This would amount to a denial of justice, so, although South Africa was the appropriate forum, the UK proceedings were not stayed on grounds of *forum non conveniens*.

[7] This was particularly so in the litigation in *Sarei v. Rio Tinto* 221 F. Supp 2d 1116 (CD Cal 2002), which arose out of the civil war in Bougainville and where the plaintiffs had a justifiable fear of returning to Papua New Guinea to bring legal proceedings against the corporation accused of complicity in international crimes by the Papua New Guinea Defence Force.

jurisdictions in the US,[8] the UK,[9] Australia,[10] and Canada.[11] There have also been an increasing number of claims brought in home jurisdictions in respect of alleged complicity by TNCs in human rights violations by host States. This development has principally taken place in the US federal courts under the 1789 Alien Torts Statute (ATS) since its revival in 1980 in *Filartiga v. Pena Irala*,[12] although claims against TNCs for human rights abuses have been brought as straight tort claims in the US as well as in the UK[13] and in Canada.[14] Claims under the ATS are founded on the commission of a tort in violation of 'the law of nations.' This nascent civil liability has been achieved by transplanting the principles under which international law imposes criminal liability on individuals into the field of civil liability in tort. These are the prohibitions on war crimes, crimes against humanity, genocide, or the norms, such as the prohibitions on piracy, the slave trade, torture, for which there is universal criminal jurisdiction under national law.

This universal civil liability has been developed by reference to the international criminal law jurisprudence that has emerged from the Nuremberg and Tokyo tribunals at the end of the second world war, the International Criminal Tribunal for the former Yugoslavia (ICTY) and the International Criminal Tribunal for Rwanda (ICTR), and the International Criminal Court established by the 1998 Rome Statute. Liability may be based on the primary wrongdoing of the corporation, such as the use of forced labour, or may be a secondary liability based on aiding and abetting an internationally wrongful act committed by a State. The

---

[8]   Such as the claims arising out of the Bhopal gas explosion. *In Re Union Carbide Gas Plant Disaster*, 634 F Supp 842 (SDNY 1986).

[9]   Such as the asbestosis claims made by South African miners in *Lubbe v. Cape plc*, [2000] UKHL 41; [2000] 1 WLR 1545.

[10]   In *Dagi v. B.H.P (No 2)*, [1997] 1 VR 428, a claim was brought before the Australian courts arising out of pollution caused by the collapse of a tailings dam in a copper mine in Papua New Guinea, and was subsequently settled.

[11]   *Recherches Internationales Quebec v. Cambior Inc*, [1998] QJ No 2554, 14 August 1998. The claim arose out of an acid spill in August 1995 from the Omai Mine tailings dam into a river in the Essequibo region of Guyana which released an estimated 4,000 000 m³ of waste laced with cyanide, other heavy metals and other pollutants. The Canadian proceedings were stayed on the ground of *forum non conveniens* due to the fact that the preponderance of evidence was located in Guyana where the damage occurred. The case was subsequently refiled in Guyana where it was dismissed in 2006.

[12]   630 F 2d 876 (2d Cir 1980).

[13]   *Guerrero v. Monterrico Metals plc*, [2009] EWHC 2475 (QB).

[14]   *Choc v. Hudbay Minerals Inc*, 2013 Carswell Ont 10514.

alleged complicity may be direct, as with the events in Ogoniland which led to the execution of Ken Saro-Wiwa and which formed the basis of the ATS claim in *Kiobel v. Royal Dutch Petroleum Co*, or may be indirect as in cases arising out of human rights violations committed by private or public security forces engaged to provide security for overseas operations of TNCs. In 'Private Empire' Steve Coll refers to the suits brought against Exxon Mobil in respect of violations of human rights by the Indonesian military that provided security for its operations in Aceh.

> Collingsworth [the plaintiffs' lawyer] crystallised why ExxonMobil was really in the dock: that it had failed to anticipate the consequences of its operations in Aceh, and had failed to move actively to protect civilians as best it might. The corporation might not have directed any of the violence, but if its leaders had exercised sufficient care and activism, torture and killings might have been avoided.[15]

We shall then move on to consider the implications of the ATS jurisprudence for the potential development of similar types of suit in jurisdictions such as the UK and Canada. In both jurisdictions claims have been brought based on violations of customary international law – in the UK claims for torture were brought in *Al Adsani v. Kuwait*[16] and *Jones v. Saudi Arabia*,[17] and in Canada a claim for torture was brought in *Bouzari v. Islamic Republic of Iran*[18] and a claim against a corporation for aiding and abetting war crimes was brought in *Bil'in (Village Council) v. Green Park Int'l Ltd*.[19] Although these claims were dismissed on grounds of sovereign immunity and in *Bil'in* on grounds of *forum non conveniens*, there has been no challenge to the bringing of a civil claim based on a violation of customary international law. The book will also consider the procedural problems that such suits have encountered, such as challenges on the grounds of act of State, sovereign immunity, or *forum non conveniens*, as well as examining those aspects of a claim based on breaches of customary international law that require analysis under national law, such as the process of ascribing to a parent corporation its subsidiary's liability for such a breach.

In the final chapter we shall conclude with an examination of non-legal methods of closing the governance gap. These comprise 'soft law' instruments such as the Global Compact, the Voluntary Principles on

---

15 Allen Lane, 2012, 404.
16 107 ILR 536 (CA.1996).
17 [2006] UKHL 26; [2007] 1 AC 270.
18 [2002] OJ No 1624; [2004] OJ No. 2800 Docket No. C38295.
19 2009 QCCS 4151.

Security and Human Rights, the OECD Guidelines for Multinational Enterprises, and the UN Guiding Principles on Business and Human Rights.

1. Corporations and international law

1. STATE RESPONSIBILITY FOR ACTS OF PRIVATE PARTIES UNDER INTERNATIONAL LAW

In this chapter we shall consider the international law background to the 'governance cap' by analysing the responsibilities under international law of its three participants: Host States where subsidiaries of multinational corporations operate; home States where their parent corporations operate; multinational corporations themselves.

A. Host State Responsibility

States are the primary bearers of obligations under human rights instruments but will also owe an obligation to exercise due diligence to ensure that those rights are not violated by private parties within their jurisdiction. However, host states are often unwilling or unable to take action against corporate wrongdoers within their jurisdiction, and indeed are themselves often the primary violators of the human rights obligations to which they have acceded.

Article 2 of the International Covenant on Civil and Political Rights (the ICCPR)[1] requires States Parties 'to respect and to ensure to all individuals within its territory and subject to its jurisdiction the rights recognised in the Covenant'. Article 2(2) provides that States Parties undertake to adopt laws and other measures necessary to give effect to the rights recognised by the ICCPR, and Article 2(3) provides that the States Parties must ensure that persons whose rights have been violated have access to an effective remedy, that access to the effective remedy is determined by competent authorities, and that such remedies are enforced when granted. Similar provisions appear in the other core UN Human Rights Treaties,[2] and also in regional Human Rights Conventions, such as

---

[1] Opened for signature 19 December 1966, 999 UNTS 171 (entered into force 23 March 1976).

[2] Such as the International Covenant on Economic, Social and Cultural Rights (ICESCR), opened for signature 16 December 1966, 999 UNTS 3

the European Convention on Human Rights,[3] and the Inter-American Court of Human Rights.[4] The State obligation of due diligence has also been applied by the African Commission on Human and Peoples Rights, although the African Charter on Human and Peoples' Rights lacks a similar express provision.[5]

A State's obligations under international human rights treaties will extend beyond its territory to any area over which the State exercises effective control. The International Court of Justice (ICJ) has held that Israel owed obligations under the ICCPR, ICESCR and the Convention on the Rights of the Child (CRC), in respect of the Palestinian occupied

---

(entered into force 3 January 1976). The Committee on Economic, Social and Cultural Rights (CESCR), which monitors its implementation, has stated that the Convention requires States Parties to prevent violations of the Convention's rights to water by private actors. CESCR, Substantive Issues Arising in the Implementation of the International Covenant on Economic, Social and Cultural Rights: General Comment 15: The Right to Water, UN ESCOR, 29th sess, Agenda Item 3, [24], UN Doc E/C.12/2002/11 (2002). Article 1 of the Convention on the Prevention and Punishment of the Crime of Genocide 78 U.N.T.S. 277, December 9, 1948, provides that the Contracting parties undertake to prevent and punish the crime of genocide. In 2007 the ICJ in *Bosnia v. Serbia-Montenegro* found that Serbia had violated its obligation to prevent genocide in relation to the massacres at Srebrenica in 1995 and had violated its obligation to punish genocide by failing to hand over Ratko Mladić, indicted for genocide and complicity in genocide, for trial by the International Criminal Tribunal for the former Yugoslavia.

   [3]   *Osman v. UK*, [1988] EHRR 101.

   [4]   *Velásquez Rodríguez v. Honduras*, [1988] Inter-Am Court HR (ser C) No 4. in which the Court held that Honduras incurred responsibility for tolerating disappearances of its citizens at the hands of private citizens. The Court held [172] that a State could be responsible for a human rights violation which was not directly imputable to it, 'not because of the act itself, but because of the lack of due diligence to prevent the violation or to respond to it'.

   [5]   *Commission Nationale des Droits de l'Homme et des Libertés v. Chad*, African Commission, Communication No 74/92 (1995). In 2001 in the 'SERAC' case Nigeria was later found to be in breach of its responsibilities under the Charter by failing to take action against pollution in Ogoniland caused by multinational oil companies operating there, the Commission referencing the decision of the Inter-American Court of Human Rights in *Velásquez Rodríguez v. Honduras*, ibid. African Commission, Communication No 155/96 (2001) ('*SERAC Case*'). In December 2012 a similar finding was made against Nigeria by the Court of Justice of the Economic Community of West African States (ECOWAS) in *SERAP v. Federal Republic of Nigeria*, Judgment N° ECW/CCJ/JUD/18/12.

territories[6], and in *Democratic Republic of Congo v. Uganda,* it found that Uganda owed obligations under the ICCPR, the CRC and the African Charter on Human and Peoples' Rights (ACHPR) in respect of its actions within the territory of the Democratic Republic of Congo.[7]

B. Home State Responsibility

Under the system of State responsibility codified by the International Law Commission in the 'Draft Articles on Responsibility of States for Internationally Wrongful Acts', there are four ways in which a State may incur responsibility for breach of an international legal obligation in respect of the actions of private parties.[8] First, in respect of the acts of private parties that are *de facto* State organs.[9] This will be the case when private parties are in a state of complete dependence on a State. Second, in relation to para-statal bodies that exercise elements of State authority, such as private bodies that operate prisons, or the conveying of police powers to private bodies.[10] The conduct of such bodies must 'concern governmental authority and not other private or commercial activity in

---

[6] *Advisory Opinion on the Legal Consequences on the Construction of a Wall in the Occupied Palestinian Territory*, (2004) 43 ILM 1009 at [107–113].

[7] *Armed Activities on the Territory of the Congo (Democratic Republic of the Congo v. Uganda),* (Merits) (2006) 45 ILM 271 at [217].

[8] Report of the International Law Commission to the General Assembly, 56 UN GAOR Supp. (No. 10) at 59, UN Doc. A/56/10 (2001), available at http://www.un.org/documents/ga/docs/56/a5610.pdf.<accessed 24 March 2015>.

[9] Article 4 of the Draft Articles: *Conduct of organs of a State:*

1. The conduct of any State organ shall be considered an act of that State under international law, whether the organ exercises legislative, executive, judicial or any other functions, whatever position it holds in the organization of the State, and whatever its character as an organ of the central Government or of a territorial unit of the State.
2. An organ includes any person or entity which has that status in accordance with the internal law of the State.

[10] Article 5 of the Draft Articles: *Conduct of persons or entities exercising elements of governmental authority:*

The conduct of a person or entity which is not an organ of the State under article 4 but which is empowered by the law of that State to exercise elements of the governmental authority shall be considered an act of the State under international law, provided the person or entity is acting in that capacity in the particular instance.

which the entity may engage'[11] for it to be attributable to the State. Third, where the private parties, although not *de facto* organs of the State, are directed or controlled by a State.[12] In *Nicaragua v. US* the ICJ set out a test whereby the US would be responsible if it were proved that it had effective control of the military or paramilitary operations in the course of which the alleged violations were committed.[13] The test was applied by the ICJ in *Bosnia v. Serbia* in which it held that the perpetrators of the Srebrenica massacres had not been under the effective control of the FRY as regards the massacres.[14] Fourth, for knowingly aiding and assisting another State in the commission of an internationally wrongful act for which that State is responsible, where that aid and assistance is given to a corporation participating in a project which will involve the other State in the commission of an internationally wrongful act.[15]

---

[11]   Commentary on the Draft Articles, p. 43[5]. The Commentary gives the following example: 'Thus, for example, the conduct of a railway company to which certain police powers have been granted will be regarded as an act of the State under international law if it concerns the exercise of those powers, but not if it concerns other activities (e.g. the sale of tickets or the purchase of rolling stock).'

[12]   Article 8 of the Draft Articles. *Conduct directed or controlled by a State*:

"The conduct of a person or group of persons shall be considered an act of a State under international law if the person or group of persons is in fact acting on the instructions of, or under the direction or control of, that State in carrying out the conduct."

[13]   *Nicaragua v. US*, 65. Unlike the position under art 4, it was not necessary to show a state of complete dependence on the part of the perpetrators.

[14]   The ICJ rejected a test of attribution for genocide, deriving from the Judgment of the International Criminal Tribunal for the former Yugoslavia (ICTY) Appeals Chamber in *Prosecutor v. Tadić*, Case (IT-94-1-A, Judgment, 15 July 1999) whereby responsibility would follow when the perpetrators were under the "overall control" of the State. In *Tadić* the ICTY was not called upon to rule on questions of State responsibility since its jurisdiction was criminal and extended over persons only and the sole question before it, to which it applied a test of "overall control", was whether the conflict was international.

[15]   Article 16 of the Draft Articles *Aid or assistance in the commission of an internationally wrongful act*:

A State which aids or assists another State in the commission of an internationally wrongful act by the latter is internationally responsible for doing so if:

(a)   that State does so with knowledge of the circumstances of the internationally wrongful act; and
(b)   the act would be internationally wrongful if committed by that State.

Accordingly, it is highly unlikely that a home State will incur responsibility for the acts of its corporations committed outside its jurisdiction. They will not be in a state of complete dependence of the State, nor will the State be in effective control of them in respect of the violations of international law which they might commit (assuming that corporations can be the subjects of obligations under international law). The only situations where State responsibility might arise would be where (a) the corporation exercises state functions, such as a private company providing security or prison services[16] or (b) the State has provided financial assistance, through export credit guarantees, to the corporation for a project which will clearly involve the host State in violations of international human rights law. An example might be a development project, such as the building of a dam that will involve the displacement of the local population.[17]

But in all the cases that have given rise to litigation in the US, and the UK, which will be considered later in this book, none of these conditions will apply. There would be no question of State responsibility being incurred in such cases. For instance, the *Unocal* litigation involved a US parent corporation, through its Bermudan subsidiary corporation, being involved in a project creating a pipeline in Burma where human rights abuses were said to have been committed by the Burmese military in the

---

The International Law Commission's (ILC) Commentary, p. 66 [1] states that art 16 is engaged:

> [w]here a State voluntarily assists or aids another State in carrying out conduct which violates the international obligations of the latter, for example, by knowingly providing an essential facility or financing the activity in question. Other examples include providing means for the closing of an international waterway, facilitating the abduction of persons on foreign soil, or assisting in the destruction of property belonging to nationals of a third country.

[16] On this basis, a State may incur responsibility for the acts of private military contractors undertaking combat missions or detention and interrogation for a State in armed conflict, such as the US occupation of Iraq. See, further, Chia Lehnardt, IILJ Working Paper 2007/2 *Private Military Companies and State Responsibility*. www.iilj.org/publications/documents/2007-2.Lehnardt. web.pdf <accessed 27 April 2015>.

[17] Robert McCorquodale and Penelope Simons, 'Responsibility Beyond Borders: State Responsibility for Extraterritorial Violations by Corporations of International Human Rights Law', 70 *Modern Law Review* 598, 612 (2007) cite the Baku-Tbilisi-Ceyhan and the Chad-Cameroon pipeline projects as instances of where the home State could be found to be aiding and assisting an internationally wrongful act.

course of providing security for the project. Neither the US parent corporation nor the Bermudan subsidiary was in a state of complete dependence on either the US or Bermuda, nor were the US or Bermuda in any way involved with the violation of international law that took place when the corporations allegedly aided and abetted forced labour by the Burmese military in the course of the construction of the pipeline.

There is also the question of which State is responsible for which corporations. Given the recognition of separate corporate personality in international law in *Barcelona Traction*[18] a State would only be responsible for the actions of corporations incorporated within its jurisdiction. So, in the *Unocal* example, the State that would be potentially responsible for the aiding and abetting of the forced labour by the Burmese military would be the US, the state of incorporation of both the parent corporation and its two subsidiary corporations which were participants in the Yadana pipeline joint venture. A further possibility would be Bermuda, due to the subsequent transfer, in 1999, of ownership of the two subsidiaries to a Bermudan corporation.[19]

Even if the necessary conditions exist for State responsibility in respect of the activities of corporations outside its territory, it is unlikely that any proceedings would be brought against the home State by the host State as the latter would be involved in those violations of human rights within its territory. Although violations of *jus cogens* norms of international law allow any state to make a claim,[20] it is difficult to conceive of any third

---

[18]   *Case Concerning the Barcelona Traction, Light and Power Co Ltd (Second Phase) (Belgium v. Spain)*, [1970] ICJ Reports 3, 42.

[19]   At one stage in the tort claims before the California Superior Court the defendant was arguing that Bermudan law should apply.

[20]   Article 48 of the Draft Articles. The Commentary states, p. 126 [2]:

Article 48 is based on the idea that in case of breaches of specific obligations protecting the collective interests of a group of States or the interests of the international community as a whole, responsibility may be invoked by States which are not themselves injured in the sense of article 42.

This reflects the statement of the ICJ in *Barcelona Traction* [33] that:

[a]n essential distinction should be drawn between the obligations of a State towards the international community as a whole, and those arising vis-à-vis another State in the field of diplomatic protection. By their very nature the former are the concern of all States. In view of the importance of the rights involved, all States can be held to have a legal interest in their protection; they are obligations erga omnes.

The ICJ then went on to state, [34]: 'Such obligations derive, for example, in contemporary international law, from the outlawing of acts of aggression, and of

State taking proceedings against another State in respect of human rights violations with which there is complicity by a corporation. To go back again to the *Unocal* example, in theory the UK, or Sweden, could have brought proceedings before the ICJ against Burma, the US, or possibly Bermuda but the prospect of this happening is virtually nil.

2. CORPORATE RESPONSIBILITY UNDER INTERNATIONAL LAW

The traditional province of international law is the regulation of relations between States and accordingly under international law private persons incur no direct responsibility for human rights violations. Such violations fall to be dealt with by their State under national law in accordance with the State's commitments under international law. In his report to the UN Human Rights Council of 19 February 2007[21] Ruggie reviewed the arguments that international human rights instruments imposed direct legal obligations on corporation but merely lacked direct accountability mechanisms, a view propounded by the United Nations Sub-Commission on the Promotion and Protection of Human Rights which underpinned the Draft Norms for Transnational Corporations. He concluded that there was no evidence for such direct corporate legal responsibility in sources such as: the International Bill of Human Rights, the Universal Declaration of Human Rights and the two Covenants (ICESCR and ICCPR) – the other core UN human rights treaties and the International Labour Organization (ILO) core conventions.[22]

The preamble to the Universal Declaration of Human Rights proclaims that 'every individual and every organ of society ... shall strive by teaching and education to promote respect for these rights and freedoms and by progressive measures, national and international, to secure their universal and effective recognition and observance'.[23] The words 'every individual and every organ of society' would suggest that the Universal

---

genocide, as also from the principles and rules concerning the basic rights of human person, including protection from slavery and racial discrimination.'

[21] A/HRC/4/35. Chapter III. 'Corporate Responsibility for other human rights violations under international law', [33–44].

[22] Ibid., [44].

[23] Adopted as General Assembly resolution 217 (III), 10 December 1948.

Declaration is directed at all humanity.[24] However, the preamble represents aspirations and moral claims and does not have legally binding effect. Ruggie then went on to note:

> Many provisions of the Universal Declaration of Human Rights have entered customary international law. While there is some debate, it is generally agreed that they currently apply only to States (and sometimes individuals) and do not include its preamble. Most of its provisions have also been incorporated in the Covenants and other United Nations human rights treaties. Do these instruments establish direct legal responsibilities for corporations? Several of them include preambular, and therefore non-binding, recognition that individuals have duties to others. But the operational paragraphs do not address the issue explicitly.[25]

Ruggie then noted an ambiguity in the commentaries of the treaty bodies charged with providing authoritative interpretations:

> Where the treaty bodies discuss corporate responsibilities, it is unclear whether they regard them as legal in nature. The most recent general comment of the Committee on Economic, Social and Cultural Rights ... on the right to work, for example, recognizes that various private actors 'have responsibilities regarding the realization of the right to work', that private enterprises – national and multinational – 'have a particular role to play in job creation, hiring policies and non-discriminatory access to work'. Fn 36[CESCR, general comment No. 18, para. 52. For similar remarks see CESCR, general comments No. 14, para. 42 and 12, para. 20. See also CRC, general comment No. 5, para. 56, which says that the State duty to respect 'extends in practice' to non-State organizations.] But then, in the same comment, the Committee appears to reiterate the traditional view that such enterprises are 'not bound' by the Covenant. Similarly, the most recent general comment of the Human Rights Committee (HRC) concludes that the treaty obligations 'do not ... have direct horizontal effect as a matter of international law' – that is, they take effect as between non-State actors only under domestic law. fn37 [HRC, general comment No. 31, para. 8.]

However, there is one area of international law which does impose direct obligations on individuals and that is with respect to international crimes for which there is universal jurisdiction. This means that a State may try

---

[24] Louis Henkin has famously written, 'Every individual includes juridical persons. Every individual and every organ of society excludes no one, no company, no market, no cyberspace. The Universal Declaration applies to them all.' 'The Universal Declaration at 50 and the Challenge of Global Markets', *Brooklyn Journal of International Law*, 17 (April 1999), 25.

[25] A/HRC/4/35, [38].

a person within its jurisdiction in respect of certain crimes committed anywhere in the world, irrespective of any connection with that State. Those crimes are: piracy, torture,[26] hijacking of aircraft, taking of hostages, slave trading, war crimes,[27] genocide,[28] crimes against humanity[29] – and aiding and abetting such crimes.[30]

The last three crimes are crimes for which an individual may be tried by an international tribunal, such as those established at Nuremberg and Tokyo after the Second World War and subsequently in the ICTY, the International Criminal Tribunal for Rwanda (the ICTR), the Special

---

[26] Universal criminal jurisdiction is obligatory for states that are parties of the Convention Against Torture and Other Cruel, Inhuman or Degrading Treatment or Punishment, UNGA Res. 39/46, 39 UN GAOR Supp. (No. 51), UN Doc. A/39/51 (1984), art 5(2) and is permitted generally under customary international law, *see Prosecutor v. Furundzija,* IT-95-17/1-T, at ¶ 156 (Dec. 10, 1998), *reprinted in* 38 *ILM* 317 (1999).

[27] Universal criminal jurisdiction is mandatory for States Parties in respect of grave breaches of the four Geneva Conventions, set out in a 8(2)(a) of the Rome Statute but is not yet established as regards the crimes set out in art 8(2)(b) of the Rome Statute.

[28] Although art 6 of the Convention on the Prevention and Punishment of the Crime of Genocide 78 UNTS 277, December 9, 1948 does not provide for universal jurisdiction, it is accepted under customary international law. *Prosecutor v. Ntuyahaga,* ICTR-90-40-T (Mar. 18, 1999); *Prosecutor v. Tadić,* IT-94-1-AR72, at ¶ 62 (Oct. 2, 1995). This rule is confirmed by State practice. See, e.g., *Attorney Gen'l of Israel v. Eichmann,* 36 ILR 277, 303–4 (Isr S Ct, 1962); *Demjanjuk v. Petrovsky,* 776 F.2d 571, 582–3 (6 th Cir. 1985), *cert. denied,* 475 US 1016 (1986); *Prosecutor v. Jorgic,* Bundesverfassungsgericht (German Federal Constitutional Court), 2 BvR 1290/99 (Decision of December 12, 2000), *reprinted in* Neue Juristische Wochenschrift 1848, 1852 (2001).

[29] Universal criminal jurisdiction exists over crimes against humanity that were recognized in art 6(2)(c) of the Nuremberg Charter of the International Military Tribunal, 8 UNTS 279, August 8, 1945, including murder, extermination, enslavement, deportation, and other inhumane acts, but is not yet established as regards the new elements of the crime listed in art 7 of the Rome Statute which includes the crimes of apartheid and forcible transfer of populations.

[30] The existence of universal criminal jurisdiction was confirmed in the Joint Separate Opinion of Judges Higgins, Kooijmans and Buergenthal in the *Case Concerning the Arrest Warrant of 11 April 2000 (Democratic Republic of the Congo v. Belgium),* February 14, 2002, [52–65].

Court for Sierra Leone (the SCSL).[31] The 1998 Rome Statute establishing the International Criminal Court (ICC) provides for criminal proceedings to be brought in respect of these three crimes when committed after 1 July 2002.[32] The Court does not have universal jurisdiction and may only exercise jurisdiction if: the accused is a national of a State Party or a State otherwise accepting the jurisdiction of the Court; the crime took place on the territory of a State Party or a State otherwise accepting the jurisdiction of the Court; or the UN Security Council has referred the situation to the Prosecutor, irrespective of the nationality of the accused or the location of the crime. The principle of complementarity means that the Court will only prosecute an individual if States are unwilling or unable to prosecute.[33] To this end, States that have ratified the Rome Statute should introduce national legislation to enable them to prosecute the three Rome Statute offences in their national courts.[34] Currently 65 of the 122 State Parties have introduced such legislation.

## A.	The Content of the Three Core International Crimes

Genocide

In 1948 the UN adopted the Convention on the Prevention and Punishment of the Crime of Genocide. Article 2 defines genocide as:

> any of the following acts committed with intent to destroy, in whole or in part, a national, ethnical, racial or religious group, as such:

---

[31]	The SCSL is a hybrid court established jointly by agreement between the UN and the government of Sierra Leone. In contrast, the ICTY and ICTR, were established as subsidiary organs of the UN by the Security Council acting pursuant to its Chapter VII powers.

[32]	Article 5 of the Rome Statute also provides for the ICC to have jurisdiction over the crime of aggression but only 'once a provision is adopted in accordance with articles 121 and 123 defining the crime and setting out the conditions under which the Court shall exercise jurisdiction with respect to this crime.' The 2010 Kampala amendments introduced a new art 8bis on the crime of aggression which has been ratified by 13 states of which four have implemented it into their national legislation. The ICC will not be able to exercise its jurisdiction over the crime of aggression until: at least 30 States Parties have ratified or accepted the amendments; and a decision is taken by two-thirds of States Parties to activate the jurisdiction at any time after 1 January 2017.

[33]	Article 17 requires the ICC to defer to investigations and prosecutions carried out genuinely by a 'State'.

[34]	Pursuant to their obligation under art 86 to co-operate with the ICC.

(a) Killing members of the group;
(b) Causing serious bodily or mental harm to members of the group;
(c) Deliberately inflicting on the group conditions of life calculated to bring about its physical destruction in whole or in part;
(d) Imposing measures intended to prevent births within the group;
(e) Forcibly transferring children of the group to another group.

The crime requires a specific intent whereby the designated acts must be done 'with intent to destroy, in whole or in part, a national, ethnical, racial or religious group, as such.'[35] Article 3 provides that the 'following acts shall be punishable':

(a)   Genocide;
(b)   Conspiracy to commit genocide;
(c)   Direct and public incitement to commit genocide;
(d)   Attempt to commit genocide;
(e)   Complicity in genocide.

The UN Security Council has adopted the 1948 Convention's definitions of genocide in the Statutes for the International Criminal Tribunals for the Former Yugoslavia and Rwanda. In addition, the 1998 Rome Statute for the International Criminal Court also adopts the Convention's definitions.

Crimes against humanity

Crimes against humanity are not the subject of any convention. The first use of the phrase 'crimes against humanity' was in 1915 when the governments of Great Britain, France and Russia employed it in condemning the Turkish government for the alleged massacres of the Armenians. The first prosecutions for crimes against humanity took place

---

[35]   *Prosecutor v. Akayesu*, Case No. ICTR-96-4-T (Trial Chamber), September 2, 1998, para 498, 517–22: 'Genocide is distinct from other crimes insomuch as it embodies a special intent or *dolus specialis*. Special intent of a crime is the specific intention, required as a constitutive element of the crime, which demands that the perpetrator clearly seeks to produce the act charged. Thus, the special intent in the crime of genocide lies in 'the intent to destroy, in whole or in part, a national, ethnical, racial or religious group.' Where the charge is complicity in genocide, the *mens rea* element requires that the accused shared the specific genocidal intent of the primary perpetrator, whereas if the charge is of aiding and abetting genocide the *mens rea* element requires only that the accused knew of the specific genocidal intent of the primary perpetrator. *Akayesu, Prosecutor v. Krstic*, ICTY Case No: IT-98-33-A 19 April 2004.

in 1945 at Nuremberg before the International Military Tribunal (IMT) whose charter defined crimes against humanity as:

> murder, extermination, enslavement, deportation, and other inhumane acts committed against any civilian population, before or during the war, or prosecutions on political, racial or religious grounds in execution or in connection with any crime within the jurisdiction of the Tribunal, whether or not in violation of the domestic law of the country where perpetrated.

The same definition was used in the Tokyo Charter of 1946, establishing the International Military Tribunal for the Far East. In 1993 the UN Security Council established the ICTY. Article 5 of the statute establishing the tribunal provides:

> The International Tribunal shall have the power to prosecute persons responsible for the following crimes when committed in armed conflict, whether international or internal in character, and directed against any civilian population:

(a) Murder;
(b) Extermination;
(c) Enslavement;
(d) Deportation;
(e) Imprisonment;
(f) Torture;
(g) Rape;
(h) Persecutions on political, racial and religious grounds;
(i) Other inhumane acts.

The list of criminal acts used in Nuremberg was here expanded to include imprisonment, torture and rape. The link with armed conflict was retained. In 1994, the UN Security Council established the ICTR. Article 3 of the ICTR Statute dropped the linkage between crimes against humanity and armed conflict provided that the inhumane acts must be part of a 'systematic or widespread attack against any civilian population on national, political, ethnic, racial or religious grounds'.

The Rome Statute provides for crimes against humanity in Article 7 which adds to the definition of crimes against humanity in the ICTY and ICTR statutes and removes any link to armed conflicts and to the requirement in the ICTR statute that that the attack was carried out 'on national, political, ethnic, racial or religious grounds'. Article 7 defines crimes against humanity as follows:

For the purpose of this Statute, 'crime against humanity' means any of the following acts when committed as part of a widespread or systematic attack directed against any civilian population, with knowledge of the attack:

(a) Murder;
(b) Extermination;
(c) Enslavement;
(d) Deportation or forcible transfer of population;
(e) Imprisonment or other severe deprivation of physical liberty in violation of fundamental rules of international law;
(f) Torture;
(g) Rape, sexual slavery, enforced prostitution, forced pregnancy, enforced sterilisation, or any other form of sexual violence of comparable gravity;
(h) Persecution against any identifiable group or collectivity on political, racial, national, ethnic, cultural, religious, gender as defined in paragraph 3, or other grounds that are universally recognised as impermissible under international law, in connection with any act referred to in this paragraph or any crime within the jurisdiction of the Court;
(i) Enforced disappearance of persons;
(j) The crime of apartheid;
(k) Other inhumane acts of a similar character intentionally causing great suffering, or serious injury to body or to mental or physical health.

Article 7(2)(a) provides: 'For the purpose of paragraph 1: 'Attack directed against any civilian population' means a course of conduct involving the multiple commission of acts referred to in paragraph 1 against any civilian population, pursuant to or in furtherance of a State or organizational policy to commit such attack;'. The reference here to the 'State or organizational policy' might suggest that the offence of crimes against humanity may be committed only by State actors, although non-State actors could incur liability for aiding and abetting the crime. However, on three occasions the ICC Pre-Trial Chamber has held that it has jurisdiction over crimes by non-State actors[36] arising out of the violence that followed the contested results of Kenya's presidential election of 27 December 2007.[37]

---

[36] The allegations were that a political party had used a criminal organization to attack rival supporters, with the passive complicity of the police. The violence saw over 1,000 murders and numerous rapes.

[37] *Situation in the Republic of Kenya*, Case No. ICC-01/09, Decision Pursuant to Article 15 of the Rome Statute on the Authorization of an Investigation into the Situation in the Republic of Kenya (Mar. 31, 2010), http://www.icccpi. int/iccdocs/doc/doc854562.pdf. The same finding was made in two subsequent decisions authorising joint summonses for the appearances of various Kenyan citizens, including the President, Uhuru Kenyatta. In all three

War crimes

These include: (i) grave breaches of the four Geneva Conventions of 12 August 1949[38] and their Additional Protocol I; (ii) other serious violations of international humanitarian law committed during an international armed conflict;[39] (iii) serious violations of the laws of war applicable in non-international armed conflicts.[40] Article 8(2)(a) of the Rome Statute covers heading (i). Article 8(2)(b) covers heading (ii) and paragraph (c) cover heading (iii). Paragraph (e) covers other serious violations of international humanitarian law committed during a non-international armed conflict. With regard to these last two headings, paragraphs (d) and (f) provide that they apply:

> [t]o armed conflicts not of an international character and thus does not apply to situations of internal disturbances and tensions, such as riots, isolated and sporadic acts of violence or other acts of a similar nature. It applies to armed conflicts that take place in the territory of a State when there is protracted armed conflict between governmental authorities and organized armed groups or between such groups.

---

decisions Judge Hans-Peter Kaul dissented on the grounds that the crime required that the group committing the widespread and systematic attack on civilians had certain State-like characteristics. See, further, Charles Chernor Jalloh 'What Makes a Crime against Humanity?' 28 *Am. U. Int'l L. Rev.* 381 (2013).

[38] 1949 Geneva Convention (I) for the Amelioration of the Condition of the Wounded and Sick in Armed Forces in the Field; 1949 Geneva Convention (II) for the Amelioration of the Condition of Wounded, Sick and Shipwrecked Members of Armed Forces at Sea; 1949 Geneva Convention (III) relative to the Treatment of Prisoners of War; 1949 Geneva Convention (IV) relative to the Protection of Civilian Persons in Time of War. https://www.icrc.org/eng/resources/documents/publication/p0173 (accessed 17 December 2014).

[39] Based primarily on the 1899 Hague Declaration, the 1907 Regulations annexed to the Hague Convention No. IV, the 1925 Geneva Protocol, the 1954 Hague Convention for the Protection of Cultural Property in the Event of Armed Conflict and its protocols, the 1989 Convention on the Rights of the Child, the 1994 Convention on the Safety of United Nations and Associated Personnel, and the Statute of the International Criminal Tribunal for the former Yugoslavia.

[40] Based primarily on art 3 common to the four Geneva Conventions of 1949, their Additional Protocol II of 1977, the 1999 Optional Protocol to the 1954 Hague Convention for the Protection of Cultural Property in the Event of Armed Conflict, the 1989 Convention on the Rights of the Child, the 1994 Convention on the Safety of United Nations and Associated Personnel, the Statutes of the International Criminal Tribunals for Rwanda and the former Yugoslavia, and the Statute of the Special Court for Sierra Leone.

Three provisions in Article 8 cover economic war crimes, which might be relevant in connection with illegal acquisition of resources in conflict zones. These are Article 8(2)(a)(iv) on the extensive destruction and appropriation of property, Article 8(2)(b)(xiii) and (e)(xii) of the ICC Statute on destroying or seizing the enemy's property, and Article 8(2)(b)(xvi) and (e)(v) on pillage. In the Nuremberg trials various German industrialists were charged with pillage in cases involving confiscation by large German companies such as IG Farben, Flick and Krupp of property in German occupied territories in Europe.[41] The crime was committed where the owner of the property was deprived of his property involuntarily and against his will. In internal conflicts, the crime of pillage is likely to be committed only by rebel groups, as the State is presumed to have ownership of natural resources in its territory.[42]

Modes of liability

As well as those who commit the actual offences, co-perpetrators and aiders and abetters may also incur criminal liability. In *Prosecutor v. Tadić*, the ICTY recognised that co-perpetrators could be held liable as participants in a joint criminal enterprise in three distinct cases, as follows:

> First, in cases of co-perpetration, where all participants in the common design possess the same criminal intent to commit a crime (and one or more of them

---

[41] *United States v. Krauch* et al. (*IG Farben Case*), Trials of War Criminals Before the Nuremberg Military Tribunals Under Control Council No. 10, Vol. VIII, 1134.

[42] See, further, Larissa Van den Herik and Daniëlla Dam, 'Revitalizing the Antique War Crime of Pillage: The Potential and Pitfalls of Using International Criminal Law to Address Illegal Resource Exploitation During Armed Conflict', 22(3) *Criminal Law Forum* (2011), who conclude:

> However, the historic crime of pillage also has serious inherent limits. Pillage, as originally included in the 1907 Hague Regulations and later in the 1949 Geneva Conventions, was not drafted with the phenomenon of illegal exploit-ation in mind. This plays out most dramatically in the situation of internal armed conflicts. In these situations, pillage appears to target one side of the armed conflict unevenly. In particular under the ICC definition, it might be difficult to address government actors that exploit 'their' natural resources to fund gruesome armed conflicts with the sole aim of clinging to power.

See, too, Professor James Stewart *Corporate War Crimes: Prosecuting Pillage of Natural Resources* available at http://www.pillageconference.org/publications/ <accessed 7 April 2015>.

actually perpetrate the crime, with intent). Secondly, in the so-called 'concentration camp' cases, where the requisite *mens rea* comprises knowledge of the nature of the system of ill-treatment and intent to further the common design of ill-treatment. Such intent may be proved either directly or as a matter of inference from the nature of the accused's authority within the camp or organisational hierarchy. With regard to the third category of cases,[43] it is appropriate to apply the notion of 'common purpose' only where the following requirements concerning *mens rea* are fulfilled: (i) the intention to take part in a joint criminal enterprise and to further – individually and jointly – the criminal purposes of that enterprise; and (ii) the foreseeability of the possible commission by other members of the group of offences that do not constitute the object of the common criminal purpose.[44]

Secondary liability may be incurred for aiding and abetting, the *actus reus* for which was set out by the ICTY Tribunal in *Prosecutor v. Furundzija* as 'practical assistance, encouragement, or moral support which has a substantial effect on the perpetration of the crime'.[45] As regards *mens rea*, there is some controversy as to whether knowing assistance or purposive assistance is required, with most of the Nuremberg decisions and those of the ICTY and ICTR pointing to the former. In 2013 there were two divergent decisions of international criminal tribunals on this issue. In *Prosecutor v. Perišić*,[46] the ICTY held that it had to be established that the defendant's assistance was 'specifically directed' to aiding the commission of the offence, whereas in *Prosecutor v. Taylor*,[47] the SCSL Appeals Chamber held that the *mens rea* of aiding and abetting was knowledge. On 23 January 2014 in *Prosecutor v. Nikola Šainović*[48] the Appeals Chamber of the ICTY concluded that 'specific direction' is not an element of aiding and abetting liability. The *mens rea*

---

[43]   'The third category concerns cases involving a common design to pursue one course of conduct where one of the perpetrators commits an act which, while outside the common design, was nevertheless a natural and foreseeable consequence of the effecting of that common purpose.' [204].

[44]   Case No.: -94-1-A 15 July 1999 at para 220. Stephen Powles draws attention to the width of the third category of joint criminal enterprise in 'Criminal Liability by Prosecutorial *Ingenuity* and Judicial Creativity,' 2(2) *Journal of International Criminal Justice* 606 (2004). See, too, Darryl Robinson, 'The Identity Crisis of International Criminal Law,' 21 *Leiden Journal of International Law* 925 (2008), *available at* < http://ssrn.com/abstract=1127851> (accessed 22 July 2010).

[45]   Case No. IT-95-17/1, Judgment, paras 195–225, 236–40.

[46]   Case No. IT-04-81-A (ICTY Feb. 28, 2013).

[47]   SCSL-03-01-A (10766-11114 Sept. 26, 2013).

[48]   ICTY, Judgment (Appeals Chamber) (Case No. IT-05-87-A), 23 January 2014.

standard required the accused to be aware of the essential elements of the specific crime committed, including the mental state of the perpetrators.

The Rome Statute of 1998 establishing the ICC would appear to point towards purposive assistance. Article 25(3) provides that a person 'shall be criminally responsible and liable for punishment for a crime' if that person '[f]or *the purpose* of facilitating the commission of such a crime, aids, abets or otherwise assists in its commission or its attempted commission, including providing the means for its commission'.[49] Article 30(1), though, points towards knowing assistance and states: '[u]nless otherwise provided, a person shall be criminally responsible and liable for punishment for a crime within the jurisdiction of the [c]ourt only if the material elements are committed with intent and knowledge'. Paragraph 2 then provides that a person has intent where: '(a) In relation to conduct, that person means to engage in the conduct; [and] (b) In relation to a consequence, that person means to cause that consequence *or is aware* that it will occur in the ordinary course of events' (emphasis added).[50] Article 25(d) deals with co-perpetration as by providing that a person shall be criminally liable if that person:

> In any other way contributes to the commission or attempted commission of such a crime by a group of persons acting with a common purpose. Such contribution shall be intentional and shall either: (i) Be made with the aim of furthering the criminal activity or criminal purpose of the group, where such activity or purpose involves the commission of a crime within the jurisdiction of the Court; or (ii) Be made in the knowledge of the intention of the group to commit the crime.

There is no provision for the third category of joint criminal enterprise set out in *Tadić* by the ICTY.

---

[49]　Rome Statute of the International Criminal Court, art 25, July 17, 1998, 2187 UNTS 90. Article 25(3) plays a prominent role in Robert Harris' thriller 'The Ghost' in which the former UK prime minister, Adam Lang, is investigated by the ICC for aiding and abetting crimes against humanity.

[50]　Paragraph 106 of the Explanatory Notes to the International Criminal Court Act 2001 states, as regards s 66 'Mental Element':

> This section reflects Article 30 of the Statute. It provides a general rule that, unless otherwise provided, the necessary mental element of an offence is present if the material elements of genocide, a crime against humanity, a war crime or an offence against the administration of justice are committed with intent and knowledge. 'Intent' and 'knowledge' are explained in subsection (3) [of art. 30].

Torture

Apart from the Rome Statute, torture has been rendered criminal under the UN Convention against Torture 1984 (UNCAT). It is a crime of universal jurisdiction both under the Convention[51] and under customary international law. Although torture can only be committed by State actors, it would be possible for a non-State actor to incur criminal liability under UNCAT by reason of its complicity and participation in torture. Article 4(1) provides that, 'Each State Party shall ensure that all acts of torture are offences under its criminal law. The same shall apply to an attempt to commit torture and *to an act by any person which constitutes complicity or participation in torture*' (emphasis added). In the case of the UK this provision has been implemented in a different manner in section 134(2) of the Criminal Justice Act 1988 which provides:

> A person not falling within subsection (1) above commits the offence of torture, whatever his nationality, if –
>
> (a) in the United Kingdom or elsewhere he intentionally inflicts severe pain or suffering on another at the instigation or with the consent or acquiescence –
>
>   (i) of a public official; or (ii) of a person acting in an official capacity; and
>
> (b) the official or other person is performing or purporting to perform his official duties when he instigates the commission of the offence or consents to or acquiesces in it.

It does not cover acts constituting complicity in torture.

Universal jurisdiction of national courts over international crimes

The principle of complementarity in the Rome Statute means that the principal avenue for prosecuting international crimes will be before national courts. International law permits, and in some cases obliges, States to prosecute international crimes wherever they are committed and without any link between the offender and the prosecuting State.[52] This is

---

51 Article 5(2) requires each State Party to '[t]ake such measures as may be necessary to establish its jurisdiction over such offences in cases where the alleged offender is present in any territory under its jurisdiction and it does not extradite him pursuant to article 8 to any of the States mentioned in paragraph 1 of this article'.

52 States are obliged to prosecute grave breaches of the Geneva Conventions and torture, pursuant to UNCAT, if they are parties to those Conventions, but there is no such obligation in relation to other cases of war crimes or crimes

universal criminal jurisdiction. The most famous universal jurisdiction statute is Belgium's 1993 Act on the Punishment of Grave Breaches of International Humanitarian Law, amended in 1999. The Act empowered Belgian courts to try cases of war crimes, crimes against humanity and genocide committed by non-Belgians outside Belgium against non-Belgians, without even the presence of the accused in Belgium. Complaints could be filed by private parties and proceeding were brought in relation to events arising out of the genocide in Rwanda, the killing of two Belgian priests in Guatemala, and crimes alleged against the former dictator of Chad, Hissène Habré.

Claims under the Act were also filed against Israel's prime minister, Ariel Sharon, in connection with his role in the Sabra and Shatila massacres of 1982, while Israeli defence minister. Other high-profile claims were filed against former US President George H.W. Bush, in connection with the bombing of Baghdad in the 1991 Gulf War, and in May 2003 a complaint was filed against US General Tommy Franks alleging that he had ordered war crimes during the invasion of Iraq in 2003. The US responded with Defense Secretary Rumsfeld threatening Belgium with the loss of its status as host to the NATO headquarters, and in August 2003 Belgium succumbed to this pressure by amending its law so that the prosecution of international crimes required some connection between the offender and Belgium. The Belgian courts' jurisdiction over international crimes would be limited to situations where: the accused is Belgian or has his primary residence in Belgium or; the victim is Belgian or has lived in Belgium for at least three years at the time the crimes were committed; or a treaty required Belgium to exercise jurisdiction over the case. In addition, the decision to proceed with a complaint now rests exclusively with the state prosecutor, unless the accused is Belgian or has his primary residence in Belgium. Some pre-existing claims, such as those against Hissène Habré, continued but in September 2003 the high-profile claims against US and Israeli officials were all dismissed by the Belgian court of cassation.

A similar process has happened in Spain where its universal jurisdiction law has twice been cut back in similar fashion.[53] In November

---

against humanity, although States probably have a right to prosecute such crimes. The Rome Statute *per se* does not stipulate a direct obligation of States to establish and exercise national jurisdiction for international crimes, although its Preamble states 'Recalling that it is the duty of every State to exercise its criminal jurisdiction over those responsible for international crimes.'

[53] Spain has been active in applying its universal jurisdiction law issuing arrest warrants against two former presidents of Guatemala, Rios Montt and

2009 Spain amended its universal jurisdiction law so that the future scope of universal jurisdiction would be limited to cases in which: (a) the victims are Spanish; (b) the alleged perpetrators are in Spain; or (c) there exists some other clear link to Spanish interests. The ability to investigate allegations of genocide, crimes against humanity and war crimes will be restricted to suspects who are either a Spanish national, a foreigner habitually resident in Spain, or a foreigner who is in Spain and whose extradition has been denied by Spanish authorities. A further amendment in April 2014 meant that with charges of torture and enforced disappearance, the suspect must be a Spanish national, or the victim must be a Spanish national at the time when the crime was committed and whose suspect is present in Spain. Otherwise, the Spanish courts can now prosecute crimes set out under international treaties only when Spain has received and denied an extradition request, in relation to a foreign suspect present in Spain. The new law provides for the closing of existing investigations which do not, retrospectively, satisfy these criteria.

The legislation implementing the Rome Statute in Canada provides for universal jurisdiction. Section 6(1) of the Crimes Against Humanity and War Crimes Act (S.C. 2000, c. 24) provides: 'Every person who, either before or after the coming into force of this section, commits outside Canada (a) genocide, (b) a crime against humanity, or (c) a war crime, is guilty of an indictable offence and may be prosecuted for that offence in accordance with section 8.' Section 8 provides:

> A person who is alleged to have committed an offence under section 6 or 7 may be prosecuted for that offence if
>
> (a) at the time the offence is alleged to have been committed
>   (i) the person was a Canadian citizen or was employed by Canada in a civilian or military capacity,
>   (ii) the person was a citizen of a state that was engaged in an armed conflict against Canada, or was employed in a civilian or military capacity by such a state,
>   (iii) the victim of the alleged offence was a Canadian citizen, or
>   (iv) the victim of the alleged offence was a citizen of a state that was allied with Canada in an armed conflict; or

---

Oscar Mejia Victores, for genocide, torture and other related crimes. In October 2013, indictments were issues against former Chinese President Hu Jintao, for allegedly committing genocide in Tibet, followed by similar indictments a month later against former Chinese President Jiang Zemin, and former Prime Minister Li Peng. China reacted angrily to these indictments and it is believed that fears of economic reprisals against Spain led to the further curtailment of the law on universal jurisdiction in 2014.

(b) after the time the offence is alleged to have been committed, the person is present in Canada.

Accordingly, the presence in Canada of the alleged offender is sufficient to ground jurisdiction and on this basis Désiré Munyaneza was prosecuted and convicted for genocide, crimes against humanity and war crimes committed in Rwanda in 1994. These crimes had all been established under customary international law by 1994, notwithstanding that the Rome Statute was only adopted on 17 July 1998.[54] On 7 May 2014 the Quebec Court of Appeal confirmed his conviction and life sentence. However, prosecutions in Canada are allowed only with the consent of the Attorney-General of Canada, which prevents the filing of politically embarrassing claims of the types that were made in Belgium under its 1993 universal jurisdiction statute.

Australia also has universal criminal jurisdiction over the three Rome Statute crimes, but, as with Canada, prosecution can only be brought with the consent of, and in the name of, the Attorney-General.[55] Universal jurisdiction also exists in relation to torture[56] and slavery[57] but where the offence occurs wholly outside Australia no proceedings may take place without the consent of the Attorney-General.

In the UK universal jurisdiction exists in respect of three international crimes. First, there is torture committed after 1988 which may be prosecuted irrespective of where it was committed and whether or not there is any connection to the UK by virtue of section 134 of the Criminal Justice Act 1988 which implements Articles 4 and 5 of the 1984 UNCAT.[58] Second, pursuant to the Taking of Hostages Act 1982,[59] there

---

[54] Judgment available at http://www.ccij.ca/programs/cases/index.php?WEBYEP_DI=12 <accessed 24 April 2015>.

[55] Section 268.121 of the Criminal Code Act 1995.

[56] Division 274 of the Criminal Code. Where the offence occurs wholly outside Australia no proceedings may take place without the consent of the Attorney-General.

[57] Division 270 of the Criminal Code. Where the offence occurs wholly outside Australia no proceedings may take place without the consent of the Attorney-General.

[58] In *R v. Bow Street Magistrates; ex parte Pinochet Ugarte (No 3)*, [2000] 1 AC 147 the House of Lords held that Pinochet was not able to claim immunity for crimes committed while he was President of Chile after 29 September 1989 when s 134 of the Criminal Justice Act 1988 brought into force the provisions of the UNCAT, which established universal criminal jurisdiction for torture. In contrast, in 2007 the Paris prosecutor dismissed a criminal complaint brought by the Center for Constitutional Rights against former US Secretary of Defense,

is hostage-taking committed after 1982. Third, pursuant to the Geneva Conventions Act 1957, there are grave breaches of the Geneva Conventions committed after 1957, but there is no jurisdiction over war crimes committed in internal armed conflicts. Suspects of these crimes can be arrested and prosecuted if they set foot in UK territory, as there is no immunity *ratione materiae* for former state officials in respect of crimes of universal jurisdiction. This has led to two embarrassing threats to arrest former Israeli officials for war crimes. In 2005 Israeli General Almog was threatened with prosecution for alleged war crimes in the Palestinian territories (an international armed conflict) under the Geneva Conventions Act 1957 after arriving in the UK for a visit and similarly former Israeli foreign minister Tzipi Livni in 2009. Since 2011 the consent of the Director of Public Prosecutions has been necessary before an arrest warrant can be issued for crimes of universal jurisdiction.

The UK courts also have extra-territorial jurisdiction over UK nationals and residents as regards the three crimes which derive from the International Criminal Court Act 2001 Act which implements the 1998 Rome Statute of the ICC.[60] First, there are war crimes committed in internal armed conflicts after 2001.[61] Second, there is genocide committed after 2001.[62] Third, there are crimes against humanity committed after 2001.[63] There is also extra-territorial jurisdiction under the War Crimes Act 1991 in respect of murder committed in Nazi-occupied

---

Donald Rumsfeld, in relation to alleged authorisation of torture on detainees at Guantanamo Bay and Abu Ghraib, in violation of UNCAT. The grounds for the dismissal were that former heads of state remained immune from prosecution in relation to official acts committed during their time in office. http://ccrjustice.org/ourcases/current-cases/french-war-crimes-complaint-against-donald-rumsfeld,-et-al. accessed 13 December 2014.

[59] This implements the 1979 International Convention Against the Taking of Hostages,

[60] The Rome Statute came into force on 1 July 2002, after 60 states had ratified it.

[61] The 1998 Rome Statute of the ICC places 'serious violations' of art 3, common to the four Geneva Conventions of 1949, on the same legal footing as 'war crimes' in international armed conflicts.

[62] The Genocide Act 1969 criminalised genocide committed in the UK, in line with the 1948 Convention on the Prevention and Punishment of the Crimes of Genocide. The Act was repealed by the International Criminal Court Act 2001.

[63] Section 70(3) of the Coroners and Justice Act 2001 inserted a new s 65A into the 2001 Act, providing for the retrospective application of the offences of genocide, crimes against humanity and war crimes and related offences to things done on or after 1 January 1991. With crimes against humanity and certain categories of war crimes under art 8(2)(b) and (e) of the Rome Statute, this is

Europe between 1939 and 1945, and under the Slave Trade Act, 1843, which criminalised participation in the slave trade by 'British subjects ... whether within the dominions of the British crown or of any foreign country'.[64]

In France there is a two-tiered system of universal jurisdiction for international crimes. Until 2010, France only asserted universal jurisdiction over international crimes where an international treaty obligated France to prosecute. This included jurisdiction over torture, pursuant to the 1984 UNCAT. The French courts also have jurisdiction over genocide, crimes against humanity, and war crimes committed in the former Yugoslavia and in Rwanda, or by Rwandan citizens in neighbouring countries, pursuant to France's implementation of United Nations Security Council Resolutions 827 and 955 establishing the ICTY and the ICTR. On August 9, 2010, the French Code of Criminal Procedure was amended to incorporate the Rome Statute and extend the jurisdiction of French courts to include genocide, crimes against humanity, and war crimes committed after that date. There are four differences between the jurisdiction over these crimes and those added in 2010. First, for the former crimes, there would be jurisdiction where the suspect is present in France at the time that a judicial investigation is opened, but for the 2010 crimes there is jurisdiction only where the accused regularly resides in France. Secondly, there is no subsidiarity requirement for torture and enforced disappearance,[65] whereas there is such a requirement for the 2010 crimes, so that prosecutors, before opening an investigation, must first verify whether any national or international court has asserted jurisdiction over a suspect or has requested their extradition. Third, the courts can exercise jurisdiction over torture, enforced disappearance and crimes committed in the former Yugoslavia and Rwanda even where the crimes were not punishable in those countries at the time they were committed. In contrast, there is a double criminality requirement for the

---

subject to the requirement that the act constituting the offence amounted to a criminal offence under international law.

 64 Section 71 of the Coroners and Justice Act 2009 creates a new offence in England and Wales and Northern Ireland of holding someone in slavery or servitude, or requiring a person to perform forced or compulsory labour. The offence is to be interpreted in accordance with art 4 of the ECHR. This offence and other offences relating to slavery in s 59A of the Sexual Offences Act 2003 and s 4 of the Asylum and Immigration (Treatment of Claimants, etc,) Act 2004 have now been consolidated in the Modern Slavery Act 2015.

 65 The French courts defer to the ICTY and ICTR which have primary jurisdiction over crimes committed in the former Yugoslavia and Rwanda.

2010 international crimes. Fourth, while criminal proceedings for serious offences can normally be initiated by prosecutors or private parties, such as victims and other affected parties, including nongovernmental organizations (NGOs), only the prosecution service may trigger prosecutions for the 2010 international crimes.

Universal jurisdiction provisions also appear in national legislation implementing the Rome Statute in: New Zealand's International Crimes and International Criminal Court Act 2000; Germany's Article 1 of its Code of Crimes Against International Law 2002, 42 ILM (2003) 995; South Africa's South African Implementation of the Rome Statute of the International Criminal Court Act 2002 section 4(3)(c); The Netherlands' International Crimes Act 2003; Ireland's International Criminal Court Act 2006 in respect of war crimes committed in international armed conflicts.

In the US, which has signed, but not ratified, the Rome Statute, universal criminal jurisdiction exists over piracy, genocide,[66] and torture. There is extra-territorial jurisdiction in respect of war crimes. Section 404 of the Restatement Third provides that there is universal jurisdiction to define and prescribe punishment for certain offences recognised by the community of nations as of universal concern, such as piracy, slave trade, attacks on or hijacking of aircraft, genocide, war crimes, and perhaps certain acts of terrorism.

Sovereign immunity and international crimes

The immunity *ratione personae* of serving Heads of State will continue to bar proceedings against such persons in respect of proceedings before national courts in respect of international crimes. In 2002 the ICJ in the *Arrest Warrant* case held that there was no rule of international law denying immunity to Heads of State in relation to criminal prosecutions before national courts in respect of international crimes.[67] However, Head of State immunity will not provide a defence where international crimes

---

[66] The 1988 Proxmire Act criminalised genocide only when 'the offense is committed within the United States' or where 'the alleged offender is a national of the United States'. Subsequently the Genocide Accountability Act of 2007, Pub L No. 110–151, 121 Stat 1821 (codified as amended at 18 USC § 1091 (2006 & Supp. IV 2010)). criminalised genocide outside the US by non-Americans, provided that they would subsequently be present in the US.

[67] *Case concerning Arrest Warrant of 1 1 April 2000 (Democratic Republic of the Congo v. Belgium)*, Judgment, ICJ Reports 2002, p. 3 ISSN 0074-(February 14, 2002). The case arose out of Belgium's issue of an arrest warrant against the serving Foreign Minister of the Democratic Republic of the Congo in respect of allegations of international crimes committed by him during the genocide in Rwanda.

are prosecuted before an international tribunal such as the Nuremberg and Tokyo tribunals, the ICC[68] or the SCSL. before which Charles Taylor was prosecuted while still the Head of State of Liberia. On May 31, 2004, the Appeals Chamber of the SCSL ruled unanimously that Charles Taylor did not enjoy any immunity from prosecution by the court although he was the serving Head of State of Liberia at the time criminal proceedings were initiated.[69] The Appeals Chamber explained the different treatment of sovereign immunity in national and international courts as being due to:

> the principle that one sovereign state does not adjudicate on the conduct of another state; the principle of state immunity derives from the equality of sovereign states and therefore has no relevance to international criminal tribunals which are not organs of a state but derive their mandate from the international community.[70]

To date the ICC has issued arrest warrants against three serving Heads of State: Sudan's Omar al Bashir in 2009; Libya's Muammar Gadaffi in 2011; Kenya's Uhuru Kenyatta in April 2011. In October 2014 Kenyatta became the first Head of State to appear before the ICC but due to problems with evidence the prosecution was dropped in December 2014.

However, the practice of national courts in criminal prosecutions for international crimes against former State officials is that such proceedings will not be barred by functional immunity, or immunity *ratione materiae*, of former State officials.[71] In *R v. Bow Street Metropolitan Stipendiary Magistrate and others, ex parte Pinochet Ugarte (Pinochet*

---

[68]   Pursuant to art 27 of the Rome Statute.

[69]   *Prosecutor v. Charles Ghankay Taylor*, Case Number SCSL-2003-01-I, Decision on Immunity from Jurisdiction, 31 May 2004. The motion was heard in the Appeals Chamber by Justices Emmanuel Ayoola, George Gelaga King, and Renate Winter. The Decision is available at http://www.eccc.gov.kh/sites/default/files/Taylor.pdf accessed 13 December 2014.

[70]   At [51].

[71]   See, criminal proceedings for crimes against humanity committed in World War Two brought by Israel against Adolf Eichmann, *Attorney General of Israel v. Eichmann*, 36 ILR (1962) 5, the numerous proceedings brought in the courts of Belgium and Spain against former heads of state. See, too, *Ferrini v. Federal Republic of Germany*, 11 March 2004, 128 ILR 659, where the Italian Court of Cassation stated that, in its view, it was 'undisputed' that State officials do not enjoy functional immunity in respect of crimes under international law. This was a civil case concerned with the immunity of the State itself, and the issue of functional immunity was not considered in the subsequent decision of the ICJ to the effect that a State's immunity in civil proceedings persisted,

(No 3))[72] the House of Lords upheld Spain's request for the extradition of the former Chilean dictator, Pinochet, on charges of torture committed during his time as Head of State after 29 September 1989 when torture became a crime in the UK with the implementation of the UNCAT to which both Chile and the UK were parties. Probably the best explanation of the decision is that a grant of immunity *ratione materiae* would have been inconsistent with those provisions of UNCAT according universal jurisdiction for torture, a crime that can only be committed by state officials. Lord Millett stated:

> The offence can be committed *only* by or at the instigation of or with the consent or acquiescence of a public official or other person acting in an official capacity. The official or governmental nature of the act, which forms the basis of the immunity, is an essential ingredient of the offence. No rational system of criminal justice can allow an immunity which is coextensive with the offence.[73]

Lord Phillips stated the position as regards international crimes in general:

> International crimes and extra-territorial jurisdiction in relation to them are both new arrivals in the field of public international law. I do not believe that State immunity *ratione materiae* can co-exist with them. The exercise of extra-territorial jurisdiction overrides the principle that one State will not intervene in the internal affairs of another. It does so because, where international crime is concerned, that principle cannot prevail ... . Once extra-territorial jurisdiction is established, it makes no sense to exclude from it acts done in an official capacity.[74]

As against these decisions of national courts, there is a dictum in the *Arrest Warrant* case where the ICJ appears to suggest that immunity *ratione materiae* would bar the prosecution of officials or former officials for international crimes committed whilst in office.[75] The Court listed four circumstances in which a criminal prosecution could be made against an incumbent or former Foreign Minister where this immunity would not act as a bar to criminal prosecution. The third of these was the

---

notwithstanding that the claims made against it involved violations of *jus cogens* norms of international law.

[72]   [2000] 1 AC 147.

[73]   Ibid., p. 277.

[74]   Ibid., p. 289.

[75]   *Case concerning Arrest Warrant of 1 April 2000 (Democratic Republic of the Congo v. Belgium)*, note 67 above, p. 3, [6.1].

prosecution of a former Foreign Minister in the courts of another State 'in respect of acts committed prior or subsequent to his or her period of office, as well as in respect of acts committed during that period of office in a private capacity'. This suggests that immunity in respect of official acts committed during the Foreign Minister's time in office continues after he or she has stepped down from office. However, the case involved the assertion of a claim to immunity *ratione personae* and in their joint separate opinion, Judges Higgins, Kooijmans and Buergenthal noted that the current trend of State practice is that former State officials are not covered by immunity *ratione materiae* when prosecuted in national courts for serious international crimes.[76] It also seems to be the case that immunity *ratione materiae* is not available in respect of an international crime committed in the territory of the forum State.[77]

International crimes and corporations
From Nuremberg onwards international tribunals have only assumed criminal jurisdiction over natural persons. Although the Nuremberg tribunals had the authority to declare an organisation to be criminal, this was with a view towards facilitating the imposition of liability on the individual members of the organisation. The tribunals had no jurisdiction to impose criminal liability on the organisation itself. The position is the same with the ICTY and ICTR which possessed jurisdiction over natural persons, but not over legal persons.[78] So too with the ICC, where Article 25(1) of the Rome Statute provides: 'The Court shall have jurisdiction over natural persons pursuant to this Statute.'

Notwithstanding this, several States that have implemented the provisions of the Rome Statute into their domestic law do not limit their jurisdiction over the three international crimes to natural persons. In the UK, section 51(1) of the International Crimes Act 2001 provides: 'It is an

---

[76] Ibid., [74] [85].

[77] In *Pinochet (No 3)*, note 58 above, Lord Millet said: 'The plea of immunity *ratione materiae* is not available in respect of an offence committed in the forum state, whether this be England or Spain.', p. 277. In 2009 an Italian court convicted, *in absentia*, various CIA agents for their abduction of Abu Omar, a suspected terrorist who was then flown to Cairo where he was allegedly tortured. See, too, the extradition from the UK of Khurts Bat, the secretary of the executive office of the Mongolian National Security Office, in relation to charges in Germany relating to the kidnapping in France and forcible transportation to Berlin of a Mongolian national, in *Khurts Bat v. Investigating Judge of the German Federal Court*, [2011] EWHC 2029 (Admin).

[78] Unlike the Nuremberg tribunals, these subsequent tribunals had not been given jurisdiction to declare organisations to be criminal.

offence against the law of England and Wales for a person to commit genocide, a crime against humanity or a war crime.' Section 52 provides for an offence in relation to conduct ancillary to these crimes. The Schedule to the Interpretation Act 1978 provides that 'person' includes 'a body of persons corporate or unincorporate'. The sections apply to acts committed in England and Wales and accordingly a company could be criminally liable if it committed one of the three Rome Statute crimes within England and Wales. However, for acts outside the UK the sections apply only to acts committed by a UK national, a UK resident or a person subject to UK service jurisdiction.[79] Accordingly there would be no jurisdiction over a company for an international crime committed outside the UK.

In Australia the three Rome Statute criminal offences were inserted into the Criminal Code as Division 268 by the International Criminal Court (Consequential Amendments) Act 2002 (Cth.). Under the Criminal Code there is a presumption that all offences therein apply equally to bodies corporate as to natural persons.[80] Division 268 offences fall in the broadest category of jurisdiction under the Criminal Code, Category D, under which anyone, anywhere, regardless of citizenship or residence, can be tried for an offence committed anywhere in the world, without the availability of a foreign law defence.[81] It would therefore be possible for Australia to prosecute a corporation of any nationality for conduct amounting to a Division 268 offence wherever in the world it is committed.

There is a divergence of approaches in national criminal laws to the attribution of knowledge to companies in offences. In the US the doctrine of *respondeat superior* is applied whereby a corporation may be held criminally liable for the illegal acts of its directors, officers, employees, and agents, provided that individual's acts were within the scope of his duties and were intended, at least in part, to benefit the corporation.[82] In

---

[79]　Section 67(3) defines a 'person subject to UK Service jurisdiction' by reference to the various Service Discipline Acts.

[80]　Part 2.5, section 12.1 of the Criminal Code.

[81]　Section 15.4 describes the extended geographical jurisdiction of Category D as follows:

'If a law of the Commonwealth provides that this section applies to a particular offence, the offence applies:

(a) whether or not the conduct constituting the alleged offence occurs in Australia; and (b) whether or not a result of the conduct constituting the alleged offence occurs in Australia.'

[82]　*New York Central & Hudson River Railroad v. US*, 212 US 481 (1909).

the UK liability is incurred due to the knowledge of directors or high level officials constituting the 'directing mind and will' of the company.[83] A wider test is now applied in relation to corporate manslaughter where the breach which causes the death must be directly attributable to a 'senior management failure'.[84] In Australia section 12(3) of the Criminal Code Act 1995 provides that, for offences of intention, knowledge or recklessness, the 'fault element must be attributed to a body corporate that expressly, tacitly or impliedly authorised or permitted the commission of the offence'. This can be shown in one of three ways. First, by 'proving that the body corporate's board of directors intentionally, knowingly or recklessly carried out the relevant conduct, or expressly, tacitly or impliedly authorised or permitted the commission of the offence'. Second, by 'proving that a high managerial agent of the body corporate intentionally, knowingly or recklessly engaged in the relevant conduct, or expressly, tacitly or impliedly authorised or permitted the commission of the offence'. Third, through 'proving that a corporate culture existed within the body corporate that directed, encouraged, tolerated or led to non-compliance with the relevant provision; or ... proving that the body corporate failed to create and maintain a corporate culture that required compliance with the relevant provision'. Sub-paragraph 6 defines 'corporate culture' as an 'attitude, policy, rule, course

---

[83] *Tesco v. Nattrass*, [1972] AC 153. The principle derives from the principle of attribution in civil cases set out in *Lennard's Carrying Co Ltd v. Asiatic Petroleum Co Ltd*, [1915] AC 705. With certain regulatory offences attribution may be determined by the construction of a particular statute, irrespective of the 'directing mind' principle, as seen in the approach of the Privy Council in *Meridian Global Funds Management Asia Ltd v. Securities Commission* [1995] 2 AC 500 (PC) and in *R v. British Steel plc*, [1995] 1 WLR 1356, regarding offences under The Health and Safety at Work Act 1974.

[84] Corporate Manslaughter and Corporate Homicide Act 2007. Section 1(1) provides: 'An organisation to which this section applies is guilty of an offence if the way in which its activities are managed or organised – (a) causes a person's death, and (b) amounts to a gross breach of a relevant duty of care owed by the organisation to the deceased.' Section 1(3) provides: 'An organisation is guilty of an offence under this section only if the way in which its activities are managed or organised by its senior management is a substantial element in the breach referred to in subsection (1).' Under s 1(4)(c) 'senior management' means 'the persons who play significant roles in – (i) the making of decisions about how the whole or a substantial part of its activities are to be managed or organised, or (ii) the actual managing or organising of the whole or a substantial part of those activities'.

of conduct or practice existing within the body corporate generally or in the part of the body corporate in which the relevant activities takes place'.

Prosecutions of corporations and corporate officials for international crimes before national courts

Many States have implemented universal jurisdiction provisions under which corporations as well as natural persons can be prosecuted in respect of international crimes. It has been argued that the appropriate focus in closing the governance gap should be on criminal, rather than civil, liability.[85] However, a survey of criminal proceedings to date against corporations or corporate officers, shows that there have been only a handful of convictions against individuals.

Australia   In October 2004, fighting took place at Kilwa, in the Democratic Republic of Congo (DRC), between government and rebel forces who had briefly occupied the town. During the fighting civilians suffered summary executions, arbitrary arrest, rape and torture at the hands of government soldiers. Anvil Mining, which had offices in Australia and Canada, operated a copper mine near Kilwa and it was alleged that it provided planes and vehicles to transport government forces during the fighting. In September 2005, the Australian Federal Police launched an investigation into Anvil's actions in relation to its possible complicity in war crimes and crimes against humanity committed by the Congolese government forces. Anvil always denied any direct involvement in these violations stating that its vehicles had been requisitioned by the Congolese authorities. Criminal proceedings were then brought before a military court in the DRC against 12 individuals, including three Anvil employees, in connection with the events at Kilwa. In June 2007 all the accused were acquitted with the tribunal also stating that Anvil Mining was not guilty, although no charges had been brought against the company. In August 2007 the Australian police closed their criminal investigation into Anvil Mining.

---

[85]   Professor James G. Stewart *'The Turn to Corporate Criminal Liability for International Crimes: Transcending the Alien Tort Statute'*, 47 *New York University Journal of International Law and Politics* (2014). Professor Stewart is a former appeals counsel for the Prosecutor of the ICTY and presently, a senior legal adviser (part-time) to appellate judges at the Extraordinary Chambers in the Courts of Cambodia.

Belgium   In 2002 a lawsuit was filed by four Burmese refugees, who alleged 'complicity in crimes against humanity' under Belgium's Universal Jurisdiction Act of June 16, 1993 relative to serious violations of international human rights against Total, its Chairman and the former president of its Burmese affiliate.[86] A claim for compensation for the victims was attached to the criminal proceedings under an *action civile*. The proceedings were subsequently dismissed by the Cour de Cassation in 2005, a ruling subsequently confirmed in 2007.[87]

France   In 2002 a further suit was filed against Total by eight Burmese nationals alleging Total's 'complicity in unlawful confinement' arising out of their submission to forced labour by the Burmese army on the construction of the Yadana pipeline. In November 2005 Total and the French NGO representing the Burmese nationals agreed a settlement involving the creation of a €5.2-million solidarity fund to compensate the eight plaintiffs as well as any other person who can demonstrate that they suffered a similar experience in the area near the pipeline construction corridor. The fund will also be used to finance humanitarian actions benefiting Myanmar refugees in the region. On March 10, 2006, Nanterre's Tribunal de Grande Instance dismissed the case.

Germany   In Germany corporations cannot be held criminally liable but senior managers may incur criminal responsibility. On 25 April 2013, two NGOs filed a criminal complaint in Germany against Olof von Gagern, a senior manager of Danzer Group, a Swiss and German timber manufacturer. The complaint arises out of claims that human rights abuses were committed by Congolese police and military during an attack on the village of Bongulu in northern DRC on 2 May 2011 and that von Gagern aided and abetted these abuses by failing to prevent these crimes from being committed. It is also alleged that the security forces received financial and logistical help from a former subsidiary of Danzer, Siforco. The allegations are denied.

The Netherlands   Three criminal proceedings have been brought in relation to alleged commission of international crimes, two against

---

[86]   Total was one of the partners in the Yadana project. Attempts to sue it in the US under the Alien Tort Statute failed due to want of jurisdiction.

[87]   The 1993 Universal Jurisdiction law was repealed by an Act of August 5, 2003. This provided a procedure for terminating certain proceedings that were under way. In June 2006 the Belgian Cour d'Arbitrage annulled this procedure. However, this did not affect the dismissal by the Cour de Cassation in 2005.

individuals, the other against a company. The first involved criminal proceedings against Frans van Anraat for complicity in genocide and in war crimes. Between 1984 and 1988 he became Saddam Hussein's sole supplier of thiodiglycol, a key component in mustard gas which the Iraqi military used against the Iranian military and civilians in its war with Iraq and also against the Kurds in Northern Iraq. Van Anraat bought the chemical from the US and Japan and then sold it on through a number of different companies located in different countries to Iraq. Van Anraat was charged with complicity in genocide and complicity in war crimes. The District Court of the Hague acquitted him of the former charge of complicity because it could not be proved that he knew of the genocidal intent of the Iraqi regime, but convicted him on the latter charge, applying the international law standard of aiding and abetting. He was sentenced to 15 years' imprisonment, a term subsequently increased to 17 years by the Court of Appeal of the Hague, which applied Dutch domestic criminal law to the issue of complicity.[88] In 2009, the Supreme Court of the Netherlands upheld Van Anraat's conviction for complicity in war crimes but reduced his sentence by six months,[89] and in 2010 the European Court of Human Rights rejected Van Anraat's claims challenging the jurisdiction of the Dutch courts and the legal certainty of the criminal acts being prosecuted.[90] In March 2012, the Dutch Prosecutor applied for the confiscation of Van Anraat's profits, of over 1 million Euros, from his sales of the chemical to Iraq. On 24 April 2013, the District Court of the Hague in the Netherlands ordered Frans van Anraat to pay compensation to 17 victims of chemical weapon attacks on the Kurdish city of Halabja by Saddam Hussein in 1988. On 7 April 2015 the Appeals Court upheld the District Court's verdict.[91]

The second case involved Guus Kouwenhoven who was charged with arms smuggling and war crimes in Liberia in the 1990s. In 2006 he was sentenced to eight years in jail for arms smuggling, but acquitted of war

---

[88]   District Court of The Hague, 23 December 2005, Case No. AX6406; Court of Appeal of The Hague, 9 May 2007, Case No. BA6734. Article 48 of the Dutch Penal Code requires that the accused provided the opportunity and/or the means to carry out the attacks described in the charges. According to previous decisions of the Supreme Court of the Netherlands the assistance need not be indispensable and it is enough that the accessory's assistance promoted the offence or made it easier to commit that offence.

[89]   Dutch Supreme Court, 30 June 2009, Case No. BG4822.

[90]   Van Anraat v. the Netherlands, Application no. 65389/09, 20 July 2010.

[91]   http://www.prakkendoliveira.nl/en/news/decision-that-van-anraat-must-pay-compensation-to-victims-of-chemical-attacks-in-iraq-confirmed/ <accessed 24 April 2015>.

crimes charges.[92] In 2008 the Court of Appeal in the Hague acquitted him of all charges and in 2010 following an appeal by the prosecution to the Supreme Court a retrial was ordered.[93] In November 2014 the court heard arguments for dismissal in the absence of available witnesses.

The third case involved a complaint filed in March 2010, by an NGO, Al Haq, against Riwal, a Dutch company, for its alleged complicity 'in the commission of war crimes and crimes against humanity ... through its supply of mobile cranes and aerial platforms for the construction of settlements and the Wall in several locations in the Occupied West Bank'.[94], in violation of the Geneva Conventions and, consequently, the Dutch International Crimes Act (Wet Internationale Misdrijven). In May 2013 the prosecutor decided not to proceed against the crane lessor or its directors as Riwal had ceased working in Israel and the occupied territories and its contribution to the building of the security barrier and settlements had been limited.[95] The Dutch government has stated that while such settlements are illegal and it discourages Dutch involvement, the involvement of Dutch companies was not prohibited.[96]

Switzerland   Two complaints have been filed against Swiss companies by NGOs. In March 2012, the European Centre for Constitutional Human Rights (ECCHR) and Colombian NGOs filed a criminal complaint with Swiss authorities against Nestlé S.A. and senior managers. They claimed that Nestlé negligently contributed to the 2005 murder of Luciano Romero, a Sinaltrainal trade unionist who worked at a Colombian subsidiary of Nestlé until 2002. In May 2013 Swiss prosecutors announced that they had decided not to prosecute because the case was

---

[92]   District Court of The Hague, 7 June 2006, Case No. AY516.

[93]   Dutch Supreme Court, 20 April 2010, Case No. BK8132.

[94]   Al Haq, Criminal Complaint Lodged Against Dutch Company for Construction of Settlements and 'The Wall' (Oct. 14, 2010), *at* http://www.alhaq.org/advocacy/targets/accountability/71-riwal/472-criminal-com plaint-lodged-against-dutch-company-for-construction-of-settlements-and-the-wall.

[95]   Openbaar Ministerie, Geen verder onderzoek naar kraanverhuurder (No further testing for crane hire) (May 14, 2013), *at* http://www.om.nl/algemene_onderdelen/uitgebreid_zoeken/@160903/verder-onderzoek/.

[96]   Press Release of the Dutch Government, Questions and Answers, Aanhangsel van de Handelingen, Tweede Kamer der Staten-Generaal (Appendix of Acts, second chamber of the states-general) (Sept. 16, 2013), *at* https://zoek.officielebekendmakingen.nl/ah-tk-20122013.

barred by the statute of limitations.[97] Since the decision, the NGOs and Romero's wife have appealed the order to the cantonal criminal court, claiming that the prosecutors engaged in improper delay in reviewing the case and that the incorrect statute of limitations was applied.[98] Romero's widow lodged her own criminal complaint and subsequently appealed against the decision of the Swiss authorities and this appeal was dismissed in December 2013. A further appeal was made before the Swiss Federal Supreme Court based on the grounds that the statute of limitations did not begin to run with the commission of the crime itself and was a continuing offence based on the corporation's failure to take any action to remedy organizational deficiencies within the firm. On 21 July 2014 the Swiss Federal Supreme Court dismissed the appeal and confirmed that time started to run from the murder of Romero and that the case was accordingly statute barred.

A second complaint was filed on 1 November 2013 by a Swiss NGO, TRIAL, against a Swiss gold refinery, Argor-Heraeus SA, in connection with allegations that it had refined gold pillaged by an illegal armed group in the DRC. The Swiss public prosecutor opened a criminal investigation into the complaint but in March 2015 the case was dropped after investigators failed to find any evidence that Argor-Heraeus SA had knowingly dealt with shipments of illegally mined gold.

US   In March 2007 Chiquita Brands International Inc. which is incorporated in New Jersey and headquartered in Cincinnati, Ohio, pleaded guilty before the US District Court for the District of Columbia to a count of engaging in transactions with a specially-designated global terrorist right-wing terrorist organisation, the 'Autodefensas Unidas de Colombia' (the AUC). The AUC had been designated by the US government as a Foreign Terrorist Organization (FTO) on September 10, 2001, and as a Specially-Designated Global Terrorist (SDGT) on October 31, 2001 which meant that it was a federal crime for a US corporation to provide money to it. Under the terms of the plea agreement, Chiquita received a $25 million criminal fine, was required to implement and maintain an effective compliance and ethics programme, and five years' probation.[99]

---

[97]   European Coalition for Corporate Justice, Update in the Nestle' Case: Prosecutor Under Court Review (June 14, 2013), *at* http://www. corporatejustice.org/UPDATE-in-the-Nestle-Case.html.

[98]   ECCHR, *Update in the Nestlé Case: Prosecutor Under Court Review*, ECCHR Special Newsletter, May 17, 2013, *at* http://www.ecchr.de/index.php/ nestle-518.html.

[99]   http://www.justice.gov/archive/opa/pr/2007/March/07_nsd_161.html.

International law and civil liability
Under international law private parties will bear obligations in respect of the crimes of universal jurisdiction. Criminal proceedings for breach of these obligations will be brought either through national courts or through international criminal tribunals. Although there have been no comparable institutions with power to award civil compensation for violations of the norms covered by the international criminal tribunals, the US courts have developed a jurisprudence on civil liability of individuals for violating norms of customary international law, either directly, or as aiders and abetters. The gateway for this development has been the Alien Tort Statute (ATS) 1789. The primary development in this area has been the voluminous litigation under the 1789 Statute since the revival of this dormant statute with the 1980 decision of the Second Circuit in *Filartiga v. Pena-Irala*.[100] Since then, the federal courts of the US have been engaged on a judicial experiment in defining the contours of civil liability for violations of international law, although claims based on violations of customary international law have also been brought before the courts of Canada[101] and of England.[102] Customary international law has thereby come to have a horizontal effect on private parties by providing norms which give rise to a cause of action in national courts.

The development of universal civil jurisdiction as a means of closing the governance gap, which will be analysed in detail in Chapters 4 and 7, has generated two controversies as to the nature of the civil liabilities imposed on private parties under customary international law. The first relates to the extra-territorial limits of universal civil jurisdiction. All ATS claims will have a foreign element – the plaintiff must be an alien. However, many ATS claims involve allegations of violations of international law occurring outside the US. Where the defendant is also an alien the result is that claims are being heard in US federal courts which have no connection with the US at all. These are so-called 'foreign

---

[100]   *See* generally, *Filartiga v. Pena-Irala*, 630 F.2d 876 (2nd Cir. 1980).

[101]   *Bouzari v. Islamic Republic of Iran*, [2002] OJ No 1624; [2004] OJ No 2800 Docket No. C38295, dismissed on grounds of sovereign immunity, and *Bil'in (Village Council) v. Green Park Int'l Ltd*, 2009 QCCS 4151, a claim alleging corporate complicity in war crimes in the occupied territories in Israel, dismissed on grounds of *forum non conveniens*.

[102]   Claims based on torture were brought in *Al-Adsani v. Kuwait*, 103 ILR 420 (QB 1995), aff'd *Al-Adsani v. Kuwait*, 107 ILR 536 (CA 1996) and *Jones v. Saudi Arabia*, [2006] UKHL 26; [2007] 1 AC 270 but were dismissed on grounds of sovereign immunity.

cubed' suits which involve claims by a foreign plaintiff against a foreign defendant in respect of events that took place in a foreign jurisdiction. Concerns have been expressed by foreign States that the ATS has seen an exorbitant exercise of jurisdiction by US federal courts that violates the permissible limits on national jurisdiction under international law.[103]

In addressing this issue, a distinction has to be made between adjudicative and prescriptive jurisdiction. Adjudicative jurisdiction is where a court hears a dispute, such as a tort claim, involving matters that took place outside the jurisdiction, but does not apply its own rules of conduct. Prescriptive jurisdiction is where a court hearing such a dispute applies its own rules of conduct. As regards adjudicative jurisdiction, a cursory look at the jurisdictional rules of the courts of England and Wales will show that there is clearly no restriction on a State as to hearing civil claims that arise out of conduct outside the jurisdiction of the UK. Under the common law, English courts may assume jurisdiction over natural persons if a claim form has been properly served on them while in England, even if they are only temporarily present in England at the time.[104] English courts may also assume jurisdiction over legal persons on the basis of service of proceedings in England.[105] Claims with no connection with the UK are likely to be stayed on grounds of *forum non conveniens* where an alternative forum can be identified, although a stay will not be granted if to do so would cause substantial injustice to the

---

[103]   *Kiobel v. Royal Dutch Petroleum Co.* Brief of the Governments of the kingdom of the Netherlands and the United Kingdom of Great Britain and Northern Ireland as *amici curiae* in Support of Neither Party. N0 10-1491. June 13 2012. 2–3, 11–18.

[104]   See, e.g., *Maharanee of Baroda v. Wildenstein*, (1972) 2 QB 283 and *Colt Indus. v. Sarlie*, [1966] 1 WLR 440 (CA). The jurisdiction of the English courts over a defendant served within the jurisdiction in respect of events occurring outside the jurisdiction was established in *Mostyn v. Fabrigas*, (1775) 1 Cowper 161.

[105]   Service could be through CPR 6.9 which provides that service of proceedings on a foreign company may be made at 'any place in the jurisdiction where the corporation carries on its activities, or at any place of business of the company within the jurisdiction' or, as regards a company registered as an overseas company, pursuant to s 1139 Companies Act 2006. The dispute need not be connected with the defendant company's activities within the jurisdiction. *Sea Assets v. PT Garuda Indonesia*, (2000) 4 All ER 371, neither must the foreign company's activity constitute a substantial part of, or be incidental to, its main objects. *South India Shipping Corp. v. Export-Import Bank of Korea*, [1985] 1 WLR 585.

claimant.[106] There have been several instances where civil claims with no connection with England have been heard before the English courts such as *Oppenheimer v. Louis Rosenthal & Co. AG*,[107] where leave was granted to serve a writ out of the jurisdiction because the Jewish plaintiff was unlikely to receive a fair hearing in proceeding in the courts of Nazi Germany, the more appropriate forum, and would risk being sent to a concentration camp were he to return to Germany.

Where a claim is made against a person domiciled in the UK, Article 2 of the Brussels Regulation requires the UK courts to accept jurisdiction, irrespective of where the conduct giving rise to the claim is situated. In this situation there is no possibility of a stay on grounds of *forum non conveniens*.[108] English courts may also assume jurisdiction over a foreign defendant in a claim involving tortious acts abroad where a co-defendant is domiciled in England.[109] Jurisdiction may also be assumed over a foreign defendant by agreement.[110] Foreign tort claims which are 'foreign cubed' suits, therefore, are not a unique feature of the US legal order. A recent example of a 'foreign cubed' suit from outside the US is provided by the decision of the courts of the Netherlands, in *Ashraf Ahmed El-Hojouj v. Harb Amer Derbal et al.,* in which damages were awarded against Libyan defendants in respect of torture of a Palestinian citizen in Libya.[111]

As regards prescriptive, or legislative, jurisdiction exercised by a State in relation to conduct taking place outside its territory, there are two views as to whether customary international law imposes any limits on such jurisdiction. The first view, based on the 1927 decision of the Permanent Court of International Justice in the *Lotus* case, is that a State

---

[106]   See, *The Vishva Ajay*, [1989] 2 Lloyd's Rep 558 (QB) a 'foreign cubed' case in which proceedings were brought in the High Court in relation to a collision between two vessels at a port in India when jurisdiction had been established by a sister-ship arrest.

[107]   [1937] 1 All ER 23.

[108]   *Owusu v. Jackson*, ECR I-1383.

[109]   See CPR PD 6B, s 3.1, and art 6(1) of the Brussels Regulation. On this basis jurisdiction was established in *Motto & Ors v. Trafigura*, [2011] EWHC 90206, over the Dutch parent company of a UK company that had chartered a vessel from which toxic waste had been dumped in Africa leading to a negligence claim being brought before the English court.

[110]   As in *Bodo Cmty.*, Claim No. HQ 11X01280, High Court (QB) where proceedings were originally issued against a UK parent company and its Nigerian subsidiary, and by agreement the claim then proceeded against the subsidiary alone in the English courts. The applicable law was that of Nigeria.

[111]   Hague District Court, No. 400882 (Mar. 21, 2012).

is entitled to extend its prescriptive jurisdiction outside its territory, subject to any rules prohibiting such prescription in certain cases.[112] The second, and more generally accepted view, is that international law imposes the requirement of a sufficiently close nexus to the forum asserting jurisdiction.[113] That nexus may be demonstrated in the following ways. First, where the offender is a national of that State (the 'active personality' principle). Second, where the victim is a national of that State (the 'passive personality' principle). Third, and more controversially, where the extra-territorial conduct has adverse effects that are felt within the territory of the State.[114] Fourth, in relation to crimes in respect of which there exists universal jurisdiction.

The position under customary international law with regard to a State's jurisdiction over extra-territorial conduct in civil cases is less clear. Some scholars deny that there are any restrictions on a State's jurisdiction[115]

---

[112]　1927 PCIJ, Series A, No 10, 19.

[113]　Sir Robert Jennings and Sir Arthur Watts, eds, *Oppenheim's International Law*, § 138, 462 (9th ed. 1992); R Y Jennings, 'Extraterritorial Jurisdiction and the United States Antitrust Laws' (1957) 33 *Brit YB Int'l L* 146, 150–61; V. Lowe, 'Jurisdiction' in *International Law* (Malcolm D. Evans ed., 2nd ed., 2006), 342 ('The best view is that it is necessary for there to be some clear connecting factor, of a kind whose use is approved by international law, between the legislating state and the conduct that it seeks to regulate. The notion of the need for a linking point ... accords closely with the actual practice of states'); § 402(2) of the US Restatement (Third) of Foreign Relations; *Blackmer v. United States*, 284 US 421, 437 (1932). In *The Nottebohm Case, (Liech. v. Guatamala),* 1955 ICJ 4, 23 (Apr. 6) the ICJ stated that this well-established principle of jurisdiction requires 'a legal bond having as its basis a social fact of attachment, a *genuine connection* of existence, interests, and sentiments, together with the existence of reciprocal rights and duties' (emphasis added).

[114]　A doctrine asserted by the US where certain overseas activities had a substantial adverse effect within the US. See, e.g., *Hartford Fire Ins Co v. Cal*, 509 US 764, 796 (1993).

[115]　See eg, Michael Akehurst, 'Jurisdiction in International Law' (1975) 46 *Brit Y B Int'l L* 145, 177 (concluding that customary international law imposes no limits on civil jurisdiction) Gerald Fitzmaurice, 'The General Principles of International Law'(1957 II) 92 *Recueil des Cours* 1, 218; Peter Manczuk, *Akehurst's Modern Introduction to Int'l Law* (7th rev ed., 1997) 110. Malcolm Shaw *International Law* 652 (CUP, 8th ed., 2008) notes that the rarity of diplomatic protests has led some writers to conclude that customary international law does not prescribe any particular regulations to restrict courts' jurisdiction in civil matters.

whereas others affirm that the restrictions on criminal proceedings apply equally to civil proceedings involving extra-territorial conduct.[116]

If there is a rule of customary international law governing the competence of States to entertain civil suits arising out of conduct committed outside the jurisdiction, what is its nature? If it mirrors the supposed rule relating to criminal suits, then claims involving domestic plaintiffs and defendants would be adjudicable under the 'passive' and 'active' nationality requirements respectively. But do the rules relating to civil suits acknowledge a further exception of universal jurisdiction? There is very little State practice on this question. What is clear is that universal jurisdiction in civil suits will not oust sovereign immunity *ratione materiae* as is the case with criminal cases. Torture claims against States and their agents were brought in Canada in *Bouzari v. Islamic Republic of Iran*, in Australia *Zhang v. Zemin*,[117] and in the UK in *Al Adsani v. Govt of Kuwait*[118] and in *Jones v. Govt of Saudi Arabia*.[119] All were dismissed on the grounds of sovereign immunity, notwithstanding that the claims arose out of violations of *jus cogens* norms of international law. The decision as to sovereign immunity in the two UK decisions was subsequently upheld by the European Court of Human Rights.[120] In the US the Supreme Court has held that the ATS is pre-empted by the Foreign Sovereign Immunity Act 28 USC, section 1330, sections 1602–11.[121] However, in both the US[122] and Canada

---

[116] See e.g., Ian Brownlie, *Principles of Public International Law* (6th ed., 2003) 298, arguing that there is no reason in principle to distinguish between the permissibility under international law of civil and criminal cases; Frederick A. Mann, 'The Doctrine of Jurisdiction in International Law' (1964 I) 111 *Recueil Des Cours* 1, 73–81, international law imposes substantial limits on civil jurisdiction; Frederick A. Mann, 'The Doctrine of Jurisdiction Revisited After Twenty Years' (1984 III) 186 *Recueil Des Cours* 19, 20–33, 67–77.

[117] [2010] 243 FLR 299.

[118] (1995) 100 ILR 465, The Times 29 March 1996.

[119] [2006] UKHL 26, [2006] 2 WLR 1424.

[120] *Al Adsani v. UK*, (2002) 34 EHRR 11; *Case of Jones and Others v. The United Kingdom* (Applications nos. 34356/06 and 40528/06) Judgment 14 January 2014.

[121] *Argentine Republic v. Amerada Hess Shipping Corp*, 488 US 428 (1989). In 1992 the Ninth Circuit held that this remained the position even where the claims were based on the violation of *jus cogens* norms, such as the prohibition on torture. *Siderman de Blake v. Republic of Argentina*, 965 F 2d 699 (9th Cir 1992).

[122] USC s 1605A.

legislation has been enacted to permit civil suits against States that are sponsors of terrorism.[123]

There is, therefore, no mandatory universal civil jurisdiction, but that does not mean that there is no permissive universal civil jurisdiction. In none of the cases referred to was it decided that extra-territorial civil jurisdiction was barred generally. Similarly in *Jurisdictional Immunities of the State (Germany v. Italy)*[124] the ICJ held that Germany could rely on sovereign immunity to prevent its being held civilly liable in the Italian courts in respect of Nazi war crimes, but did not hold that there was a general bar on extra-territorial jurisdiction in civil cases. In any event, the recognition by any particular State of a cause of action deriving from a universal prohibition of international law applicable to non-State parties could not be said to be an exercise of prescriptive jurisdiction by that State as it would not involve the application of its own domestic law, but rather that of a universal norm of international law. The position under the ATS has now been resolved by the Supreme Court's decision in *Kiobel v. Royal Dutch Petroleum Co* that the statute had no extra-territorial application, based on the application of a US canon of statutory interpretation, a decision which has put an end to litigation of 'foreign cubed' cases under the ATS.[125] However, *Kiobel* was not decided on the basis of any rule of international law precluding a State from asserting jurisdiction over 'foreign cubed' civil claims that have no connection with that State.

The second controversy is as to the type of persons subject to universal civil jurisdiction and whether legal persons can be regarded as subjects of customary international law. The contours of this nascent international civil law have been developed in the US federal courts by transplanting the principles under which international law imposes criminal liability on individuals into the field of civil liability in tort. However, from the Nuremberg and Tokyo tribunals to the ICC civil liability under customary international law is evidenced by the sources which established criminal liability, and the jurisdiction of every international criminal tribunal has been expressly limited to a jurisdiction over natural persons. Therefore, the argument goes, if universal civil jurisdiction derives from universal criminal jurisdiction it must follow that its effect is also limited to natural persons and that legal persons are subject to no obligations under customary international law. In September 2010 this reasoning led the

---

[123]   The Justice for Victims of Terrorism Act 2012.
[124]   Judgment, paras 91–97 (Feb. 3, 2012).
[125]   133 S Ct 1659 (2013).

Second Circuit in *Kiobel v. Royal Dutch Petroleum Co* to decide that suits under the ATS could not be brought against corporations.[126]

However, subsequent decisions in other Circuits have affirmed that corporations can incur liability under the ATS, reasoning that customary international law provides the prohibitive norms and it is then left to each State to determine how to apply them within their domestic legal order. Domestic law would then determine the issue of corporate liability. This is the approach taken by Judge Leval, dissenting, in *Kiobel*[127] and by Judge Possner in *Flomo v. Firestone Natural Rubber Co.*[128] Although it has never been possible to bring criminal proceedings against a corporation before an international tribunal, that does not necessarily mean that the prohibition against conduct is limited to natural persons. Volker Nehrlich has addressed this point as follows:

> A norm of criminal law describing a crime may be understood as comprising two sub-norms: the first, most elementary, sub-norm consists of a prohibition of certain conduct, such as the prohibition to kill another person. To make it a norm of criminal law, however, a second sub-norm is required, which provides that the consequence of any contravention of the first sub-norm is criminal punishment. In international criminal law, this structure can best be observed in respect of war crimes, where the prohibition of certain conduct is generally contained in a rule of international humanitarian law, be it customary or conventional in nature; the second sub-norm is often grounded in international custom.[129]

Thus, international criminal proceedings against individuals evidences the prohibition of international law that binds all persons, natural or juridical, even though no international tribunals have been established with power to hear criminal cases against non-natural persons. This argument is supported by Judge Schwarz's analysis of the point in *Presbyterian Church of Sudan v. Talisman Energy* in which he noted that the IMT in the *Farben* and *Krupp* cases spoke of the corporations as having violated international law, even though the proceedings were against their individual executives.[130] It is also echoed in the observations

---

[126]   621 F 3d 111 (2d Cir 2010).

[127]   *Ibid.*, 173–6.

[128]   643 F 3d 1013, 1020–21 (7th Cir 2011)

[129]   Volker Nehrlich, 'Core Crimes and Transnational Business Corporations', 8 *J. Int'l Crim. Just.* 895, 898 (2010).

[130]   244 F Supp. 2d 289, 315–6 (SDNY 2003).). At Nuremberg the heads of major German corporations were prosecuted for, inter alia, war crimes and crimes against humanity. In each of these cases, individuals, and not corporate entities, were put on trial, but the court consistently spoke in terms of corporate

of Judge Shahabudeen in his separate opinion in *Certain Phosphate Lands in Nauru*:

> In international law a right may well exist even in the absence of any juridical method of enforcing it … Thus, whether there is a right to contribution does not necessarily depend on whether there exists a juridical method of enforcing contribution.[131]

This is an issue that can only be resolved by national courts when faced with a civil claim based on a violation of customary international law. In the US the issue is still unresolved and there remains a Circuit split. Although this question was referred to the US Supreme Court in *Kiobel* when the Supreme Court which gave judgment on 17 April 2013 it said nothing about this issue, instead deciding the claim on the basis of the territorial limits of the cause of action that could be created under federal common law pursuant to the grant of jurisdiction under the ATS.

---

liability. In *United States v. Krauch*, 8 Trials of War Criminals before the Nuremberg Military Tribunals under Control Council Law No. 10, 1081, 1140 (1952): it stated:

> With reference to the charges in the present indictment concerning Farben's [a German corporation] activities in Poland, Norway, Alsace-Lorraine, and France, we find that the proof establishes beyond a reasonable doubt that offenses against property as defined in Control Council Law No. 10 *were committed by Farben,* and that these offenses were connected with, and an inextricable part of the German policy for occupied countries. […]. The *action of Farben* and its representatives, under these circumstances, cannot be differentiated from acts of plunder or pillage committed by officers, soldiers, or public officials of the German Reich. […] Such *action on the part of Farben* constituted a violation of the Hague Regulations [on the conduct of warfare] (emphases added).

Similarly in *United States v. Krupp*: '[T]he confiscation of the Austin plant [a tractor factory owned by the Rothschilds] […] and its subsequent detention by the Krupp firm constitute a violation of Article 43 of the Hague Regulations [… and] the Krupp firm, through defendants[, …] voluntarily and without duress participated in these violations.' 9 Trials of War Criminals Before the Nuernberg Military Tribunals Under Control Council Law No. 10 , 1327, 1352–53 (1950).

[131] *Certain Phosphate Lands in Nauru (Nauru v. Australia), Preliminary Objections, Judgment (sep. op. Shahabuddeen)*, ICJR (1992), 240, 290.

3. CORPORATE RIGHTS UNDER INTERNATIONAL LAW

With the rise of globalisation corporations have obtained, under international law, extensive legal rights against States matching their economic power.[132] Foreign investors have obtained these rights through the investor-state dispute settlement (ISDS) provisions of both bilateral investment treaties (BITs) and multilateral investment treaties between States. Since the 1990s there has been a huge increase in the conclusion of BITs[133] and multilateral trade and investment agreements such as the North American Free Trade Agreement, (NAFTA) between the US, Canada and Mexico, which came into force on 1 January 1994, the 2004 Central American Free Trade Agreement (CAFTA)[134] and the 1994 Energy Charter Treaty (ECT).[135] The EU is about to ratify the Comprehensive Economic and Trade Agreement (CETA) with Canada which contains ISDS provisions[136] and is currently negotiating the Transatlantic

---

[132] Business interests have also been indirect beneficiaries of the binding trade disciplines set up by the World Trade Organisation (WTO). Although the WTO agreements contemplate State-to-State arbitration, States have been quite willing to initiate proceedings to protect the interests of their corporations. Indeed, Philip Morris has funded various States, such as Ukraine, in bringing proceedings under the WTO against Australia in respect of its plain packaging law for cigarettes.

[133] The first BIT was signed on 26 November 1959 between West Germany and Pakistan, coming into force on 28 November 1962. More than 2,000 of these BITs have now been concluded. The UK is currently party to 84 BITs, the US to 37.

[134] The parties to the treaty are the US and Costa Rica, El Salvador, Guatemala, Honduras, Nicaragua, as well as the Dominican Republic, and entered into force for the US, El Salvador, Guatemala, Honduras, and Nicaragua in 2006, for the Dominican Republic in 2007, and for Costa Rica in 2009. The text of the treaty is available at https://ustr.gov/trade-agreements/free-trade-agreements/cafta-dr-dominican-republic-central-america-fta/final-text <accessed 8 April 2015>.

[135] The ECT controls the transnational environment for trade, transfer and protection of investment in the energy sector. It entered into force in 1998, was signed by 51 states, including the EU and Euratom (Eastern and Western European states, the former Soviet Union, Japan, Australia). Part III, arts. 10–17 contain provisions for the protection of foreign investors in the energy sector.

[136] Negotiations for CETA concluded in October 2013 with ratification due in 2015. However, in January 2015 France and Germany issued a joint declaration asking the European Commission to examine 'all the options for modifying' the ISDS clause in the agreement.

Trade and Investment Partnership (TTIP) with the US which is also scheduled to contain ISDS provisions.[137] On 13 January 2015 negotiations with the US on ISDS were suspended and will only resume once the Commission has come to the assessment that its new proposals guarantee among other things that the jurisdiction of courts in the EU Member States will not be limited by special regimes for investor-to-state-disputes.[138] In the US on 22 April 2015, the Senate Finance Committee approved a bill to fast-track TTIP.

These investment treaties between States have privatised the international protection of investors by treaties giving investors of one party a direct right of action, through closed-door arbitration, against the government of the other country in the event of a violation of various provisions designed to protect investors, which extend beyond the prohibition on expropriation under international law. Common to nearly all these agreements are variants of the following provisions: 'national treatment' and 'most favoured nation treatment' provisions which extend the WTO disciplines on trade into the field of investment; provisions entitling the investor to fair and equitable treatment in accordance with international law; provisions entitling the investor to compensation in the event of expropriation or measures tantamount to expropriation.

Over the last 20 years corporations have woken up to the opportunities offered by these treaties to claim compensation from States when they are adversely affected by national and municipal laws, regulations, and even court decisions. Although investment treaties protect foreign investors, it has proved very easy for domestic investors to reorganise their corporate structure to turn themselves into foreign investors in advance of regulation that is likely to affect their business. A notable example is the ongoing arbitration brought by Philip Morris Asia (PMA) against Australia in connection with Australia's 2011 plain packaging laws for cigarettes.[139] Having challenged the legislation in the Australian courts, and lost, PMA commenced arbitration under the Australia's BIT with

---

[137]   The Commission conducted a public consultation between 27 March and 13 July 2014. The Commission's summary of the responses received in the consultation is available at *trade.ec.europa.eu/doclib/docs/2015/january/tradoc_153044.pdf* <accessed 8 April 2015>.

[138]   http://europa.eu/rapid/press-release_MEMO-15-3202_en.htm <accessed 8 April 2015>.

[139]   A similar challenge is being made to Uruguay's tobacco packaging laws under Uruguay's BIT with Switzerland. A detailed legal analysis of the claims by Todd Weiler is available http://www.smoke-free.ca/eng_home/2010/PMIvs Uruguay/Opinion-PMI-Uruguay.pdf <accessed 16 April 2015>.

Hong Kong.[140] It was able to make use of this BIT by reorganising its corporate structure, through PMA acquiring a large number of shares in Philip Morris Ltd (Australia) shortly after the Australian government announced it was considering a plain packaging measure.[141] Philip Morris is also funding various governments, such as Ukraine, in challenging Australia's measure in the WTO.[142] Australia is vigorously resisting these challenges to its plain packaging measures.

Other noteworthy examples are: the arbitration initiated under the ECT by Swedish company Vattenfall challenging Germany's phase out of nuclear power following the Fukushima reactor disaster in 2011;[143] the arbitration initiated under NAFTA against Canada by a Delaware Corporation, Lone Pine, challenging Quebec's moratorium on fracking;[144] the arbitration initiated by a US corporation, Pacific Rim, under CAFTA against El Salvador in respect of its moratorium on gold mining;[145] the arbitration initiated by Chevron against Ecuador in respect of a court judgment in Ecuador which awarded nearly $10 billion against Chevron in compensation for oil pollution in the Amazon basin caused by a consortium in which Texaco, whose interest it acquired in 2001,

---

[140] PMA claims that the measure constitutes an expropriation of its investments, is in breach of Australia's obligations to accord fair and equitable treatment to PMA's investments, that its investments have been deprived of fair and equitable treatment and that its investments have been deprived of full protection and security. Further details of the arbitration available at http://www.ag.gov.au/tobaccoplainpackaging <accessed 16 April 2015>.

[141] http://www.tobaccotactics.org/index.php/Australia:_Challenging_Legisla tion <accessed 16 April 2015>. In 2004 Australia concluded a free trade agreement with the US but public pressure entailed that the agreement did not include investor-state dispute settlement provisions.

[142] For an informative, and humorous, analysis of the suit see https://www.youtube.com/watch?v=6UsHHOCH4q8 <accessed 16 April 2015>.

[143] For further details of the suit, see http://www.tni.org/briefing/nuclear-phase-out-put-test <accessed 8 April 2015>. The claim is for €1.4 billion to cover lost profits.

[144] For further details of the suit, see http://content.sierraclub.org/press-releases/2013/10/lone-pine-resources-files-outrageous-nafta-lawsuit-against-fracking-ban <accessed 8 April 2015>. The claim is for US $250 million to cover anticipated lost future profits.

[145] For further details of the suit, see https://www.citizen.org/documents/Pacific_Rim_Backgrounder1.pdf <accessed 8 April 2015>. The claim is for US $315 million to cover anticipated lost future profits.

was a participant.[146] The Pacific Rim arbitration[147] and the Lone Pine arbitration[148] involve Canadian-based businesses who have arranged their corporate structures so that there is a US corporation which is able to constitute the foreign investor which is able to bring suit under CAFTA and NAFTA respectively.[149]

The existence of bilateral investment treaties can contribute to the governance gap by providing a disincentive for host States to legislate to strengthen environmental and human rights standards. This is particularly the case where such agreements include 'stabilisation clauses', common in long-term investments in the extractive industries, which oblige the host State to freeze its existing regulatory structure for the length of the project, which may be for up to 50 years. In a report in 2008 Professor Ruggie drew attention to this in where he states:

> To attract foreign investment, host States offer protection through bilateral investment treaties and host government agreements. They promise to treat investors fairly, equitably, and without discrimination, and to make no unilateral changes to investment conditions. But investor protections have expanded with little regard to States' duties to protect, skewing the balance between the two. Consequently, host States can find it difficult to strengthen domestic social and environmental standards, including those related to human rights, without fear of foreign investor challenge, which can take place under binding international arbitration.[150]

A subsequent study for Professor Ruggie and the International Finance Corporation noted:

---

[146]   See, further, discussion of the litigation in Chapter 2.

[147]   In December 2007, a subsidiary of Pacific Rim Mining Corp based in the Cayman Islands reincorporated in Nevada under the name Pac Rim Cayman LLC (Pac Rim) and this US subsidiary is the party bringing the suit under CAFTA, to which Canada is not a party.

[148]   The company bringing the suit has its headquarters in Calgary, but is incorporated in the US, so enabling it to proceed under NAFTA against Canada as a foreign investor. Until September of 2010, Lone Pine Resources had been a wholly owned subsidiary of a US company, Forest Oil Corporation. In September 2010, Lone Pine Resources became incorporated under the laws of the State of Delaware and after completion of an initial public offering on 1 June 2011 the company became a stand-alone corporate entity. In November 2012 the Delaware company commenced suit under NAFTA.

[149]   For further details of this strategy, see Richard G. Dearden and Wendy J. Wagner *Bilateral Investment Treaty Considerations in Structuring Natural Resource Investments* February 2013 http://www.gowlings.com/Knowledge Centre/article.asp?pubID=2776 <accessed 8 April 2015>.

[150]   A/HRC/8/5 7 April 2008 [34].

135. The results of this study suggest that investors and governments continue to conclude investment contracts in which they agree to exempt the investor from – or compensate the investor for the costs of – the application of new laws. Further, it is clear that in a number of cases the stabilization clauses are in fact drafted in a way that may allow the investor to avoid compliance with, or seek compensation for compliance with, laws designed to promote environmental, social, or human rights goals. Assuming the validity of using social and environmental laws as a surrogate for human rights, it is possible to infer further that some stabilization clauses in modern contracts may negatively impact the host state's implementation of its human rights obligations.

136. In the sample from this study, the stabilization clauses in non-OECD countries are more likely than those in OECD countries to limit the application of new social and environmental laws to the investments.[151]

The effect of BITs on State regulatory competence has led some States to give notice of withdrawal from their BITs. South Africa's Black Economic Empowerment policy gave rise to claims from investors in Luxembourg and Italy in 2007 claiming it amounted to an expropriation of their mineral rights. This has led to South Africa progressively terminating its BITs to avoid investor-state arbitration proceedings claiming compensation for economic expropriation.[152] In 2013 it gave notice of termination of its BITs with the UK, the Netherlands, Belgium and Germany. In March 2014 Indonesia terminated its BIT with the Netherlands, the start of a process by which it will withdraw from all its BITs. However, many BITs contain 'survival clauses' which mean that for a period of ten to 15 years after termination their provisions will continue to apply to investments made while the treaty was in force.

---

[151] *Stabilization Clauses and Human Rights.* A research project conducted for IFC and the United Nations Special Representative of the Secretary-General on Business and Human Rights 27 May 2009.

[152] Such a claim was brought in 2007 by investors from Luxembourg and Italy, arguing that South Africa's Mining and Petroleum Resources Development Act (MPRDA) contained provisions that expropriated their mineral rights. http://hsfnotes.com/arbitration/2013/08/21/south-africa-terminates-its-bilateral-investment-treaty-with-spain-second-bit-terminated-as-part-of-south-africas-planned-review-of-its-investment-treaties/ <accessed 7 March 2015>. See, too, https://www.dlapiper.com/en/uk/insights/publications/2014/12/international-arbitration-newsletter-q4-2014/challenging-the-status-quo/ <accessed 14 April 2015>.

2. Suing in the US (1): Jurisdiction

The first hurdle for the plaintiff wishing to bring a transnational tort claim against a TNC in the US will be establishing jurisdiction in one of the federal courts of the US or in a state court. Litigation is expensive in the US. There is no legal aid for plaintiffs, but suits against TNCs are funded either through the contingency fee basis, under which plaintiffs will not pay lawyers' fees but will agree to allow their lawyers to recover a percentage of any amount ultimately awarded or settled, or through lawyers acting pro bono.

1. ESTABLISHING JURISDICTION IN THE FEDERAL COURTS

Article III (2) of the US Constitution defines the jurisdiction of the federal courts as follows:

> The judicial power shall extend to all cases, in law and equity, arising under this Constitution, the laws of the United States, and treaties made, or which shall be made, under their authority; to all cases affecting ambassadors, other public ministers and consuls; to all cases of admiralty and maritime jurisdiction; to controversies to which the United States shall be a party; to controversies between two or more states; between a state and citizens of another state; between citizens of different states; between citizens of the same state claiming lands under grants of different states, and between a state, or the citizens thereof, and foreign states, citizens or subjects.

There are two main ways in which a tort claim may be brought in the federal courts. The first is under 28 USC s. 1332, which allows claims to be brought before the federal courts in 'diversity cases'. These are claims involving 'controversies between ... citizens of different states' where the amount claimed exceeds \$75,000.[1] Complete diversity of all plaintiffs and all defendants is required, and is determined at the time the action is

---

[1]   Diversity jurisdiction will not exist where one or more of the co-plaintiffs is a US citizen, nor will it exist where the plaintiffs are Stateless.

brought. With a corporation, citizenship is determined by the place of incorporation or the location of its principal place of business.[2] The law applied in a diversity case is determined by the choice of law rules of the state in which the action was filed.[3] Second, a claim may be brought under 28 USC s. 1350 under the Alien Tort Statute.[4] Third, a claim may be brought under 28 USC § 1331 which gives federal courts jurisdiction over matters arising under the Constitution and federal laws.

A. Service of Proceedings

The defendant may be served where it is present in the jurisdiction or where it submits to jurisdiction by agreement. It may also be served out of the jurisdiction pursuant to the 'long arm' provisions of the state in which proceedings are commenced. Such provisions must conform with the requirements of 'due process' stipulated in the fifth and 14th amendments of the US Constitution.[5] Service may be based on the

---

[2] In *Doe v. Exxon Mobil Corporation*, WL 4746256 (DDC) (2014) there was no complete diversity as regards one of the defendants, an Indonesian subsidiary of Exxon's which was initially incorporated in Delaware but was reincorporated in the Cayman Islands, prior to the filing of the suit. The defendant was dismissed under Rule 21 of the Federal Rule of Civil Procedure which allows the court to dismiss parties whose presence in the litigation destroys jurisdiction, so-called 'jurisdictional spoilers'.

[3] *Erie Railroad Co v. Tompkins*, (1938) 304 US 64, 58 S Ct 817, 82 L Ed 1188.

[4] Claims under the ATS may be brought only in the federal courts, although this does not preclude bringing a parallel claim on the same facts, but pleaded in tort, before a state court. This dual approach was adopted by the plaintiffs in the *Unocal* litigation.

[5] The fifth amendment provides:

No person shall be held to answer for a capital, or otherwise infamous crime, unless on a presentment or indictment of a grand jury, except in cases arising in the land or naval forces, or in the militia, when in actual service in time of war or public danger; nor shall any person be subject for the same offense to be twice put in jeopardy of life or limb; nor shall be compelled in any criminal case to be a witness against himself, nor be deprived of life, liberty, or property, without due process of law; nor shall private property be taken for public use, without just compensation.

The 14th amendment provides:

All persons born or naturalized in the United States, and subject to the jurisdiction thereof, are citizens of the United States and of the state wherein they reside. No state shall make or enforce any law which shall abridge the privileges or immunities of citizens of the United States; nor shall any state

defendant's presence within the jurisdiction, its domicile within the jurisdiction, or its consent to the service of proceedings. Where none of these requirements are satisfied, the defendant may be served if it has dealings or affiliations with the forum jurisdiction which make it reasonable to require it to defend a lawsuit there. It is, therefore, possible to serve proceedings on a foreign defendant by reason of its contacts with the US forum. For this reason, several ATS cases, such as *Kiobe v. Royal Dutch Petroleum Co*;[6] *Sarei v. Rio Tinto*;[7] and *Presbyterian Church of Sudan v. Talisman Energy*,[8] have been brought against foreign corporate defendants, the so-called 'foreign cubed' cases.

In *International Shoe Co v. Washington*[9] the US Supreme Court set out four principles to assess whether or not there existed minimum contacts to justify subjecting the defendant to the jurisdiction of the forum. First, jurisdiction is permissible when the defendant's activity in the forum is continuous and systematic and the cause of action is related to that activity. Secondly, sporadic or casual activity of the defendant in the forum does not justify assertion of jurisdiction on a cause of action unrelated to that forum activity. Thirdly a court may assert jurisdiction over a defendant whose continuous activities in the forum are unrelated to the cause of action sued upon when the defendant's contacts are sufficiently substantial and of such a nature as to make the state's assertion of jurisdiction reasonable. This is known as 'general jurisdiction'. Fourthly, even a defendant whose activity in the forum is sporadic, or consists only of a single act, may be subject to the jurisdiction of the forum's courts when the cause of action arises out of that activity or act. This is known as 'specific jurisdiction'.[10]

Most cases against corporate defendants have involved assertion of general jurisdiction through service on some entity within the jurisdiction that is connected in some way with the defendant. This has been the means by which 'foreign cubed' cases have come before the federal

---

deprive any person of life, liberty, or property, without due process of law; nor deny to any person within its jurisdiction the equal protection of the laws.

   [6]   621 F 3d 111 (2d Cir 2010). 133 S Ct 1659 (2013).

   [7]   221 F Supp 2d 1116 (CD Cal 2002).

   [8]   244 F Supp 2d 289 (SDNY 2003). 582 F 3d 244 (2d Cir 2009).

   [9]   *International Shoe Co. v. Washington*, 326 US 310, 66 S Ct 154, 90 L Ed 95 (1945).

   [10]   Dismissal for lack of personal jurisdiction falls under Fed R Civ P 12(b)(2), under which the plaintiff bears the burden of establishing a *prima facie* case that the court has personal jurisdiction over a defendant.

courts. An example is *Wiwa v. Royal Dutch Petroleum Co*,[11] a companion suit to *Kiobel*.[12] The ATS claim alleged that Shell Nigeria, under the direction of the defendants, Royal Dutch, a Netherlands corporation, and Shell Transport, an English holding company, had instigated, orchestrated, planned and facilitated human rights abuses by the Nigerian government in suppressing opposition to oil exploration and development in the Ogoni region. The validity of service on the defendants depended on whether the defendants had been 'present' in New York through their Investment Relations Office (IRO) which was run by Mr Grapsi. The Second Circuit held that the IRO's activities in the jurisdiction had been sufficiently important to justify a finding of agency.[13]

The nature of general jurisdiction has recently been reviewed on two occasions by the Supreme Court, and these are likely to be as significant in limiting 'foreign cubed' cases coming before the federal courts as the Supreme Court's decision in *Kiobel* on the extra-territorial reach of the ATS. In 2011 *Goodyear Dunlop Tires Operations, SA v. Brown*,[14] the Supreme Court addressed the distinction between general or all-purpose jurisdiction, and specific or conduct-linked jurisdiction. It held that a court may assert jurisdiction over a foreign corporation 'to hear any and all claims against [it]' only when the corporation's affiliations with the state in which suit is brought were so constant and pervasive 'as to render

---

[11] 226 F 3d (2d Cir 2000).

[12] In *Kiobel v. Royal Dutch Petroleum Co*, 02 Civ 7618 (KMW) (HBP), Slip op. (SDNY June 21, 2010), an attempt was made to join the Shell Petroleum Development Company of Nigeria (SPDC), a Shell Nigerian subsidiary which was to prove unsuccessful as there were insufficient contacts between the subsidiary and the US.

[13] See, too, *Presbyterian Church of Sudan v. Talisman Energy*, 244 F Supp 2d 289 (SDNY 2003). A similar analysis was applied there by Judge Schwarz, in finding that the Canadian defendant could be served in New York because of significant operations conducted for it there by its wholly owned subsidiary. However, in contrast, in *Doe v. Unocal*, *(1998)* 27 F Supp 2d 1174 (CD Cal 1998). Aff'd 248 F 3d 915. (9th Cir 2001), Judge Paez held that neither specific nor general jurisdiction could be asserted against Total SA, a French corporation that was part of the consortium involved in the Yadana project. Total SA had no direct contacts with the US beyond the listing of its stock on various exchanges and promoting sales of stock in the US and its contract with Unocal, a Californian corporation, was an insufficient basis for specific jurisdiction, as it was a contract made out of the jurisdiction, in respect of oil from the Yadana project that would not go to the US. Nor could due process as regards 'general jurisdiction' be established through the presence in California of Total's subsidiary corporations.

[14] 564 US (2011) 131 S Ct 2846.

[it] essentially at home in the forum State.' The Supreme Court noted that, 'For an individual, the paradigm forum for the exercise of general jurisdiction is the individual's domicile; for a corporation, it is an equivalent place, one in which the corporation is fairly regarded as at home.'[15] The claim arose from a bus accident outside Paris that killed two boys from North Carolina and the boys' parents brought a wrongful-death suit in North Carolina state court alleging that the bus's tyre was defectively manufactured. As well as suing the parent corporation, Goodyear, an Ohio corporation, the plaintiffs also sued Goodyear's Turkish, French, and Luxembourgian subsidiaries which manufactured tyres for sale in Europe and Asia, a small percentage of which were distributed in North Carolina. The Supreme Court reversed the finding of the North Carolina Court of Appeals held that this rendered the subsidiaries amenable to the general jurisdiction of North Carolina courts. Placing a product into 'the stream of commerce' did not warrant a determination that there was general jurisdiction over the defendants who were not 'essentially at home' in North Carolina.

The second claim, decided in January 2014, was *Daimler AG v. Bauman*[16] which arose out of an allegation that during Argentina's 1976–83 'Dirty War,' Daimler's Argentinian subsidiary, Mercedes-Benz Argentina (MB Argentina) had collaborated with the Argentinian security forces to kidnap, detain, torture, and kill certain Argentinian workers. Jurisdiction was based on the California contacts of Mercedes-Benz USA, LLC (MBUSA), a Daimler subsidiary incorporated in Delaware with its principal place of business in New Jersey.[17] MBUSA distributed Daimler-manufactured vehicles to independent dealerships throughout the US, including California. The Ninth Circuit imputed MBUSA's California contacts[18] to Daimler on an agency theory[19] whereby a subsidiary would be the agent of the parent corporation where it 'performs services that are sufficiently important to the foreign corporation that if it did not

---

[15]   Ibid., 2851 (citing Brilmayer et al., 'A General Look at General Juris-diction', 66 *Texas L. Rev.* 721, 728 (1988)).

[16]   571 US (2014), 134 S Ct 746.

[17]   Daimler was sued pursuant to California's long-arm statute, under which California state courts may exercise personal jurisdiction 'on any basis not inconsistent with the Constitution of this state or of the United States.' Cal Civ Proc Code Ann §410.10 (West 2004).

[18]   Which were assumed to be sufficient to make MBUSA 'at home' in California, a point not challenged by the defendant.

[19]   The district court had held that Daimler's own contacts with California were, by themselves, too sporadic to justify the exercise of general jurisdiction and this was not challenged on appeal.

have a representative to perform them, the corporation's own officials would undertake to perform substantially similar services.'[20] On this basis, the Ninth Circuit found that there was general jurisdiction given the importance of MBUSA's services to Daimler, given Daimler's hypothetical readiness to perform those services itself if MBUSA did not exist.[21] However, the Supreme Court reversed. Even if the subsidiary, MBUSA, was at home in California and its contacts there could be imputed to its parent, Daimler, it was necessary for Daimler to be 'at home' in California. Given its slim contacts with that state, this was not the case. The Supreme Court rejected the plaintiffs' argument that general jurisdiction could be exercised in every state in which a corporation 'engages in a substantial, continuous, and systematic course of business.'[22] Neither Daimler nor MBUSA was incorporated in California, nor did either corporation have its principal place of business there.

The effect of the two decisions is to make it very unlikely to serve a foreign defendant through a branch or subsidiary in the US, as happened in *Wiwa*, on grounds of general jurisdiction. Only if the defendant corporation can be regarded as 'essentially at home' in the state in which suit is brought will there be general jurisdiction. This, *Kiobel* apart, would be sufficient to close down future 'foreign cubed' ATS suits.

2. PRUDENTIAL GROUNDS OF ABSTENTION

Having established jurisdiction against the defendant in the US, the plaintiff must be prepared to resist a challenge to jurisdiction which can be on one or more of the following grounds. These are judge-made rules which constitute the so-called 'prudential limitations' on the jurisdiction conferred on the federal courts by Article III of the US Constitution. These are: *forum non conveniens*; sovereign immunity; indispensible parties; act of state; political question; comity; foreign affairs doctrine; suits by non-resident aliens, other than under the ATS. Success in dismissing the case on these non-merits grounds will mean the case will not be heard in the US and has therefore become the principal battleground for transnational tort claims in the US. These grounds of abstention, other than some form of *forum non conveniens*, do not apply to claims brought before a state court.

---

[20] 644 F 3d, at 920 (quoting *Doe v. Unocal Corp*, 248 F 3d 915, 928 (9th Cir 2001)).

[21] The plaintiffs had never asserted specific jurisdiction.

[22] Brief for Respondents 16–17, and nn. 7–8.

Donald Earl Childress III has recorded that between 2007 and 2012 the average dismissal rate on grounds of *forum non conveniens* in reported and unreported cases involving foreign plaintiffs was 62 per cent, with an average of 78.5 per cent recognising foreign law as an important factor in dismissal.[23] A study of claims under the ATS by Michael Goldhaber shows that of 167 suits against corporate defendants between 1980–2012, 17 suits have settled, four proceeded to trial and 99 were dismissed of which five were on grounds of *forum non conveniens*, three on grounds of political question, two on grounds of sovereign immunity, and one on grounds of state secrets.

A.   *Forum Non Conveniens*

Once a plaintiff has managed to commence proceedings against the defendant in a US forum, it faces the prospect of the defendant applying for the case to be dismissed[24] on grounds of *forum non conveniens*.[25] In 1946 the Supreme Court in *Gulf Oil Corp v. Gilbert* set out the principles that should be applied to the issue of *forum non conveniens* in federal courts.[26] These principles are also generally, but not universally, applied in the state courts.[27] The defendant must first establish that there exists an adequate alternative forum. Once this has been established, the court should then undertake a balancing exercise involving two factors. First, there are the private interests of litigants, principally the ease and cost of access to documents and witnesses. In most litigation against multi-national parent corporations, these factors will weigh heavily in favour of dismissal of the suit. Secondly, there are the public interest factors, such

---

[23]   'The Search for a Convenient Forum in Transnational Cases', 53 *Virginia Journal of International Law* 157. (2012).

[24]   Unlike the position in the UK, *forum non conveniens* results in dismissal of the suit, rather than a stay, so once granted there is no possibility of the case coming back before the US court.

[25]   *Forum non conveniens* is a non-merits ground for dismissal and a district court may dismiss a case on this ground without first determining that it has jurisdiction over the cause (subject-matter jurisdiction) and the parties (personal jurisdiction) whether it has subject-matter and personal jurisdiction. *Sinochem Int'l Co Ltd v. Malaysia Int'l Shipping Corp*, 549 US 422, 429 (2007).

[26]   *Gulf Oil Corp v. Gilbert*, 330 US 501, 508–9, 67 S Ct 839, 843-44, 91 L Ed 1055 (1947).

[27]   However, this has not invariably been the case. In *Dow Chemicals v. Castro Alfaro*, 786 SW 2d 674 (S Ct Tex 1990) the Supreme Court of Texas held that *forum non conveniens* formed no part of the law of Texas. Legislation was subsequently introduced to reverse this position.

as the interest of the forum state, the burden on the courts, and notions of judicial comity.

In 1981 in *Piper Aircraft v. Reyno*[28] these principles were applied for the first time to a claim involving foreign plaintiffs and where the wrong complained of had occurred outside the US. The Court added a gloss to the *Gilbert* principles by suggesting that little deference should be given to the plaintiff's choice of forum in a US court in such circumstances. In *Wiwa* the Circuit Court for the Second Circuit noted that, 'While any plaintiff's selection of a forum is entitled to deference, that deference increases as the plaintiff's ties to the forum increase'. This was because '[t]he greater the plaintiff's ties to the plaintiff's chosen forum, the more likely it is that the plaintiff would be inconvenienced by a requirement to bring the claim in a foreign jurisdiction'. For these purposes, the plaintiffs only needed to be US residents, and did not also have to be resident in the Southern District of New York where they had filed suit.[29]

Forum non conveniens operates whether the claim is a tort claim brought in the federal courts under diversity jurisdiction or for violations of the law of nations under the ATS. In *Wiwa*[30] the Second Circuit reversed the District Court's dismissal on grounds of *forum non conveniens* in favour of the courts of the UK and remanded the case to the District Court for a more careful examination of the *forum non conveniens* factors. It stated that in passing the Torture Victims Protection Act 1991 (TVPA), 'Congress has expressed a policy of US law favoring the adjudication of such suits in US courts.' However TVPA has not nullified 'or even significantly diminished' the doctrine of *forum non conveniens*.

> The statute has, however, communicated a policy that such suits should not be facilely dismissed on the assumption that the ostensibly foreign controversy is not our business. The TVPA in our view expresses a policy favoring our courts' exercise of the jurisdiction conferred by the ATS in cases of torture unless the defendant has fully met the burden of showing that the *Gilbert* factors tilt strongly in favour of trial in the foreign forum.[31]

---

[28] *Piper Aircraft v. Reyno*, 454 US 235 (1981).

[29] A foreign plaintiff will be treated in the same way where there is a treaty between the US and the country of the foreign plaintiff which accords its nationals access to US courts equivalent to that provided to US citizens. ATS claims may also be treated in the same way.

[30] *Wiwa v. Royal Dutch Petroleum Co*, note 11 above.

[31] 226 F 3d 888 (2nd Cir 2000) 106.

Subsequently, in both *Flores v. SPCC*[32] and *Aguinda v. Texaco Inc*
(Aguinda)[33] it has been held that ATS claims enjoy no special immunity
from the effects of the doctrine. The statement in *Wiwa* is really no more
than a caution against 'facile' dismissals on the ground of the foreign
nature of the controversy and a reminder that where torture is involved,
the US does have a public interest in hearing the case. However, that
interest is still capable of being outweighed by other factors in the case
that point to the dismissal of the case in favour of the courts of the
alternative forum.

Identifying an available alternative forum

Before the court begins to weigh the private and public interests in favour
of dismissal, it must first be satisfied of the adequacy of the courts in the
alternative forum. This will usually be the place of the plaintiff's
residence, or the place where the wrong was committed. In *Bank of
Credit and Commerce International (Overseas) Ltd v. State Bank of
Pakistan*[34] it was said that an alternative forum is generally regarded as
adequate when: (1) the defendant is subject to the service of process
there[35] and; (2) the forum permits litigation of the subject-matter of the
dispute.

As regards the first requirement, a stay will only be granted where the
defendant agrees to accept the jurisdiction of the alternative forum,
although it can delay giving such agreement to the time of the hearing.
This was one of three conditions which Judge Keenan attached to the
stay of the New York tort proceedings arising out of the Bhopal disaster
in *In re Union Carbide Corp Gas Plant Disaster at Bhopal (Union
Carbide)*.[36] Judge Keenan also required that Union Carbide agree to
honour the judgment of the Indian courts, and to use US discovery rules
in the Indian proceedings. In 1987 the Second Circuit upheld Judge

---

[32]   *Flores v. SPCC*, 253 F Supp 2d 510 (SDNY 2002). Aff'd 343 F.3d 140
(2d Cir 2003).
[33]   *Aguinda v. Texaco Inc*, 142 F Supp 2d 534 (SDNY 2001), aff'd 303 F 3d
470 (2d Cir 2002).
[34]   *Bank of Credit and Commerce International (Overseas) Ltd v. State Bank
of Pakistan*, 273 F 3d 242, 246 (2d Cir 2001).
[35]   All defendants must be amenable to process in the alternative forum for it
to be regarded as an available alternative forum. In *Doe v. Exxon Mobil
Corporation*, note 2 above, [18], one of the defendants, Exxon specifically
denied that it was amenable to process in Indonesia and therefore the district
court could not dismiss on grounds of *forum non conveniens*.
[36]   *In re: Union Carbide Corp Gas Plant Disaster*, F Supp 842 (SDNY
1986).

Keenan's stay but lifted the last two conditions.[37] Courts may also condition the dismissal on the defendant agreeing to waive any statute of limitations' defence in the alternative forum and to agree to satisfy any final judgment of the alternative forum. In *Carijano v. Occidental Petroleum Corp* the Ninth Circuit overturned the District Court's dismissal of a mass tort claim finding that it had abused its discretion by failing to impose conditions on its dismissal that were warranted by facts in the record showing justifiable reasons to doubt the defendant's full cooperation in the foreign forum.[38]

As regards the second requirement, there are various reasons why a claim may not be litigated in the alternative forum: the type of claim brought before the US forum would not be cognisable in the alternative forum;[39] the plaintiffs may be subject to reduced legal rights in the alternative forum by reason of their religion;[40] evidence of corruption in the alternative forum that is so pervasive that it will prove practically impossible for the claim to be litigated there. However, a failure of the courts of the alternative forum to provide for punitive damages,[41] or the

---

[37] In 1987 the Second Circuit upheld Judge Keenan's stay but lifted these two conditions, 809 F 2d 195 (2d Cir 1987).

[38] 643 F 3d 1216 (9th Cir 2011). The claims arose out of alleged pollution in Peru during the US defendant's operation of oil extraction until 2000 when it sold its interest. Questions were raised about what assets might be available in Peru to satisfy any ultimate judgment there. Judge Wardlaw stated [17]:

Because the district court did not require Occidental to agree that any Peruvian judgment could be enforced against it in the United States, or anywhere else it held assets, as a condition for dismissal, Occidental remains free to attack any Peruvian judgment on due process grounds under California's foreign judgments statute. The private factor of the enforceability of judgments thus weighs against dismissal.

The case was closed in a sealed proceeding on September 16, 2013 and on 5 March 2015 it was announced that a settlement had been reached.

[39] In *Sarei v. Rio Tinto*, note 7 above, Judge Morrow held that Australia was not an adequate forum because the Australian courts did not recognise independent tort claims based on violations of customary international law. A similar finding was made in *Presbyterian Church of Sudan v. Talisman Energy (Talisman)*, 244 F Supp 2d 289 (SDNY 2003) by reason of doubts as to whether an action based on violations on the law of nations could be brought before the courts of Canada.

[40] In *Talisman* the plaintiffs produced evidence showing that the system of Islamic law in place in Sudan accorded greatly reduced legal rights to non-Muslims.

[41] *Flores v. SPCC*, note 32 above. Peru was held to be an alternative forum, even though its courts did not award punitive damages.

absence of any class action procedure in the alternative forum[42] does not mean that the alternative forum is inadequate.

Balancing the private interest and public interest factors

Having established that there exists an adequate alternative forum, the court will now proceed to weigh the private and public interests in favour of retaining or vacating the suit in the US jurisdiction. Under *Gulf Oil Corp v. Gilbert*,[43] the 'private interest' factors include: the relative ease of access to sources of proof; the cost of obtaining the attendance of willing witnesses; the availability of compulsory process for obtaining attendance of unwilling witnesses; the possibility of viewing the relevant premises, and other such practical concerns. However, in most tort suits against a multinational corporation where the tort occurred outside the US, these factors will weigh heavily against the retention of the suit, even if the plaintiff's choice of US forum is not subject to the 'lesser deference' discount set out in *Piper Aircraft v. Reyno*.

As regards the public interest factors the Supreme Court in *Piper Aircraft v. Reyno* synthesised the *Gulf Oil Corp v. Gilbert* factors as follows: the local interest in having localised controversies decided at home; the interest in having the trial of a diversity case in a forum that is at home with the law that must govern the action; the avoidance of unnecessary problems in conflicts of law or in the application of foreign law; the unfairness of burdening citizens in an unrelated jurisdiction with jury duty. In considering these factors the court would need to strike a balance between the interests of the home and host States. In the two major environmental tort cases, *Union Carbide*, arising out of the Bhopal gas explosion in December 1984, and *Aguinda*, arising out of allegations of pollution in Ecuador from an oil pipeline, the interest of the host State in regulating activity within its jurisdiction has been held to outweigh the interest of the US as the home State.

However, these competing interests are likely to be weighed differently where the claim involves alleged complicity of a subsidiary corporation in human rights abuses by a foreign government. In *Wiwa v. Royal Dutch Petroleum Co*[44] the Second Circuit observed that *forum non conveniens* dismissals in torture cases were a huge setback to the plaintiff. The plaintiff would need to start again in the courts of another nation and obtain not only new counsel but also, maybe, a new residence. The

---

42   *Aguinda*, note 33 above and *Sarei v. Rio Tinto*, note 7 above.
43   *Gulf Oil Corp v. Gilbert*, note 26 above.
44   *Wiwa v. Royal Dutch Petroleum Co*, note 11 above.

plaintiff could generally not sue in the place where the abuse had taken place, due to dangers it would face in returning there. It would face difficulty in suing in the courts of other nations who would find such suits time-consuming, burdensome, and difficult to administer. Such suits might also embarrass the government of the forum in which suit had been brought. 'Finally, because characteristically neither the plaintiff nor the defendant are ostensibly either protected by the domestic law of the forum nations, courts often regard such suits as "not our business".'

In *Wiwa* the defendants argued that England was the alternative forum, rather than Nigeria, where the alleged abuses had occurred. The Second Circuit found that England was not an obviously better suited foreign forum than the courts of New York. There was no substantial physical evidence that was difficult or expensive to transport as in *Union Carbide*. For a non-party witness, trial in New York would not be significantly more inconvenient than a trial in England.[45] The extra costs of shipping documents and flying witnesses to New York, rather than London, would not be excessively burdensome, given the defendant's vast resources. Any inconvenience would be fully counter-balanced by the cost and inconvenience to the plaintiff of having to reinstigate litigation in England, especially given their minimal resources compared to the defendants' vast ones. The court noted that the plaintiffs had obtained excellent pro bono counsel in New York and had no guarantee of getting equivalent representation in London without incurring substantial expenses. There was also the cost to a US resident plaintiff of being uprooted to England for the duration of the trial and being required to replicate in England the large amounts of time, money and energy already expended on the suit in the US.

This removes a powerful private interest factor in favour of the defendant, the desirability of having the claim heard in the jurisdiction in which the alleged wrong occurred. On the facts of *Wiwa* the inconvenience to the defendant in litigating in New York as opposed to London would be considerably less than in cases in such as *Union Carbide* where the alternative forum would be the jurisdiction in which the disaster occurred and in which the bulk of the evidence was located, including evidence that would be difficult or impossible to remove to another jurisdiction. There was also a US public interest in such cases evidenced by the fact that in 1991 Congress saw fit to pass the TVPA.

---

[45]   The second defendant was in any case, Dutch. The fact that Nigeria was a member of the Commonwealth was of no particular significance. These factors argued equally against dismissal in favour of the courts of the Netherlands.

In ATS cases a powerful argument against a stay on grounds of *forum non conveniens* is that the plaintiffs should not be required to bring their claim in the place where the violations occurred due to the risks likely to be faced by them in litigating there, given the nature of their claims. For this reason in *Wiwa* the plaintiffs could not be expected to litigate in Nigeria, and a similar decision was reached in *Sarei v. Rio Tinto*.[46] Their claim arose out of allegations of human rights abuses during the ten-year civil uprising on Bougainville. The plaintiffs objected to Papua New Guinea as an alternative forum because of the risk to their personal safety if they were forced to litigate there. Given that the plaintiffs and other Bougainvilleans had been engaged in a civil war with the Papua New Guinea government for the past ten years, this was a well-founded apprehension.[47] Although Papua New Guinea was still an available alternative jurisdiction, this factor tipped the balance of private interest factors in favour of retention of the suit, together with the doubts raised as to whether the plaintiffs would be able to identify counsel willing to represent them on a contingency fee basis in Papua New Guinea.[48]

Where the plaintiff's claim is wholly based on an environmental tort, without any accompanying allegations of other human rights abuses, their chances of resisting the defendant's application to dismiss on grounds of *forum non conveniens* will be slim. Cases such as *Union Carbide* and *Aguinda* are predicated on the lack of a strong US connection, both as regards private and public interest factors, to counteract the strong pull of the jurisdiction in which the claim arose. In particular, the choice of law analysis adopted pointed to the application of the law of the country in which the tort was committed, India and Ecuador respectively.[49] This factor will be absent in an ATS case as there will be no choice of law

---

[46]   See, note 7 above.

[47]   In *Doe I v. Exxon Mobil Corp*, 393 F Supp 2d 20 (D DC 2005) this factor prevented tort claims from being stayed on the ground of *forum non conveniens*.

[48]   A similar argument was raised in *Aldana v. Del Monte Fresh Produce*, 578 F 3d 1283 (11th Cir 2009) but the Eleventh Circuit upheld the district court's decision to dismiss the ATS claim for *forum non conveniens*, noting that both the state court's and the district court's *forum non conveniens* dismissals contained an express proviso that the appellants' motions would be reconsidered if there is ever any indication that they might be required to return to Guatemala.

[49]   Where foreign tort claims have been made against US defendants, some courts have factored into the public interest analysis the US public interest in having the claims heard in the defendant's home state. See, *Dow Chemicals v. Castro Alfaro*, note 27 above. A similar analysis as regards choice of US law was adopted in a tort case arising out of allegations of complicity of a US corporation in violations of human rights by security forces in Indonesia. *Doe v. Exxon Corp*

issues before the US court, as the governing law will be customary international law, as delimited by *Sosa*.[50]

B. Foreign Sovereign Immunity

Immunity of foreign states

Foreign States, their agencies and instrumentalities, are immune from suit under the Foreign Sovereign Immunity Act 28 USC, s. 1330, ss 1602–11. In *Argentine Republic v. Amerada Hess Shipping Corporation* the Supreme Court held that the Act pre-empted claims under the ATS and accordingly claims against a foreign State would not be possible under the statute.[51] In 1992 the Ninth Circuit held that this remained the position even where the claims was based on the violation of *jus cogens* norms, such as the prohibition on torture.[52]

An exception to foreign sovereign immunity exists when the action is based on: (1) a commercial activity carried on in the US by the foreign State or; (2) an act performed in the US in connection with a commercial activity of the foreign State elsewhere or; (3) an act outside the US in connection with a commercial activity of the foreign State elsewhere and that act causes a direct effect in the US. In *Doe v. Unocal Corporation*[53] the plaintiffs argued that the Burmese government and MOGE, a State corporation, fell within the third exception. Judge Lew rejected this argument. First, the pipeline may have been a commercial activity, but the human rights violations associated with it were not because they derived from abuse of the State's police powers and, as such, were peculiarly sovereign in nature. Secondly, there were no direct effects in the US. The plaintiffs had provided no allegation to support their allegation that the violations reduced the cost of the project and so gave Unocal an unfair competitive advantage in the US gas market. The Ninth Circuit upheld the decision but on the second ground only.[54] They held that Judge Lew had been in error on the first ground of his decision in that an abuse of police powers in connection with commercial activity

---

(Plaintiffs' motion to amend complaint). Not Reported in F.Supp.2d, 2 March 2006, WL 516744 (DDC), Rev'd on appeal.

[50] However, conflicts of law issues may still arise on issues of vicarious liability as in *In Re South African Apartheid Litigation*, 617 F Supp 2d 228, (SD NY 2009).

[51] 488 U.S. 428 (1989).

[52] *Siderman de Blake v. Republic of Argentina*, 965 F 2d 699 (9th Cir 1992).

[53] 110 F Supp 2d 1294 (CD Cal 2000).

[54] 395 F 3d 932 (2002), 957–8.

could fall within the second and third exceptions. The words of these exceptions were 'in connection with' rather than 'based on'.

Immunity of officials of foreign States

The position as regards claims against foreign officials was clarified in 2010 in *Yousuf v. Samantar* when the Supreme Court held that a foreign official did not fall under either s. 1603(a) which referred to a 'foreign state' or section 1603(b) which referred to an 'agency or instrumentality of a foreign state'.[55] Instead, the immunity of State officials is determined by the common law, under which there are two types of immunity. First, there is Head of State immunity which is an absolute immunity for serving Heads of State and applies even against *jus cogens* claims.[56] Second there is conduct-based immunity of foreign officials arising out of their official acts when in office. In *Samantar* the Fourth Circuit held that this may not be asserted in respect of private acts or acts involving an alleged violation of a *jus cogens* norm of international law or the commission of an international crime – such as torture in *Filartiga*.[57] This *jus cogens* restriction of conduct-based immunity has not been accepted by the Second Circuit in *Matar v. Dichter*[58] nor outside the US.[59]

Immunity of the US and its officials

Claims against the US and its officials are also liable to be met with a plea of sovereign immunity unless it has been waived. In *Al-Aulaqi v. Obama* there was held to be no waiver in a suit against the US President in respect of a threatened extra-territorial killing of the father of a US citizen.[60] The Federal Tort Claims Act 1948 (the FTCA) provides a

---

55   560 US 305, 130 SCt 2278 (2010).

56   *Tachiona v. Mugabe*, 169 F Supp 2d 259 (SDNY 2001).

57   *Yousuf v. Samantar* 699 F 3d 763 (C A 4 (Va) 2012).

58   563 F 3d 9 (2nd Cir 2009). Claims were brought under the ATS and TVPA against the former Israeli intelligence chief in connection with the bombing of Gaza in 2002.

59   See, the UK decisions in *Al-Adsani v. Kuwait*, 103 ILR 420 (QB 1995), *aff'd Al-Adsani v. Kuwait*, 107 ILR 536 (CA 1996), as regards a civil claim against a State, and *Jones v. Saudi Arabia* [2006] UKHL 26, [2007] 1 AC 270, as regards a civil claim against a State official, and in the related decisions of the European Court of Human Rights. *Al Adsani v. UK* (2002) 34 EHRR 11, *Case of Jones and Others v. UK*, (Applications nos. 34356/06 and 40528/06) Judgment 14 January 2014.

60   727 F Supp 2d 1 (DDC 2010). The ATS 'itself does not provide a waiver of sovereign immunity,' *Industria Panificadora, S.A. v. United States*, 957 F 2d

waiver of immunity that permits private parties to sue the US in a federal court for most torts committed by persons acting on behalf of the US.[61] This limited waiver of sovereign immunity is subject to the 'combat exception' contained in 28 US Code § 2680(j) withdrawing the waiver in respect of, 'Any claim arising out of the combatant activities of the military or naval forces, or the Coast Guard, during time of war.'

The Act and the 'combat exception' waiver has been held to cover the activities of private military contractors when they are integrated into combatant activities over which the military retained command authority. This was decided in *Saleh v. Titan Corporation Ltd*[62] where the Court of Appeals for the District of Columbia held that both state law tort claims and claims under the ATS were pre-empted by the combat exception to the waiver of US sovereign immunity conferred by the FTCA. The claim was made by Iraqi nationals, or their widows, who sued two American companies that had been contracted to provide interrogators or interpreters for the US military at Abu Ghraib. The claim arose out of the alleged infliction of abusive treatment or torture while plaintiffs, or their decedents, were detained by US military forces there during the US occupation of Iraq. In 1988 in *Boyle v. United Technologies Corporation*,[63] the Supreme Court had held that State law tort claims could be pre-empted when (a) they implicated uniquely federal interests and (b) there was a significant conflict between those interests and State law. The FTCA exceptions to the waiver of sovereign immunity determined that the conflict was significant and measured the boundaries of the conflict.[64] Accordingly, the majority held that during wartime, where a private

---

886, 887 (DC Cir 1992); accord *Sanchez-Espinoza v. Reagan*, 770 F 2d 202, 207 (DC Cir 1985).

[61]   (June 25, 1948, ch. 646, Title IV, 62 Stat. 982, '28 USC Pt.VI Ch.171' and 28 USC § 1346(b)).

[62]   580 F 3d 1(CADC 2009). The district court had held that private military contractors would be immune only when the contractor's 'employees were acting under the direct command and exclusive operational control of the military chain of command.' *Ibrahim v. Titan Corporation*, 556 F Supp. 2d 1 (DDC. 2007).

[63]   487 US 500 (1988).

[64]   In *Boyle* the Supreme Court had refrained from deciding whether the government contractor could rely on sovereign immunity and in *Saleh* the Court of Appeals also made no finding on this point.

service contractor is integrated into combatant activities over which the military retains command authority, a tort claim arising out of the contractor's engagement in such activities shall be preempted.[65]

Private companies that are sued in connection with their activities with the US government and its agencies may also escape liability by relying on the State secrets doctrine. In *Mohamed v. Jeppesen Dataplan* the plaintiff sued a private company in connection with providing the aircraft by which the plaintiff was taken to US-run detention centres in countries such as Morocco, Egypt, Afghanistan, as part of the extraordinary rendition programme of the CIA.[66] The Ninth Circuit affirmed the District Court's dismissal of action brought under the ATS. The US government's valid assertion of the State secrets privilege warranted dismissal of the litigation under *United States v. Reynolds*,[67] because there was no feasible way to litigate the defendant's alleged liability without creating an unjustifiable risk of divulging State secrets.

Claims by inmates of Guantanamo Bay against US authorities are pre-empted by the Military Commissions Act.[68] Claims by inmates in respect of post-clearance deprivations are pre-empted by the FTCA.[69]

---

[65] The same finding was made in another case against a private military contractor on similar facts in *Al Shimari v. CACI Int'l, Inc*, 658 F 3d 413, 415 (4th Cir 2011). The plaintiffs in that case then filed a petition for rehearing of the case en banc, which was granted, 679 F 3d 205, 212 (4th Cir 2012). On May 11, 2012, the Fourth Circuit then vacated its earlier holding and remanded the case back to the district court to proceed with discovery and summary judgment. In doing so, it did not address whether or not the contractors should prevail on the merits. The district court then dismissed the ATS claims in the light of the Supreme Court's finding in *Kiobel* and held that the tort claims were subject to Iraqi law and were barred thereby. The Fourth Circuit has now reversed the dismissal of the ATS claims and remanded the case back to the district court to determine whether the claims should be dismissed as raising non-justiciable political questions, 2014 WL 2922840 (CA 4 (Va)).

[66] En Banc Order: 614 F 3d 1070 (9th Cir 2010).

[67] 345 US 1, 11 (1953).

[68] *Allaithi v. Rumsfeld*, 753 F 3d 1327 (CADC 2014). A provision of the Military Commissions Act (MCA) stripping courts of jurisdiction over any action other than an application for habeas corpus brought by an alien enemy combatant against the US relating to detention, treatment, trial, or conditions of confinement was held to be severable from invalidated MCA provision stripping courts of jurisdiction over habeas proceedings brought by alien enemy combatants. *Hamad v. Gates*, 732 F 3d 990 (9th Cir 2013).

[69] *Janko v. Gates* 741 F 3d 136 (CA DC 2014).

C. Indispensible Parties

Rule 19 of the Federal Rules of Civil Procedure provides that in certain circumstances proceedings may be dismissed because of the absence of an indispensable party. It must first be established that the absent party is necessary and unable to be joined. Section (a) provides that a party is 'necessary' if '(1) in the person's absence complete relief cannot be accorded among those already parties or (2) the person claims an interest relating to the subject matter of the action'. If an absent party is 'necessary', section (b) then directs the court to consider 'whether in equity and good conscience the action should proceed among the parties before it, or should be dismissed'. In considering this issue the court should balance: the prejudice to any party or to the absent party; whether relief could be shaped to lessen that prejudice; whether an adequate remedy, even if not complete, could be awarded without the absent party; whether there existed an alternative forum. If the necessary party is immune, its immunity may be a compelling factor and dispense with the need to undertake a balancing inquiry.

In *Doe v. Unocal Corporation*[70] the defendants argued that the case should be dismissed because of the absence of SLORC and MOGE, who, as organs of the Burmese State, would have been entitled to rely on the doctrine of foreign sovereign immunity. This is an argument that could be raised in all ATS claims based on aiding and abetting, as the primary violation will have been committed by State organs. Judge Paez rejected this plea. If the plaintiffs could show that the defendants were joint tortfeasors, complete relief might still be awarded among the remaining parties.[71]

D. Act of State

The doctrine of Act of State precludes a US court from adjudicating claims which would require the court to invalidate a foreign sovereign's official acts within its own territory – so leading to interference with executive branch foreign policy decisions. The defendant bears the initial burden of showing that the claim involves: an official act of a foreign sovereign; performed within its own territory, and; a claim for relief that

---

[70]   963 F Supp 880 (CD Cal 1997).

[71]   A similar finding was made in *Doe v. Exxon Mobil Corporation*, note 2 above. where the Indonesian subsidiary's presence in the suit destroyed diversity and it was dismissed from the suit, but the proceedings against the other defendants, as alleged joint tortfeasors, were able to continue in its absence.

would require the court to declare the foreign sovereign's act invalid. The doctrine was considered in *Sarei v. Rio Tinto*.[72] The ATS claims were brought by plaintiffs from the island of Bougainville and related to violations of international law allegedly committed by the defendant and the Papua New Guinea Defence Force (the PNGDF) during the ten-year civil uprising on the island. Judge Morrow held that the doctrine did not cover the claims in respect of war crimes and crimes against humanity. These were allegedly illegal acts and could not be regarded as the official act of a foreign sovereign. Although orders given by military commanders during wartime were commonly viewed as official sovereign acts, the actions of the PNGDF referred to by the plaintiffs did not involve acts of legitimate warfare. In contrast the claims for racial discrimination, and environmental torts involving breaches of UNCLOS, did fall within the doctrine.[73]

If the defendant discharges the initial burden, the court will then consider four factors in determining whether or not to abstain from jurisdiction on this ground.[74] First, was there any international consensus regarding the claims in issue? In *Unocal* the Ninth Circuit held that an allegation of a breach of a *jus cogens* norm[75] would weigh against the application of the doctrine as such norms were, by definition, supported by a high degree of international consensus.[76] Secondly, what would the impact of any judgment be on US foreign relations? The submission of a Statement of Interest by the US State Department is likely to be accorded very great weight, but the courts are not bound to follow it. Thirdly, had there been a change in government since the time of the alleged abuses? In *Unocal* where there had been no change of government since the abuses were committed, the Ninth Circuit held that this factor on its own was not enough to justify dismissal of the claims. Fourthly, was the conduct in question undertaken for a public purpose? Applying these

---

[72]   *Sarei v. Rio Tinto*, note 7 above.

[73]   The Ninth Circuit reversed this finding as regards the claims for racial discrimination, as these involved the violation of a *jus cogens* norm and such acts could not be regarded as the official acts of a sovereign. *Sarei v. Rio Tinto*, F 3d 2006 WL 2242146 (9th Cir Aug 7, 2006).

[74]   The first three factors were set out in *Sabbatino*, 376 US 398 (S Ct 1964) at 428. The fourth was set out in *Liu v. Republic of China*, 892 F 2d 1419 (9th Cir 1989).

[75]   A *jus cogens* norm of customary international law is one that has received such widespread acceptance among the community of nations that it binds even those States which are persistent objectors to its application.

[76]   *Unocal (2002). John Doe I v. Unocal Corporation*, 395 F 3d 932 (9th Cir 2002).

tests, claims involving allegations of complicity in international crimes by state actors will not be dismissed on grounds of act of state, but may well be dismissed under the next ground of abstention, that of 'political question'.

E. Political Question

The political question doctrine derives from the US constitutional principles of the separation of powers, so as to restrict the justiciability of certain issues. However, not every case implicating US foreign relations involves a non-justiciable political question.[77] The doctrine involves an examination of the following six factors set out in *Baker v. Carr*.[78]

(1) the existence of any textually demonstrable constitutional commitment of the issue to a coordinate political department;
(2) a lack of judicially discoverable and manageable standards for resolving the claims;
(3) the impossibility of deciding without an initial, non-judicial, policy determination;
(4) the impossibility of a court's undertaking independent resolution without expressing lack of the respect for the coordinate branches of government;
(5) an unusual need for unquestioning adherence to a political decision already made;
(6) the potentiality of embarrassment from multifarious pronouncements by various departments on one question.

The political question doctrine has resulted in dismissals of ATS suits on the grounds that the claims involve allegations which implead the conduct of a foreign government and implicate the foreign policy objectives of the executive. Unlike the act of State doctrine, the courts have been prepared to dismiss suits where there are allegations of complicity in international crimes by foreign State actors. In *Doe I v. Exxon Mobil Corporation*[79] ATS claims had been made against the

---

[77] *Klinghoffer v. SNC Achille Lauro*, 937 F 2d 44,49 (2d Cir 1991) where it was stated that, 'The fact that the issues… arise in a politically charged context does not convert what is essentially an ordinary tort suit into a non-justiciable political question … .'

[78] *Baker v. Carr*, 369 US 186, 210, 82 S Ct 691, 7 L Ed 2d 663 (1962).

[79] *Doe I v. Exxon Mobil Corporation*, 393 F Supp 2d 20 (DDC 2005). Aff'd 473 F 3d 345 (CADC 2007).

defendant in respect of its activities in Aceh, Indonesia, and its alleged complicity in human rights abuses that were said to have been carried out there by the Indonesian security forces. The Bush administration submitted a Statement of Interest arguing that continuance of the suit would hinder US actions against Islamic terrorists in Aceh. Judge Oberdorfer held that the Statement of Interest justified the dismissal of the ATS claims. *Sosa* meant that courts needed to be aware of the 'collateral consequences' of interfering with US foreign relations that the use of the statute entailed. Proper concern for Indonesia's sovereignty required the dismissal of claims against the Indonesian corporate defendant in which Pertamina, Indonesia's state-owned oil and gas company, had a 55 per cent holding. However, the claims could still proceed as transitory tort claims against the US corporate defendants, subject to the condition that discovery be conducted in such a manner so as to avoid intrusion into Indonesian sovereignty.

In *Corrie v. Caterpillar Inc*[80] an action was brought against manufacturer of bulldozers by family members of individuals killed or injured when Israeli Defence Forces (IDF) used bulldozers, which were paid for by US, to demolish homes in Palestinian Territories. The decisive factor was that sales of the bulldozers to Israel were paid for by the executive branch of the US pursuant to a congressionally enacted programme calling for executive discretion as to what lies in the foreign policy and national security interests of the US. Allowing the action to proceed would necessarily require the judiciary to question the executive's decision to grant extensive military aid to Israel. Similarly, in *Du Daobin v. Cisco Systems*[81] the claim was dismissed because adjudication of this question would entail the judiciary determining whether the US rules and regulations surrounding the export of products to China were sound.[82]

However, the submission of a Statement of Interest did not lead to dismissal on this ground in *In re South African Apartheid Litigation*.[83] Claims under the ATS were brought alleging that various corporations had aided and abetted violations of international law by the South African government during apartheid. Both the US and South Africa argued that the case should not proceed on the grounds that it would interfere with the policy embodied by the Truth and Reconciliation

---

[80]   503 F 3d 974 (9th Cir 2007).

[81]   Case 8:11-cv-01538-PJM Document 63 Filed 02/24/14

[82]   The claim arose out of the transfer of computer technology to China, which was not prohibited by US trade regulations, which was then allegedly used to perpetrate violations of human rights on its citizens.

[83]   See note 50 above, 284–5.

Commission in respect of conduct committed under the apartheid regime. Judge Schiendlin held that the claims would not be dismissed on grounds of political question. In her view the first three *Baker* factors would almost never apply in an ATS action. Such suits are committed to the judiciary by statute and utilise standards set by universally recognised norms of customary international law. As regards the fourth to sixth factors these would be relevant only if judicial resolution of a question would contradict prior decisions taken by a political branch in those limited contexts where such contradiction would seriously interfere with important governmental interests. The claims brought did not challenge the political branches' policy of constructive engagement with apartheid-era South Africa or aim to hold defendants liable for engaging in commerce consistent with those policies. To survive this motion to dismiss, plaintiffs must plausibly allege that defendants 'substantially assisted' violations of the law of nations and knew that their assistance would be substantial. Merely engaging in commerce would be insufficient. The Ninth Circuit's decision in *Corrie* was distinguishable because there the US Government paid for the bulldozers, and finding Caterpillar liable for the sales would necessarily require the judiciary to question the executive's decision to grant extensive military aid to Israel. The resolution of the present case did not require the court to pass judgment on the US policy of constructive engagement with apartheid era South Africa.

F. Comity

The doctrine of comity is based on 'the recognition which one nation allows within its territory to the legislative, executive or judicial acts of another nation'.[84] The doctrine gives the courts a discretion to defer to the laws or interests of a foreign country and decline to exercise the jurisdiction they otherwise have. The Restatement Third at s. 403(2) sets out seven factors relating to this issue.[85] These considerations will

---

[84] *Hilton v. Guyot*, 159 US 113, at 164, 16 S Ct 139, 40 L Ed 95 (1895).

[85]

  (a) the link of the activity to the territory of the regulating state, i.e., the extent to which the activity takes place within the territory, or has substantial, direct, and foreseeable effect upon or in the territory; (b) the connections, such as nationality, residence, or economic activity, between the regulating state and the person principally responsible for the activity to be regulated, or between that state and those whom the regulation is designed to protect; (c) the character of the activity to be regulated, the importance of regulation to the regulating state, the extent to which other

generally overlap with those that are relevant to the public interest analysis under *forum non conveniens*.

G. The Foreign Affairs Doctrine

The doctrine involves two related doctrines, 'field pre-emption' and 'conflict pre-emption.'[86] Field pre-emption considers whether state law intrudes upon federal prerogatives in the field of foreign policy, even in the absence of a conflict with any federal act having the power of law, and conflict pre-emption considers whether State law interferes with an affirmative federal act. In *Galvis Mujica v. Occidental Petroleum Corporation*[87] State law tort claims were dismissed on ground of conflict pre-emption. The claim arose out of bombings that took place in Santo Domingo, Colombia, in December 1998 which, it was alleged, had been carried out to provide security for the defendant in protecting its pipeline, with the defendants having assisted the Colombian military in carrying out the raid. The district Court dismissed on this ground finding that California was found to have only a weak interest in the claims, which was overcome by the policy concerns stated in the State Department's Supplemental Statement of Interest to the effect that to preserve its diplomatic relationship with Colombia, it preferred the case to be

---

states regulate such activities, and the degree to which the desirability of such regulation is generally accepted; (d) the existence of justified expectations that might be protected or hurt by the regulation; (e) the importance of the regulation to the international political, legal, or economic system; (f) the extent to which the regulation is consistent with the traditions of the international system; (g) the extent to which another state may have an interest in regulating the activity; and (h) the likelihood of conflict with regulation by another state.

The seventh factor has been held to amount to a prerequisite to dismissal on this ground. *Hartford Fire Ins Co v. California*, 509 US 764, 113 S Ct 2891, 125 L Ed 2d 612 (1993), applied in *Sarei v. Rio Tinto*, note 7 above. However, in *Mujica v. Airsca*, 771 F 3d 580 (9th Cir 2014) the Ninth Circuit has held that proof of a true conflict is not a prerequisite when considering *adjudicatory* comity, as opposed to *prescriptive* comity is at where a party claims that it is subject to conflicting regulatory schemes that apply extraterritorially.

[86]   *American Insurance Association v. Garamendi*, 539 US 396 (2003).

[87]   381 F Supp 2d 1164, (CD Cal 2005). The district court had declined to dismiss on grounds of act of state and political question and had previously found that Colombia was not an available forum and declined to dismiss on grounds of *forum non conveniens* and comity, 381 F Supp 2d 1134 (CD Cal 2005).

handled exclusively by the Colombian justice system, a position confirmed by a Statement of Interest by Colombia. The Ninth Circuit
subsequently affirmed the dismissal, but on grounds of comity.[88] In
contrast, in, *Doe v. Exxon Mobil Corporation*,[89] a State law tort claim
subject to Indonesian law was held not to involve any foreign policy
concerns.

H.   Suits by Non-resident Aliens

In *Berlin Democratic Club*, a general rule was propounded that non-
resident aliens have no standing to sue in US courts, subject to three
exceptions: (1) where the *res* is in the US; (2) where the statutory scheme
allows suits by non-resident aliens; and (3) where a non-resident alien is
seized abroad and transported back to the US for prosecution.[90] In *Doe v.
Exxon*[91] claims were made against a US corporation in connection with
allegations of human rights abuses committed by the Indonesian military
that were providing security for it in the Arun natural gas field in Aceh.
Judge Royce C. Lamberth dismissed the proceedings on the basis of the
general rule in *Berlin Democratic Club*, as the plaintiffs had failed to
show they came within any of the three exceptions. This ruling would
block off most tort claims brought by foreign plaintiffs, a diversity
jurisdiction equivalent to *Kiobel*. However, in 2011 the Court of Appeals
for the District of Columbia reversed the dismissal of the non-federal tort
claims, holding that prudential standing is to be analysed on a case-by-
case basis based on the zone of interests of the law applicable to the
plaintiff's cause of action, and that no special rule applies to claims by
non-resident aliens.[92]

---

[88]   See note 85 above.

[89]   See note 2 above.

[90]   410 F Supp 144, 152 (DCDC 1976). Since then US courts have also
allowed non-resident aliens to bring certain constitutional challenges, as in
Boumediene v. Bush, US 128 S Ct 2229, 2262, (2008) in which it was held that
detainees at Guantanamo Bay 'are entitled to the privilege of habeas corpus to
challenge the legality of their detention'.

[91]   658 F Supp 2d 131 (2009).

[92]   654 F 3d 11 (CADC 2011).

3. SUING IN STATE COURTS

Another avenue of suit would be for plaintiffs to bring their claims in tort, or under customary international law,[93] in the state courts. 'Transitory' tort claims, that is, claims involving torts committed outside the US, may be brought before the state courts, provided the actions impugned would constitute a tort in the foreign state.[94] A claim can be advanced on two fronts, as an ATS claim in the district courts and as a tort claim in either the district courts or in state courts. A tort claim in a state court may be joined to parallel proceedings in the district courts under section 1367. This provides that: 'the district courts shall have supplemental jurisdiction over all other claims that are so related to claims in the action within such original jurisdiction that they form part of the same case or controversy under Article III of the United States Constitution.' In *Doe v. Unocal* Judge Paez held that the district court had jurisdiction over plaintiffs' supplemental state law tort claims.[95] When Judge Lew dismissed the ATS claim in 2000[96] he declined to retain jurisdiction over these claims which were then refiled in the California Superior Court.[97]

---

[93]   See, Julian G. Ku, *Customary International Law in State Courts*, 42 VA. J. INT'L L. 265 (2001); Curtis A. Bradley and Jack Goldsmith, *Customary International Law as Federal Common Law: A Critique of the Modern Position*, 110 HARV. L. REV. 815, 834, 870 (1997) Paul Hoffman and Beth Stephens *International Human Rights Cases Under State Law and in State Courts* 3 U.C. IRVINE L. REV. 9, 13–15 (2013). In *Namba v. McCourt*, 204 P 2d 569, 579 (Or 1949), the Supreme Court of Oregon held that a statute preventing Japanese Americans from owning agricultural land violated the Fourteenth Amendment, looking in part to the human rights provisions of the UN Charter to support its decision. "When our nation signed the Charter of the United Nations we thereby became bound to the following principles (Article 55c, and see Article 56): 'Universal respect for, and observance of human rights and fundamental freedoms for all without distinction as to race, sex, language, or religion.'"

[94]   *Cuba R. Co. v. Crosby*, 222 US 473, 479 (1912) where the Supreme Court explained '[t]he only justification for allowing a party to recover when the cause of action arose in another civilized jurisdiction is a well founded belief that it was a cause of action in that place..'

[95]   963 F Supp 880 (CD Cal1997).

[96]   *Doe v. Unocal*, 110 F Supp 2d 1294, 1307 (CD Cal 2000).

[97]   USC 28 Section 1441(c) provides that:

The district courts may decline to exercise supplemental jurisdiction over a claim under subsection

(a) if –

 (1) the claim raises a novel or complex issue of State law,

Claims in state courts are not subject to dismissal on grounds of act of State, comity, or political question, as these are all grounds for dismissal of proceedings in the district courts. They may also not be subject to dismissal on grounds of *forum non conveniens* depending on the state in question. Removal of proceedings in state courts to federal courts is possible under 28 USC s. 1441 but para (b)(2) provides, 'A civil action otherwise removable solely on the basis of the jurisdiction under section 1332 (a) of this title may not be removed if any of the parties in interest properly joined and served as defendants is a citizen of the State in which such action is brought.'[98]

There should therefore be no removal where the ground of federal jurisdiction is the diversity of the parties, as where a US defendant is sued by a foreign plaintiff in a state court. However, removal is possible where the case raises issues implicating the foreign relations of the US, in which case the citizenship of the parties is immaterial. Federal question jurisdiction will exist if the plaintiffs' suit 'arises under' the 'Constitution, treaties or laws of the United States.'[99] In general, a case 'arises under' federal law if federal law creates the cause of action, or if a substantial disputed issue of federal law is a necessary element of a state law claim. In some cases, removal has been ordered when the state suit implicated foreign policy concerns. The foreign affairs doctrine provides that state laws may not intrude 'into the field of foreign affairs which the Constitution entrusts to the President and the Congress.'[100] An example is *Torres v. Southern Peru Corporation.*[101] Peruvian plaintiffs sued a US defendant mining company (SPCC) in Texas state court alleging that they had been harmed by the SPCC's copper smelting operations conducted in Peru. The Fifth Circuit removed the suit, concluding that '[t]his action therefore strikes not only at vital economic

---

    (2) the claim substantially predominates over the claim or claims over which the district court has original jurisdiction,
    (3) the district court has dismissed all claims over which it has original jurisdiction, or
    (4) in exceptional circumstances, there are other compelling reasons for declining jurisdiction.

[98] Section 1441 (f) provides: 'The court to which a civil action is removed under this section is not precluded from hearing and determining any claim in such civil action because the State court from which such civil action is removed did not have jurisdiction over that claim.'

[99] 28 USC § 1331

[100] *Zschernig v. Miller*, 389 US 429, 432, 88 SCt 664, 19 L Ed 2d 683 (1968).

[101] 113 F 3d 540, 542–3 (5th Cir 1997).

interests but also at Peru's sovereign interests by seeking damages for activities and policies in which the government actively has been engaged.' The Fifth Circuit noted the importance of the mining industry to Peru's economy and its government's participation in some of the activities that formed the basis of the suit. Because the plaintiffs' complaint implicated foreign-policy concerns, the court found that substantial questions of federal common law were raised, which made the exercise of federal-question jurisdiction appropriate.[102] Following removal to the federal courts, the case was subsequently dismissed on grounds of *forum non conveniens*. However, the Ninth Circuit in *Patrickson v. Dole Food Co*[103] refused to remand a state law tort suit involving alleged harm sustained by Latin American banana workers from exposure to a toxic pesticide. The common law of foreign relations would become an issue only when, and if, it was raised as a defence and the plaintiff's case did not require the court to evaluate any act of state or apply any principle of international law.

4. ENFORCEMENT OF FOREIGN JUDGMENTS

The fate of most foreign mass tort claims brought against US TNCs has been to be dismissed on the grounds of *forum non conveniens*. The dismissal will be conditional on the US defendant agreeing to accept service of proceedings in the alternative forum, and may also be subject to a condition that the defendants agree to the enforcement in the US of any final judgment in the alternative forum. This condition is not applied when the suit is dismissed on the other prudential grounds of abstention. A study by Professor David Robertson of the University of Texas School of Law, *Forum non conveniens in America and England: 'A rather fantastic fiction'* attempted to discover the subsequent history of each reported transnational case dismissed under *forum non conveniens* from *Gulf Oil v. Gilbert* in 1946 to the end of 1984. He found that less than 4 per cent of cases dismissed under the doctrine of *forum non conveniens* ever reach trial in a foreign court. Data was received on 55 personal

---

[102]   This analysis was adopted by the Eleventh Circuit in *Pacheco de Perez v. AT&T Co*, 139 F 3d 1368, (11th Cir 1998), although it found that a suit against a US company in respect of a gas explosion in Venezuela did not impinge on US foreign relations, and that Venezuela's interests in the action was not enough to confer federal jurisdiction over the case.

[103]   251 F 3d 795, 803 (9th Cir 2001), *aff'd in part on other grounds*, 538 US 468 (2003).

injury cases and 30 commercial cases. Only one of the personal injury cases and two of the commercial cases actually reached trial in a foreign court. The rate of refiling in the alternative forum has increased from 2000 onwards with an increasing number of dismissed US suits being heard in alternative fora in courts in Latin America which have become more receptive to hearing such suits,[104] which has led to led to the phrase 'forum shopper's remorse.'

Enforcement of such foreign judgments is another matter. The defendant will probably have ensured the removal of its assets from that jurisdiction prior to any final judgment, leaving the victorious plaintiffs to seek enforcement of the judgment in the US. They may, however, find that the US court refuses to recognise their judgment because of concerns about the judicial process in the foreign forum. States which were hostile to plaintiffs at the time of the initial *forum non conveniens* application before the US courts, may have changed to being hostile to defendants, as seems to have been the case with Ecuador and Nicaragua in the enforcement proceedings discussed below.

In the US the recognition and enforcement of foreign money judgements is governed by the law of the state in which recognition is sought. Most states have codified the Uniform Foreign Money Judgment Recognition Act of 1962 or have adopted the Uniform Foreign-Country Money Judgments Recognition Act of 2005. Florida's recognition Act is based on the 1962 Recognition Act. Under both Acts there are three mandatory grounds for non-recognition: (1) the judgment was rendered under a system which does not provide impartial tribunals or procedures compatible with the requirements of due process of law; (2) the foreign court did not have personal jurisdiction over the defendant; or (3) the foreign court did not have jurisdiction over the subject matter. There are a further six discretionary grounds in both Acts: (1) the defendant in the proceedings in the foreign court did not receive notice of the proceedings in sufficient time to enable him to defend; (2) the judgment was obtained by fraud; (3) the [cause of action]... on which the judgment is based is repugnant to the public policy of this state; (4) the judgment conflicts with another final and conclusive judgment; (5) the proceeding in the foreign court was contrary to an agreement between the parties under which the dispute in question was to be settled otherwise than by proceedings in that court; or (6) in the case of jurisdiction based only on personal

---

[104]   See, M. Ryan Casey and Barrett Ristroph, 'Boomerang Litigation: How Convenient Is Forum Non Conveniens in Transnational Litigation?', 4 *Byu Int'l L. and Mgmt. Rev.* 21, 21 (2007).

service, the foreign court was a seriously inconvenient forum for the trial of the action. Christopher Whytock in *Forum Non Conveniens and Enforcement of Foreign Judgments* has shown how different standards regarding assessment by US courts of foreign courts in *forum non conveniens* dismissals[105] and applications for recognition of a foreign judgment have created an 'access-to-justice' gap.

> In summary, the forum non conveniens doctrine has a lenient, plaintiff-focused foreign judicial adequacy standard that US courts necessarily apply ex ante, whereas the judgment enforcement doctrine has a stricter, defendant-focused foreign judicial adequacy standard that US courts apply ex post. When these two doctrines are applied in the same dispute, they can interact in a way that produces a transnational access-to-justice gap. Specifically, a US court may deny a plaintiff access to the US legal system if the foreign judiciary is deemed adequate ex ante under the lenient standard, but then decline to give effect to a remedy obtained in the same foreign judiciary because it is deemed inadequate ex post under the stricter standard. A transnational access-to-justice gap may also arise if a suit is dismissed in favor of a foreign court on forum non conveniens grounds, but enforcement is denied on public policy or reciprocity grounds.[106]

Two high-profile sets of mass tort litigation by foreign plaintiffs against US TNCs illustrate the enforcement problems that faced down the line from a dismissal of US proceedings on grounds of *forum non conveniens*. Both sets of litigation involved widespread use of the media by the plaintiff's lawyers to publicise their claims, as a means of exerting pressure on the defendants, including the production of two films 'Crude' and 'Bananas'[107], the first of which was to prove the undoing of the plaintiffs' attempts to enforce their foreign judgment in the US.

---

[105]   Michael T. Lii, 'An Empirical Examination of the Adequate Alternative Forum in the Doctrine of Forum Non Conveniens,' 8 *Rich. J. Global L. and Bus.* 513, 526 tbls. 4 and 5 (2009), presents empirical study of published *forum non conveniens* decisions between 1982 and 2006, showing that courts deem alternative forums adequate 82 per cent of the time, and deny *forum non conveniens* motions on adequacy grounds only 18 per cent of the time.

[106]   Columbia Law Review Vol. 111 (2011), 1441, 1481. See, too, Jonathan C. Drimmer and Sarah R. Lamoree, 'Think Globally, Sue Locally: Trends and Out-of-Court Tactics in Transnational Tort Actions', 29 *Berkeley J. Int'l Law* 456 (2011).

[107]   The film was a 2009 documentary about the DBCP litigation in Nicaragua by Swedish director, Fredrik Gertten, who was sued for defamation by Dole after the film's screening at the Los Angeles film festival in June 2009. In 2010 a Los Angeles court found for Gertten which allowed the film to be released in the US. A subsequent film was released by Gertten in 2011, Big Boys Gone Bananas,

A. The Ecuador Oil Pollution Claims

The first piece of litigation is *Aguinda v. Texaco Inc* where claims arose out of environmental damage and personal injuries that were alleged to have arisen out of negligent management of oil pipelines in Ecuador in the 1960s and 1970s. The pipelines ran over land owned by the government of Ecuador and were operated by a consortium in which a fourth-tier subsidiary of Texaco, Tex-Pet, participated until 1992. Two class actions were brought against Texaco in New York, its home state. In 2001 Judge Rakoff dismissed the claims on grounds of *forum non conveniens*.[108] Texaco agreed to accept service in Ecuador and to waive any statute of limitations-based defences that might have accrued since the filing of the complaint in the US. Texaco also agreed to satisfy any judgments in favour of the plaintiffs, reserving its right to contest their validity only in the limited circumstances permitted by New York's Recognition of Foreign Country Money Judgments Act.

The case was then brought before the courts in Ecuador against Chevron who had acquired Texaco in 2001. The litigation was co-ordinated by a US lawyer, Steven Donziger. The case, now known as the 'Lago Agrio' case after the oil town at the centre of the alleged pollution, was now based on a violation of Article 19(2) of the Ecuadorian constitution creating a diffuse right to live in a healthy environment. The 1999 Environmental Management Act gave private individuals the standing to sue under the article. After proceedings were commenced in Ecuador, in 2007 Chevron removed all its assets from that jurisdiction. In 2009, Chevron, speaking through a spokesman, stated that Chevron intended to contest the judgment if Chevron lost. He said: 'We're going to fight this until hell freezes over. And then we'll fight it out on the ice.' Judgment was given against Chevron in 2011 for approximately $18 billion, including an award of punitive damages.[109]

---

about the lawsuit brought by Dole. The film is not to be confused with the 1971 film of that name by Woody Allen.

[108] F Supp 2D 534 (SDNY 2001), aff'd 3d 470 (2d Circuit, 2002).

[109] Chevron denied that there had been a merger with Texaco. In its final decision on the merits, the Nueva Loja court dismissed this defence and held that under art 17 of Ecuador's Corporations' Law (Ley de Compañías) Texaco and Chevron would both be jointly liable. In the event that Texaco and Chevron were still separate entities, the corporations' corporate veils could be lifted and they could be considered as a single entity for purposes of the trial. See *Aguinda v. Chevron Corp*, No. 002-2003 (Super Ct of Nueva Loja, Feb. 14, 2011), 11, 15.

True to its words, Chevron then moved heaven and earth to prevent enforcement of the judgment, aided by out-takes from Joe Berlinger's film, 'Crude', about the Lago Agrio litigation. A scene in the final cut showed Donziger and the plaintiffs' lawyers working with Carlos Beristain, a physician and psychologist, before the Ecuadorean court appointed him to serve as an independent expert for the environmental report in the case. Donziger asked for the scene to be cut, but Berlinger initially refused and the film was shown at Sundance with the scene included, although it was excised for the subsequent DVD release. Chevron's lawyers, Gibson, Dunn and Crutcher, picked up on the scene in the film shown at Sundance and obtained a court order against Berlinger ordering discovery of all the 500 hours of out-takes for the film. These then formed the basis for Chevron's application for a pre-emptive order denying enforcement in the US of any judgment in the Lago Agrio case. Judge Kaplan initially granted the order but was overruled by the Second Circuit.[110] In November 2013 the Court of Cassation in Ecuador upheld the judgment but reduced the damages to US\$9.51 million, allowing Chevron's appeal with regard to punitive damages. In March 2014 Judge Kaplan in the Southern District of New York Chevron held that Steve Donziger, the US lawyer who co-ordinated the litigation in Ecuador, and two of his Ecuadorean clients, had procured the Ecuador judgment by fraud,[111] and through violation of the The Racketeer Influenced and Corrupt Organisations Act (RICO),[112] and ordered that the defendants not be allowed to profit from that judgment in any way. The decision, which is being appealed, effectively prevents enforcement of the Ecuador judgment in the US.

The claimants have since sought to enforce the judgment in Argentina,[113] Brazil and Canada.[114] In Canada, Chevron argued that the Ontario

---

[110]   *Chevron Corp v. Donziger*, 768 F Supp 2d 581 (SDNY 2011); overruled *Chevron Corporation v. Naranjo*, 667 F 3d 232 (2d Cir 2012).

[111]   *Chevron Corp. v. Donziger*, 974 F Supp 2d 362 (SDNY 2014). Judge Kaplan found that the judgment had been secured by bribing a judge and ghostwriting court documents which involved violations of the Foreign Corrupt Practices Act and the Racketeer Influenced and Corrupt Organizations Act.

[112]   18 USC s 1962 (2002). The Statute was enacted to deal with organised crime.

[113]   In June 2013 Argentina's Supreme Court lifted a previous court order freezing Chevron's assets in Argentina. Enforcement proceedings are still continuing in Argentina.

[114]   It is possible that Chevron may soon have assets within Ecuador available for attachment in satisfaction of the judgment. Texaco had a long-standing dispute with Ecuador about the amount taken by the government under the

court had no jurisdiction to enforce a foreign judgment in a case where the claim had no real and substantial connection with Ontario. At first instance Brown J of the Superior Court of Justice rejected this argument and held that the Ontario court had jurisdiction to hear the action. However, he stayed the action on the basis that Chevron had no assets within the jurisdiction and there was no hope of piercing the veil of Chevron's 100 per cent owned Canadian subsidiary, Chevron Canada, and executing the judgment against its assets to satisfy the judgment against its ultimate parent. The Court of Appeal held that there was jurisdiction in the case in that in enforcing foreign judgments the focus of the 'real and substantial' test was solely on the foreign jurisdiction, Ecuador, and there was no further enquiry into the relationship between the dispute and the domestic Canadian court being asked to enforce the foreign judgment. The Court of Appeal then went on to hold that although Chevron Canada was entitled to dispute that its assets were exigible for the judgment debts of its ultimate parent, that argument was not availing at the jurisdictional stage of the enforcement proceedings and could be appropriately addressed after Chevron Canada had had the opportunity to file a defence. Accordingly, the stay of the enforcement proceedings was set aside. On 4 September 2015 the decision on jurisdiction was upheld by the Canadian Supreme Court, although this does not mean that the judgment will ultimately be enforced against Chevron Canada. Chevron is still free to argue against enforcement on the ground that a parent corporation is not enforceable against the assets of its subsidiary.[115]

Chevron's second line of attack has been to commence proceedings against Ecuador itself under the investor-state arbitration provisions of the 1993 US-Ecuador bi-lateral investment treaty, which entered into force in 1997. The arbitration is proceeding on two tracks. The first track is to do with the effect of the 1995 settlement between the government of Ecuador and Texaco and the type of claims subject to the settlement and whether the release extended to Chevron. The second track is to do with

---

original oil production sharing agreement set up in the 1970s. Chevron commenced arbitration through the Permanent Court of Arbitration in the Hague which ruled in its favour. Ecuador appealed through the Dutch courts. On September 26 2014 the Dutch Supreme Court ruled in Chevron's favour and ordered the government of Ecuador to pay Chevron $106 million plus interest.

[115] *Chevron Corp. v. Yaiguaje* (SCC 35682), available at http://www.canada-usblog.com/2015/09/04/supreme-court-of-canadas-decision-in-chevron-enforcement-of-ecuadorian-court-judgment-can-proceed/ <accessed 17 September 2015>.

alleged corruption in the Ecuadorean judiciary during the Lago Agrio case, and has yet to be decided.

In the first track of the arbitration Chevron sought a declaration: that Ecuador's actions had breached the US-Ecuador BIT, including its obligations to afford fair and equitable treatment, full protection and security, effective means of enforcing rights, and to observe obligations it entered into under the overall investment agreements; that enforcement of the Lago Agrio Judgment within or without Ecuador would be inconsistent with Ecuador's obligations under the Settlement Agreements, the BIT and international law; that the Lago Agrio Judgment was a nullity as a matter of international law. The source of their complaint was an agreement made between Ecuador and Tex-Pet, in 1995 releasing Tex-Pet from any diffuse claim for environmental harm under Article 19.2 in return for remediation measures to be undertaken by Tex-Pet. In September 2013 the tribunal made a partial award to this effect construing the agreement as extending to unnamed releasees, such as successors in title to Tex-Pet. The agreement, however, did not bar claims by private citizens in respect of loss or damage they had personally suffered as a result of the alleged pollution caused by the activities of the Consortium which had formed the basis of the initial US claims in *Aguinda* and *Jota.*

On 12 March 2015 the tribunal decided that some of the claims were individual claims and so not subject to the 1995 settlement agreement.[116] The case had been ambiguously pleaded, alleging relief of collective rights while being in the name of the individual plaintiffs in the US *Aguinda* proceedings, which were individual claims brought as a class action. The tribunal concluded that under the law of Ecuador a claim could be individual even if the remedy sought was one of environmental remediation for widespread environmental damage. The tribunal, therefore, concluded that the Lago Agrio pleadings contained some claims that were materially equivalent to the claims brought in *Aguinda* before the Second Circuit and these claims were not barred by the 1995 settlement agreement.

B.   The Nicaragua DBCP Claims

The second example is provided by the enforcement proceedings in respect of judgments in Nicaragua in two cases involving mass personal

---

[116]   http://business-humanrights.org/en/hague-tribunal-rules-for-ecuador-in-investment-arbitration-with-chevron-govt%E2%80%99s-settlement-with-firm-did-not-preclude-oil-pollution-case-by-ecuadorian-plaintiffs <accessed 5 April 2015>

injury claims by workers on banana plantations alleging injuries sustained in the 1970s and 1980s through handling of the pesticide dibromochloropropane (DBCP). A series of claims have come before the US courts arising out of the use of DBCP by US corporations in banana plantations in Costa Rica, Nicaragua, El Salvador, Ecuador, the Philippines, after its use within the US had been banned by the Environmental Protection Agency in the late 1970s. The claims alleged that workers on the plantations suffered injury, particularly male sterility, as a result of being required to handle DBCP. The initial battleground was that of *forum non conveniens* and in one early suit the plaintiffs obtained a ruling that the doctrine no longer formed part of the law of Texas.[117] Subsequently, Texas legislated to reinstate the doctrine and subsequent cases were dismissed on this ground.[118]

The next development was the passing of 'retaliatory legislation' in the alternative forum designed to make it unavailable and so block dismissal of US suits on grounds of *forum non conveniens*. The effect of such legislation was considered in *Martinez v. Dow Chemicals*.[119] The plaintiffs were agricultural workers in several different countries who claimed in respect of injuries sustained as a result of exposure to a pesticide manufactured by the defendants. Their claims before a Texas court were dismissed for *forum non conveniens*. They then attempted to recommence suit in Costa Rica, Honduras and the Philippines but found that retaliatory legislation had the effect of preventing their claims being heard there, given their decision to file suit first in the US. Judge Barbier held that in such circumstances their claims should not be dismissed on grounds of *forum non conveniens*.

Similar legislation was introduced in Nicaragua in late 2000 with Special Law 364 which was specifically directed at claims for DBCP injuries on banana plantations, with retrospective effect. The law contained various plaintiff-friendly provisions such as an irrefutable presumption of causation on presentation of medical test results as proof of injuries, a requirement that defendants put up a guarantee for approximately US$14.5 million, curtailed prospects of appeal, and the non-application of the statute of limitations. The law allowed defendants to opt out of Nicaraguan jurisdiction if they agreed to accept jurisdiction in the US courts. In one action under Special Law 364 on behalf of 201 plaintiffs, filed in Chinandega, Nicaragua in 2002, judgment was given in

---

[117] *Dow Chemicals v. Castro Alfaro*, note 27 above.
[118] *Delgado v. Shell Oil Co*, 890 F Supp 1324, 1362 (SD Tex 1995).
[119] *Martinez v. Dow Chemicals*, 219 F Supp 2d 719 (ED La 2002).

favour of 150 plaintiffs for a total of $97.4 million. The plaintiffs then sought recognition of the judgment in the US and the case ended up in Federal District Court for the Southern District of Florida.

Florida's recognition Act is based on the 1962 Recognition Act. And in *Osorio v. Dole Food Co* Judge Huck refused to recognise the Nicaraguan judgment on the first and third of the mandatory grounds, and also on the third discretionary grounds.[120] There was persuasive evidence of wide-spread direct political interference and judicial corruption in Nicaragua, based on the evidence regarding the operation of the Nicaraguan judicial system as a whole, and not the particulars of the case. Additionally the Nicaraguan court had no jurisdiction over the defendants. Special Law 364 requires the posting of a bond as a 'procedural prerequisite for being able to take part in the lawsuit,' and if defendants do not do so within ninety days, they 'must subject themselves unconditionally to the jurisdiction of the courts of the United States of America'. The defendants, Dole and Dow, had refused to post the bond, Judge Huck found that the defendants had 'effectively invoked their opt-out rights,' which divested the trial court of both personal and subject-matter jurisdiction. The plaintiffs claimed that Article 7 of Special Law 364 did not give defendants a right to opt out of Nicaragua's jurisdiction by refusing to make the deposits, but, rather, precluded them from arguing *forum non conveniens* if the plaintiffs decided to sue in the US. Judge Huck was also persuaded[121] by a dictum of the Ninth Circuit in *Dow Chemical v. Calderon*, that Article 7 'is most reasonably read to provide DBCP defendants with a right to elect jurisdiction'.[122] Finally, recognition of the judgment would be contrary to public policy because of Special Law 364's provisions as to bond and deposit requirements, minimum damages, irrefutable presumptions of knowledge and causation, abolition of statutes of limitations, and effective curtailment of appellate review.

On appeal, the Eleventh Circuit agreed with the district court that the Nicaraguan court lacked jurisdiction over the defendants; that the judgment was 'rendered under a system which does not provide … procedures compatible with the requirements of due process of law'; and that enforcing the Nicaraguan court's judgment would be repugnant to Florida public policy.[123] But the Eleventh Circuit declined to address the district court's finding that the Nicaraguan court's judgment could not be enforced because it 'was rendered under a system which does not provide

---

[120]   665 F. Supp 2d 1307 (SD Fla 2009),
[121]   Ibid., 1326.
[122]   *Dow Chem. v. Calderon*, 422 F 3d 827, 832–3 (9th Cir 2005).
[123]   635 F 3d 1277 (11th Cir 2011).

impartial tribunals' and declined to adopt the district court's holding on this question.

Further DBCP cases involving Nicaragua were brought against Dole before the Los Angeles County Superior Court in *Mejia v. Dole Food Co*, *Rivera v. Dole Food Co*, and *Tellez v. Dole Food Co*. The latter was designated a test case and proceeded to trial and in November 2007 the jury found for six of the 12 plaintiffs, awarding $5 million in damages, including $2.5 million in punitive damages against Dole, an award subsequently reduced to $1.58 million compensatory damages with the elimination of punitive damages. Subsequently, evidence came to light of widespread fraud in the plaintiff's evidence in the *Mejia* and *Rivera* suits, with claims being made on behalf of persons who had never been employed by Dole, while others had faked sterility. Judge Chaney stayed proceedings and in April 2009 after a three-day hearing dismissed the claims with prejudice, awarding costs to the defendants.[124] She noted:

> Because of the pervasive nature of the fraud that permeates the DBCP cases from Nicaragua, the Court questions the authenticity and reliability of any documentary evidence presented by plaintiffs that comes out of Nicaragua, and it has serious doubts about the bona fides of any plaintiff claiming to have been injured as a result of exposure to DBCP, while employed on a Nicaraguan banana plantation associated with Dole. Sadly, this means that if there are people who have been injured in Nicaragua due to DBCP exposure, it is extremely difficult if not impossible for them credibly to litigate their claims.[125]

In July 2010 Judge Chaney dismissed the *Tellez* suit for the same reasons.[126]

The allegations of fraud may tend to cloud the issue on the enforcement of the Chevron and Dole judgments. However, the public policy exception could render unenforceable a foreign judgment that is reached in an impeccable manner but which applies substantive law which the US court regards as incompatible with US standards. An example might be a foreign judgment under which a US parent corporation is held liable by applying a theory of single economic enterprise. In the Bhopal litigation

---

[124] *Mejia v. Dole* Case No.BD40049; Judgment available at *online.wsj.com/ public/resources/…/WSJ-Dole_Chaney_ruling.pdf* <accessed 8 April 2015>.

[125] Ibid., [8].

[126] In September 2012 Dole reached a final settlement of five DBCP suits brought in the US and 33 in Nicaragua with plaintiffs represented by Texas personal injury lawyers, Provost Umphrey. DBCP suits would continue against other defendants, including Dow, Shell, Occidental, Del Monte and Chiquita.

in India, Deo J in an unreported interlocutory judgment on 17 December 1987 awarded interim compensation of US$270 million, on the basis that Union Carbide would end up being found liable under *Rylands v. Fletcher*, and its liability, as a parent company, would be by virtue of the control it had over its subsidiary through its majority holding in it.[127] On 4 April 1988 Seth J in the Madhya Pradesh High Court upheld the interim award of damages, on the same grounds, but reduced the amount to US$195 million. On 14/15 February 1989, while its challenge to Seth J's decision was still pending before the Indian Supreme Court, Union Carbide settled with the Indian government for US$470 million. Had the case run its course in India, an ultimate judgment on this basis may well have proved unenforceable in the US on public policy grounds.

---

[127] Applying *DHN Food Distribution Ltd v. London Borough of Tower Hamlets*, [1976] 1 WLR 852, CA.

3. Suing in the US (2): The Alien Tort Statute 1789 and statutory causes of action

In this chapter we shall consider statutory provisions in the US which provide a cause of action in relation to conduct that violates international law. The first, and most famous provision, is the Alien Tort Statute 1789 (ATS) whose jurisdictional grant has been held to allow the development of a cause of action based on violations of a limited category of *jus cogens* norms of customary international law. The scope of the statute has recently been restricted by the Supreme Court's ruling in *Kiobel* that it does not have extra-territorial reach. Second, there is the Torture Victims Protection Act 1991 (TVPA) which gives a civil right of action to any national in respect of torture. Third, there are two statutory provisions which give US nationals civil rights of action in respect of injuries or death sustained as a result of terrorism. Fourth, there is a statutory right of action granted to the victims of human trafficking.

1. THE ALIEN TORT STATUTE 1789

The statute provides that: 'The district courts shall have original jurisdiction of any civil action by an alien for a tort only, committed in violation of the law of nations or a treaty of the United States.' The statute was probably enacted in response to the Marbois incident of 1784 involving verbal and physical assaults on the French Ambassador, Longchamps, by a French citizen. There was concern that a claim for a violation of the law of nations might not be admissible in the state courts, notwithstanding Congress's exhortation in 1781 that state courts entertain such claims. The Act lay dormant for nearly two centuries until 1980 when it was successfully invoked in a claim for damages in *Filartiga v. Pena-Irala*.[1] The plaintiff, the sister of a Peruvian who had been tortured in Peru, successfully invoked the Act to obtain an award of damages

---

[1]   *Filartiga v. Pena-Irala*, 630 F 2d 876 (2d Cir 1980).

against her brother's torturer, who was then living in Brooklyn. The decision in *Filartiga* has generated a flood of cases by aliens before the federal courts of the United States, in which claims for compensation against individuals have been based on alleged violations of international law.[2]

The ATS claims need to establish that there has been a 'violation of the laws of nations',[3] which has been construed as a reference to norms of customary international law, and may be challenged either on jurisdictional grounds or on grounds that the plaintiff has failed to state an arguable claim.[4] Most of the ATS jurisprudence arises out of these preliminary challenges by defendants, and only four cases have proceeded to trial. With a motion to dismiss for lack of subject matter under Rule 12(b)(1) it is for the plaintiff to establish jurisdiction by a preponderance of the evidence.[5] The court may consider materials outside the pleadings and should construe the complaint liberally in favour of the plaintiffs and accept all factual allegations as true. However, the court 'need not accept inferences drawn by the plaintiffs if those inferences are unsupported by facts alleged in the complaint; nor must the Court accept plaintiffs' legal conclusions'.[6] With a motion to dismiss for failure to state a claim under Rule 12(b)(6) a complaint must 'state a claim to relief that is plausible on its face'.[7] The plaintiff must plead sufficient factual content that allows a court to draw a 'reasonable

---

[2]   In 1991 the Torture Victims Protection Act took the ATS as its inspiration in creating a cause of action under US law where under 'color of law of any foreign nation' an individual was subject to torture or extra-judicial killing. The reference to an 'individual' meant that the cause of action created was also available to US citizens, and not, as is the case with the ATS, restricted to aliens.

[3]   A claim for a violation of a treaty of the US under the ATS will only be possible if the treaty is self-executing. In *Jogi v. Voges*, 425 F 3d 367 (7th Cir 2005) such a claim was advanced in relation to an alleged violation of art 36 of the Vienna Convention on Consular Relations (Vienna Convention), Apr. 24, 1963, 21 UST 77, TIAS No. 6820. The 7th Circuit subsequently reconsidered its opinion and decided not to rest subject-matter jurisdiction on the ATS, since it was unclear whether the treaty violation constituted a 'tort', but deciding that jurisdiction was secure under 28 USC § 1331, 480 F 3d 822 (7th Cir 2007).

[4]   In the *Unocal* litigation the defendants first challenged the claim on jurisdictional grounds in *Unocal (1997)*, 963 F Supp 880, and then applied for summary judgment in *Unocal (2000)*, 110 F Supp 2d 1294.

[5]   *Bradshaw v. Office of the Architect of the Capitol*, 856 F Supp 2d 126, 134 (DDC 2012).

[6]   *Speelman v. United States*, 461 F Supp 2d 71, 73 (DDC 2006).

[7]   *Ashcroft v. Iqbal*, 556 US at 677–8 (2009) (quoting *Bell Atlantic Corp. v. Twombly*, 550 US 544, 570 (2007). Under Federal Rule of Civil Procedure

inference' of liability. A court must accept as true all of the factual allegations contained in the complaint and 'draw all reasonable inferences in the plaintiff's favor'.[8] The plaintiff need not provide 'detailed factual allegations', but must provide some factual allegations to render the claim plausible.[9] These pleading standards have been held to apply to ATS claims.[10]

Before considering the nature of US jurisprudence under the ATS that has emerged over the last 30 years, one should pause to consider why such suits are being brought. Violations of international law will involve tortious conduct. Torture, for example, will constitute trespass to the person. Why, then, do victims of such violations choose to base their suits in the US on violations of customary international law? First, there is the jurisdictional gateway to the federal courts that is given under the ATS where there is a civil action by an alien for a tort committed in violation of the law of nations. For example, in the landmark decision of *Filartiga*,[11] the plaintiff and the defendant were both Paraguayan and therefore the plaintiff would have been unable to sue under the diversity jurisdiction created under 28 USC § 1332. Indeed, many claims against corporations under the ATS have no connection with the US, other than the fact that the corporation conducts some form of business activity there, enabling the foreign corporation to be served with proceedings. This was the case in *Kiobel* which involved Dutch and English corporations being sued by Nigerian plaintiffs in respect of events which took place in Nigeria. Second, it may be easier to resist an application to stay proceedings on grounds of *forum non conveniens* if the claim is brought under the ATS rather than as an ordinary tort claim.[12] Third, the substantive law of liability is determined by international law, as developed through the jurisprudence of the international criminal tribunals, rather than by reference to the law of the State in which the violations occurred. Fourth, the courts are free to develop limitation periods other

---

8(a)(2), a complaint must contain a 'short and plain statement of the claim showing that the pleader is entitled to relief'.

   [8]   *Ofori-Tenkorang v. American Int'l Group, Inc* 460 F 3d 296, 298 (2d Cir 2006).

   [9]   *Bell Atlantic Corp. v. Twombly*, 550 U.S 544, 127 S Ct 1955,1970.

   [10]   *Sinaltrainal v. Coca Cola*, 578 F 3d 1252, 1261 (11th Cir 2009).

   [11]   *See*, note 1 above.

   [12]   This seems to have been the view expressed in *Wiwa v. Royal Dutch Petroleum Co*, 226 F 3d 88 (2nd Cir 2000), although in *Aguinda v. Texaco, Inc*, 142 F Supp 2d 534 (SDNY 2001) it was held that ATS claims are to be treated in the same way as any other claims when applying a *forum non conveniens* analysis.

than those applicable in tort actions. For example, in ATS suits, a ten-year period of limitation has been applied, by analogy with the limitation period contained in the TVPA.[13] Finally, there is the greater adverse publicity for a corporation in being held liable for complicity in a breach of customary international law as opposed to incurring liability for a 'garden variety tort'.

Three landmark decisions opened up the scope of the ATS as a means of proceeding against corporations in respect of their involvement with violations of the customary international law. The first was the Second Circuit's decision in 1995 in *Kadic v. Karadzic*[14] that the ATS could grant jurisdiction over claims against non-State actors, individuals who were not acting in an official capacity. The second was Judge Paez's 1997 decision in *Doe v. Unocal* that the ATS granted jurisdiction for a claim against a corporation in respect of its alleged complicity in forced labour practiced by the security forces of the Burmese state.[15] The third was Judge Schwarz's 2003 decision in *Presbyterian Church of Sudan v. Talisman Energy* in which he rejected the defendant's argument that corporations could not be the subjects of customary international law.[16]

Since then, a variety of claims have been brought against corporate defendants under the ATS. However, despite the plethora of ATS claims against corporations, only four cases have proceeded to trial. In two the

---

[13]   *Papa v. United States*, 281 F 3d 1004, (9th Cir 2002). The ATS itself contains no express limitation period. The time for bringing proceedings may be extended through equitable tolling. When determining whether equitable tolling is applicable, a district court must consider whether the person seeking application of the equitable tolling doctrine: (1) has acted with reasonable diligence during the time period she seeks to have tolled; and (2) has proved that the circumstances are so extraordinary that the doctrine should apply. *Zerilli-Edelglass v. New York City Transit Auth*, 333 F 3d 74, 80–81 (2d Cir 2003). Equitable tolling was applied in *In re South African Apartheid Litigation*, 617 F Supp 2d 228, 286–8 (2009 SDNY) where the actions complained of took place in the 1970s and 1980s but suit was not commenced until 2002. However, equitable tolling prevented the claims being barred by limitation because there was no practical, safe or effective way for them to bring these claims without risk of retaliation by the apartheid state prior to 1994.

[14]   70 F 3d. 232 (2d Cir 1995).

[15]   963 F Supp. 880 (CD Cal 1997). Claims had previously been brought against corporations under ATS in *Amlon Metals v. FMC*, 775 F Supp 668 (SNDY 1991) but had been dismissed on the ground that the plaintiffs had failed to state a violation of the law of nations.

[16]   244 F Supp 2d 289 (SDNY 2003). The defendants in the *Unocal* litigation did not challenge the reach of ATS to corporations.

jury found for the plaintiffs,[17] and in two the defendants prevailed.[18] The reach of the ATS has been shaped by two decisions of the Supreme Court, first in *Sosa v. Alvarez-Machain* in 2004 which placed limits on the actionable norms of international law under the statute and second in *Kiobel v. Royal Dutch Petroleum Co* in 2013 which found that the statute had no extra-territorial reach.

A. *Sosa v. Alvarez-Machain*

In 2004 the Supreme Court considered the scope of ATS for the first time in *Sosa v. Alvarez-Machain*.[19] Until then, only a handful of dissenting judgments had challenged the view that the ATS was not only to do with the jurisdiction of the federal courts, but also created causes of action based on violations of customary international law.[20] The Department of State, alarmed at the prospect of the ATS being used against anti-terrorist measures adopted by the US and its allies, submitted an amicus brief arguing that ATS had only procedural effect and created no new causes of action.[21]

Sosa v. Alvarez Machain provided the Supreme Court with its first opportunity to review the operation of the ATS.[22] The plaintiff's claim was based on an allegation that he had been unlawfully abducted from Mexico for 24 hours to bring him back to the US to face trial. Justice Souter, giving the principal majority opinion, held that the Act was

---

[17]   In *Chowdhury v. Worldtel Bangladesh Holding, Ltd*, 588 F Supp 2d 375 (EDNY 2008), the plaintiff was awarded $1.5 million. On appeal the ATS claim was dismissed but the award of damages was upheld under the TVPA. 746 F 3d (2nd Cir 2014); *Licea v. Curacao Drydock Co*, 584 F Supp 2d 1355, 1366 (SD Fla 2008) ($80 million ATS judgment in default against corporate defendant).

[18]   *Romero v. Drummond* in 2007 and *Bowoto v. Chevron* in 2008.

[19]   *Sosa v. Alvarez Machain*. 542 US 692, 124 S Ct 2739.

[20]   Customary international law was held to be the applicable law in *Filartiga v. Pena-Irala 577* (1984) F Supp. 860, *Xuncax v. Gramajo*, and *Doe v. Unocal (2002)* 395 F 3d 932 (9th Cir 2002). In contrast, in *Tachiona v. Mugabe*, (2002) 234 F Supp 2d 401 at 418, it was suggested that the law of the foreign *situs* might be applied where that is not out of line with international law or the policy behind ATS Another possibility, applied in Judge Reinhardt's minority opinion in *Doe v. Unocal (2002)* is that the substantive law should be that of the *lex fori*.

[21]   Brief for the US as Respondent in *Sosa v. Alvarez-Machain*, No. 03-339 (Jan.2004).

[22]   In *Argentine Republic v. Amerada Hess*, 488 US 428 (1989), 109 S Ct 683 the Supreme Court held that the Foreign Sovereign Immunities Act applied to ATS claims but did not examine the operation of the statute itself.

jurisdictional and created no new causes of action. It was not, however, stillborn, as it was understood by the drafters of the Act that common law would provide a cause of action for the three violations of international law thought to carry personal liability at the time – offences against ambassadors, violation of safe conducts, piracy. No developments over the next 200 years precluded the development of common law expanding this category but a federal court should exercise restraint in considering such a new cause of action. At the time the statute was passed the assumption of the first Congress would be that a cause of action for violation of customary international law would be provided by the general common law. Since then the prevailing conception of the US common law had changed with the 1938 decision in *Erie R. Co v. Tompkins,* in which the Supreme Court denied the existence of any federal 'general' common law.[23] Judicial creation of federal common law then largely withdrew to specialised areas, some of them defined by express congressional authorisation to devise a body of law directly, or in interstitial areas of particular federal interest, with the general practice being to look for legislative guidance before exercising innovative authority over substantive law. The majority of the Supreme Court held that federal common law could provide a cause of action by reference to the presumed intent of the first Congress in introducing the statute.

Accordingly, the federal courts should recognise private claims under federal common law only for violations of those international law norms which had the same definite content and acceptance among civilised nations as did the three historical paradigms at the time the ATS was enacted. A related consideration was whether international law extends the scope of liability for a violation of a given norm to the perpetrator being sued, if the defendant is a private actor such as a corporation or individual.[24] This restriction was generally consistent with the reasoning of many of the previous decisions on the reach of the ATS. Justice Souter referred with approval to the following references in previous ATS decisions: in *Filartiga* that 'For the purposes of civil liability, the torturer has become – like the pirate and slave trader before him *hostis humanis generis*, an enemy of all mankind';[25] in *Tel-Oren* that the ATS was limited to only 'a handful of heinous actions – each of which violates

---

[23] 304 US 64, 58 S Ct. 817, 82 L Ed 1188 (1938).
[24] *Sosa*, note 19.
[25] *Filartiga*, note 1 above, 890.

definable and universal and obligatory norms';[26] and in *In re estate of Marcos* to a norm that is 'specific, universal and obligatory'.[27]

The determination of whether a norm was sufficiently definite to support a cause of action 'should (and, indeed, inevitably must) involve an element of judgment about the practical consequences of making that cause available to litigants in the federal courts'.[28] Other factors that might limit the availability of relief in the federal courts for violations of customary international law could be a requirement of prior exhaustion of domestic remedies, as well as policy of case-specific deference to the political branches.[29] Justice Souter then concluded that Alvarez's relatively brief period of detention in excess of positive authority did not show a violation of any international law norm which met this standard.

Justice Breyer substantially agreed with Justice Souter but pointed out that substantive uniformity on a norm of international law would not automatically lead to universal jurisdiction. The eighteenth century consensus on piracy, for instance, was not only that it was wrong but also that any nation could prosecute any pirate:

Today international law will sometimes similarly reflect not only substantive agreement as to certain universally condemned behavior but also procedural agreement that universal jurisdiction exists to prosecute a subset of that behavior ... That subset includes torture, genocide, crimes against humanity, and war crimes ... The fact that this procedural consensus exists suggests that recognition of universal jurisdiction in respect to a limited set of norms is consistent with principles of international comity. That is, allowing every nation's courts to adjudicate foreign conduct involving foreign parties in such cases will not significantly threaten the practical harmony that comity principles seek to protect. That consensus concerns criminal jurisdiction, but consensus as to universal criminal jurisdiction itself suggests that universal tort jurisdiction would be no more threatening ... That is because the criminal courts of many nations combine civil and criminal proceedings, allowing

---

[26] *Tel-Oren v. Libyan Arab Republic,* 726 F 2d 774, (CADC 1984) Edwards J 781.

[27] *In re Estate of Marcos,* 25 F 3d 1467 (CA 1994), 1475.

[28] *Sosa,* note 19, 733.

[29] Ibid., fn 21. In cases such as *In re South African Apartheid Litigation,* 238 F Supp 2d 1379 (JPML 2002) 'there is a strong argument that federal courts should give serious weight to the Executive Branch's view of the case's impact on foreign policy'.

those injured by criminal conduct to be represented, and to recover damages, in the criminal proceeding itself.[30]

The upshot of *Sosa* is that although the ATS is a jurisdictional grant, that grant determines the substantive claims that could be heard in the district courts pursuant to the grant. In *Sarei v. Rio Tinto* Justice Schroeder analysed the nature of the cause of action under the ATS as follows:

> Thus, it is by now widely recognized that the norms *Sosa* recognizes as actionable under the ATS *begin* as part of international law – which, without more, would not be considered federal law for Article III purposes – but they *become* federal common law once recognized to have the particular characteristics required to be enforceable under the ATS.[31]

Therefore, it is the jurisdictional grant under the ATS that enables the federal courts to develop federal common law to recognise an action for damages for violations of those norms of customary international law that have the characteristics specified in *Sosa*. After *Erie* it would not be possible for the federal courts to admit new causes of action based on violations of norms of customary international law on the basis of general common law.[32] However, the jurisdictional grant of the ATS enabled the federal courts to do so by developing federal common law, subject to the demanding limits set out by the majority in *Sosa*.

B. *Kiobel v. Royal Dutch Petroleum Co*

All ATS claims will have a foreign element – the plaintiff must be an alien. However, many ATS claims involve allegations of violations of international law occurring outside the US. Where the defendant is resident in the US these suits involve two foreign elements and have been referred to as 'foreign squared' suits. Where the defendant is also an alien there are three foreign elements: claims by a foreign plaintiff against a foreign defendant in respect of events that took place in a foreign jurisdiction. These are so-called 'foreign cubed' suits which involve claims that are being heard in US federal courts which have no connection

---

[30]   Ibid., 762–3. Justice Scalia, with whom Justice Thomas agreed, dissented on the basis that the Supreme Court's decision in *Erie* left the federal courts with no discretion to create federal common law.

[31]   *Sarei v. Rio Tinto*, 671 F 3d 736 (9th Cir 2011).

[32]   For this reason under diversity jurisdiction it would not be possible to develop causes of action in the federal courts based on customary international law as there would be no legislative mandate to do so.

with the US at all. Concerns have been expressed by foreign States that the ATS has seen an exorbitant exercise of jurisdiction by US federal courts that violates the permissible limits on national jurisdiction under international law.[33] In 2013 the issue of the territorial reach of the ATS came before the Supreme Court in *Kiobel v. Royal Dutch Petroleum Co*.[34]

In 2010 the Second Circuit, by a majority, held that there was no jurisdiction under the ATS to hear a claim against a corporation for an alleged violation of a norm of customary international law.[35] In 2011, the Supreme Court granted certiorari to consider the corporate liability question. After oral argument in February 2012, the Supreme Court directed the parties to file supplemental briefs addressing an additional question: 'Whether and under what circumstances the [ATS] allows courts to recognize a cause of action for violations of the law of nations occurring within the territory of a sovereign other than the United States.' The Supreme Court heard oral argument on this issue in October 2012 and on 17 April 2013 unanimously upheld the Second Circuit's dismissal of the complaint. Its judgment was based entirely on its answer to the second question. The decision is likely to call a halt to the elucidation of civil liability of non-State actors under customary international law through ATS suits in the US federal courts.

The majority opinion was based on the application of a canon of statutory interpretation known as the presumption against extra-territorial application which provides that '[w]hen a statute gives no clear indication of an extraterritorial application, it has none'.[36] The presumption was typically applied to discern whether an Act of Congress regulating conduct applies abroad. Chief Justice Roberts held that the question was not whether a proper claim had been stated under the ATS, but whether a claim may reach conduct occurring in the territory of a foreign sovereign.[37] In *Morrison*, the Supreme Court had noted that the question of

---

[33] *Kiobel v. Royal Dutch Petroleum Co*, Brief of the Governments of the Kingdom of the Netherlands and the United Kingdom of Great Britain and Northern Ireland as *amicus curiae* in support of neither party. N0 10-1491. June 13 2012. 2–3, 11–18.

[34] *Kiobel v. Royal Dutch Petroleum Co*, 133 S Ct. 1659 (2013), Roberts, CJ, delivered the opinion of the Court, in which Scalia, Kennedy, Thomas, and Alito, JJ, joined Kennedy, J, filed a concurring opinion. Alito, J, filed a concurring opinion, in which Thomas, J joined. Breyer, J, filed an opinion concurring in the judgment, in which Ginsburg, Sotomayor, and Kagan, JJ, joined.

[35] 621 F 3d 111 (2d Cir 2010).

[36] Ibid., 1664 (quoting *Morrison v. Nat'l Australia Bank Ltd.*, 130 S Ct 2869, 2878 (2010).

[37] Ibid., 1664.

extra-territorial application was a 'merits question', not a question of subject-matter jurisdiction. The ATS, on the other hand, was 'strictly jurisdictional'.[38] Chief Justice Roberts then went on to say:

> It does not directly regulate conduct or afford relief. It instead allows federal courts to recognize certain causes of action based on sufficiently definite norms of international law. But we think the principles underlying the canon of interpretation similarly constrain courts considering causes of action that may be brought under the ATS.[39]

Thus, the majority opinion in *Kiobel* seems to be a merits dismissal, rather than a dismissal for lack of subject-matter jurisdiction, as seen by Chief Justice Roberts' statement that:

> The question under *Sosa* is not whether a federal court has jurisdiction to entertain a cause of action provided by foreign or even international law. The question is instead whether the court has authority to recognize a cause of action under US law to enforce a norm of international law.[40]

The answer to that merits question is determined by the initial congressional intent behind the enactment of the ATS in 1789. To rebut the presumption the ATS would need to evince a 'clear indication of extraterritoriality',[41] which it did not. Although the ATS covered actions by aliens for violations of the law of nations, that did not imply extra-territorial reach, for violations affecting aliens could occur either within or outside the US. At the time of its enactment there were 'three principal offenses against the law of nations' that had been identified by Blackstone: violation of safe conducts; infringement of the rights of ambassadors; and piracy. The first two offences had no necessary extra-territorial application. The third, piracy, typically occurred on the high seas, beyond the territorial jurisdiction of the US or any other country. Although the Supreme Court had generally treated the high seas the same as foreign soil for purposes of the presumption against extraterritorial application, applying US law to pirates did not involve the imposition of the sovereign will of the US on to conduct occurring within the territorial jurisdiction of another sovereign. 'Pirates were fair game wherever found, by any nation, because they generally did not operate

---

[38]   Ibid., 1664 (quoting Sosa, note 19 above, 713).
[39]   Ibid., 1664.
[40]   Ibid., 1666.
[41]   Ibid., 1665 (quoting *Morrison*, 130 S Ct, 2883).

within any jurisdiction.'[42] As regards Attorney-General Bradford's 1795 opinion, that was said to defy a definitive meaning:

> Whatever its precise meaning, it deals with U. S. citizens who, by participating in an attack taking place both on the high seas and on a foreign shore, violated a treaty between the United States and Great Britain. The opinion hardly suffices to counter the weighty concerns underlying the presumption against extraterritoriality.[43]

Chief Justice Roberts concluded by stating that on the facts all the relevant conduct took place outside the US. Even where the claims did touch and concern the territory of the US, they had to do so with sufficient force to displace the presumption against extra-territorial application.[44] Mere corporate presence would not suffice. Justice Kennedy concurred but noted that it was proper for the Court:

> to leave open a number of significant questions regarding the reach and interpretation of the Alien Tort Statute [...] Other cases may arise with allegations of serious violations of international law principles protecting persons, cases covered neither by the TVPA nor by the reasoning and holding of today's case; and in those disputes the proper implementation of the presumption against extraterritorial application may require some further elaboration and explanation.[45]

Justice Alito in his concurrence stated:

> [a]s a result, a putative ATS cause of action will fall within the scope of the presumption against extra territoriality – and will therefore be barred – unless the domestic conduct is sufficient to violate an international law norm that satisfies *Sosa*'s requirements of definiteness and acceptance among civilized nations.[46]

---

[42] Ibid., 1667.

[43] Ibid., 1668. Bradford was proposing an ATS action for incidents that arose out of American participation in a French raid on the British Sierra Leone colony. His opinion concludes that the US had a duty to provide a remedy because 'committing, aiding, or abetting hostilities' like those in Sierra Leone 'render[ed the perpetrators] liable to punishment under the law of nations'. Bradford expressed 'no doubt that the company or individuals who have been injured by these acts of hostility have a remedy by a *civil* suit in the courts of the United States; jurisdiction being expressly given to these courts in all cases where an alien sues for a tort only, in violation of the law of nations'.

[44] *Morrison*, 130 S Ct, 2883–8.

[45] *Kiobel*, note 35 above, 1669.

[46] Ibid., 1670, Justice Thomas joined in Justice Alito's concurrence.

His is the most stringent approach to the presumption against extra-territorial application. Not only would it mean that there would be no cause of action under the ATS in cases like *Filartiga* where the violation of the international law norm prohibiting torture took place in Peru, but it would deny an action against pirates where the violation of the international law norm takes place on the high seas.

Justice Breyer agreed with the result but did not invoke the presumption against extra-territoriality. He framed the question in *Sosa* as follows:

> *Sosa* essentially leads today's judges to ask: Who are today's pirates? ... We provided a framework for answering that question by setting down principles drawn from international norms and designed to limit ATS claims to those that are similar in character and specificity to piracy. ... In this case we must decide the extent to which this jurisdictional statute opens a federal court's doors to those harmed by activities belonging to the limited class that *Sosa* set forth *when those activities take place abroad* (emphasis added).[47]

The ATS was enacted with 'foreign matters' in mind, given the explicit reference in its text to 'alien[s]', 'treat[ies]', and 'the law of nations'. The ATS was intended to cover violations of three norms of international law for which a cause of action would be provided by common law. Piracy was one of these and necessarily involved conduct occurring abroad. Justice Breyer stated:

> The majority cannot wish this piracy example away by emphasizing that piracy takes place on the high seas ... That is because the robbery and murder that make up piracy do not normally take place in the water; they take place on a ship. And a ship is like land, in that it falls within the jurisdiction of the nation whose flag it flies.[48]

Justice Breyer then continued:

> In applying the ATS to acts 'occurring within the territory of a[nother] sovereign,' I would assume that Congress intended the statute's jurisdictional reach to match the statute's underlying substantive grasp. That grasp, defined by the statute's purposes set forth in *Sosa*, includes compensation for those injured by piracy and its modern day equivalents, at least where allowing such compensation avoids 'serious' negative international 'consequences' for the United States ... .[49]

---

[47]   Ibid., 1671 (internal citations omitted) (emphasis in the original).
[48]   Ibid., 1672.
[49]   Ibid., 1673.

Justice Breyer concluded that there would be jurisdiction under the ATS where: (1) the alleged tort occurs on American soil, and (2) the defendant is an American national; or (3) the defendant's conduct substantially and adversely affects an important American national interest, including a distinct interest in preventing the US from becoming a safe harbour (free of civil as well as criminal liability) for a torturer or other common enemy of mankind.[50] The second element would cover cases such as *Filartiga* and *In re Estate of Marcos, Human Rights Litigation*.[51] This jurisdictional approach was analogous to, and consistent with, the approaches of a number of other nations as well as being consistent with the substantive view of the statute taken in *Sosa*.

In the end *Kiobel* was not decided on the basis of any rule of international law either as regards the civil liability of corporations for violations of customary international law or as regards a rule precluded a State from asserting jurisdiction over 'foreign cubed' civil claims that had no connection with that State. Rather the Supreme Court decided it on the application of a US canon of statutory interpretation which restricted the causes of action that could arise in the federal courts under the grant of jurisdiction under the ATS. However, the Supreme Court's decision in *Kiobel* has sounded the death knell for 'foreign cubed' suits proceeding in the federal courts under the ATS, other than cases of piracy.[52]

What is less clear is whether the decision will close off 'foreign squared' suits under the ATS. These involve an alien plaintiff suing a US defendant in respect of a violation of international law that took place in a foreign jurisdiction, as was the case in *Unocal*.[53] Under Justice Breyer's

---

[50]   Ibid., 1674. In doing so Justice Breyer referred to Restatement (Third) Of Foreign Relations Law §§ 402, 403 and 404 (1986). The latter is particularly significant in that it explains that a 'state has jurisdiction to define and prescribe punishment for certain offenses recognized by the community of nations as of universal concern, such as piracy, slave trade', and analogous behaviour. Ibid., 1673.

[51]   25 F 3d 1467, (9th Cir 1994).

[52]   *Institute of Cetacean Research v. Sea Shepherd Conservation Society*, (2013) 725 F 3d 940 (9th Cir.) The Ninth Circuit held that held that 'private ends' include those pursued on personal, moral or philosophical grounds. The case involved an environmental group that aimed to disrupt what it considered illegal whaling by Japanese vessels by confronting the whalers with its two vessels from which it threw glass bottles filled with paint or butyric acid at the whaling ships. These activities, which took place on the high seas, were held to constitute piracy and gave rise to a claim under the ATS.

[53]   *Doe v. Unocal*, note 20 above.

analysis in *Kiobel*,[54] the most favourable to the continued viability of
ATS suits, a case like *Unocal*[55] would involve his second element, the
defendant being an American national, but not the first, the alleged tort
occurring on American soil. That leaves the third element of Justice
Breyer's analysis, the distinct national interest in preventing the US from
becoming a safe haven for a torturer or other common enemy of
mankind. It is arguable that this would be satisfied where a US
corporation is charged with aiding and abetting an international crime
and that Justice Breyer would have found jurisdiction under the ATS had
the *Kiobel* defendants been American corporations. The majority opinion
and in particular Justice Alito's statement that a putative ATS action
would be barred 'unless the *domestic conduct* is sufficient to violate an
international law norm that satisfies *Sosa*'s requirements of definiteness
and acceptance among civilized nations' is less conducive to such a
view.[56] In most ATS cases involving US corporations, the aiding and
abetting has taken place outside the US – in *Unocal* it was in Burma –
and such cases would therefore not give rise to a cause of action under
the ATS, given the presumption against extra-territorial application of the
statute. Chief Justice Roberts' opinion leaves this question open. The
claims must 'touch and concern' the territory of the US, and do so with
sufficient force to displace the presumption against extra-territorial
application. No indication is given as to what force is necessary to
displace the presumption other than that mere geographical presence in
the US will not be enough.

C. After *Kiobel*

Decisions in the wake of *Kiobel* show that claims may be brought under
the ATS where the violation of the law of nations takes place on US
territory, or on US territory abroad, such as an embassy. However, where
a US defendant is sued in relation to a violation of the law of nations that
takes place outside the US, there has been a divergence of views in
analysing the effect of the presumption against extra-territorial application and Chief Justice Roberts' 'touch and concern' wording. In the
first case, the question of whether the presumption is rebutted is purely a
question of analysis of the statute itself. The presumption is not rebutted
with the ATS which did not show a clear indication of extra-territoriality
and there is no room for any judicial discretion. In the latter two cases,

---

[54]   *Kiobel v. Royal Dutch Petroleum Co,* note 34 above, 1671.
[55]   *Doe v. Unocal,* note 20 above.
[56]   *Kiobel v. Royal Dutch Petroleum* Co, note 34 above, 1671.

there appears to be room for judicial discretion as regards jurisdiction under the ATS for claims involving conduct outside the US where the claims 'touch and concern' the territory of the US with sufficient force.

In *Balintulo v. Daimler AG*,[57] another case arising out of complicity of US companies in violations of the law of nations by the South African apartheid regime, the Second Circuit rejected the plaintiffs' argument that whether the relevant conduct occurred abroad is simply one prong of a multi-factor test, and the ATS still reaches extra-territorial conduct when the defendant is an American national. In no cases did the ATS permit claims based on illegal conduct that occurred entirely in the territory of another sovereign and there was no room for judicial discretion. The Supreme Court in *Kiobel* had expressly held that claims under the ATS could be brought only for violations of the law of nations occurring within the territory of the US. In this case all the human rights violations took place in South Africa. The complaint alleged that the US defendant parent corporations were vicariously liable for aiding and abetting violations of the laws of nations committed within South Africa by their South African subsidiaries. None of those acts took place within the US and therefore the US parent corporations could not be vicariously liable for that conduct under the ATS. Claims of derivative liability depended on the viability of the underlying claim.[58]

The same approach was shown by the Eleventh Circuit in *Cardona v. Chiquita Brands International Inc*[59] where the majority dismissed the ATS claims because the acts alleged all arose outside the US and the ATS

---

[57]   727 F 3d 174 (2d Cir 2013).

[58]   See, e.g., *S.E.C. v. Obus*, 693 F 3d 276, 292 (2d Cir.2012); *Homoki v. Conversion Servs Inc*, 717 F 3d 388 402 (5th Cir 2013); *Rivera v. Centro Medico de Turabo, Inc*, 575 F 3d 10, 24 (1st Cir 2009); *David P. Coldesina, DDS v. Estate of Simper*, 407 F 3d 1126, 1138 (10th Cir 2005). In related proceedings in *In re South African Apartheid Litigation*, No. 02 MDL 1499, 2013 WL 6813877, at *1–2 (Dec. 26, 2013). Judge Schiendlin dismissed the suits against the non-US corporate defendants but as regards the claims against the US corporate defendants she allowed the plaintiffs to brief the issue of whether a corporation may be liable for a violation of the ATS.

[59]   Similarly, in *Cardona v. Chiquita Brands International Inc*, Case No. 12-14898 on 24 July 2014 the Eleventh Circuit dismissed a claim against a US corporation that had allegedly been involved in torture and death inflicted by paramilitary forces employed as security forces in Colombia. Judge Sentelle: 'There is no allegation that any torture occurred on US territory, or that any other act constituting a tort in terms of the ATS touched or concerned the territory of the United States with any force.'

contained nothing to rebut the presumption against extra-territorial application of a US statute. They also doubted whether a claim for torture by
non-State actors fell outside the category of cognisable ATS claims as set
out in *Sosa*.[60] Judge Martin dissented. First, the *Bradford* opinion pointed
to the fact that the statute provided a remedy for extra-territorial
violations of the laws of nations committed by US citizens. Secondly,
Kiobel could be distinguished because the relevant conduct for which the
plaintiffs sought to hold Chiquita liable did not occur on foreign soil:

> Critically, the plaintiffs instead have alleged that Chiquita's corporate officers
> reviewed, approved, and concealed payments and weapons transfers to
> Colombian terrorist organizations from their offices in the United States with
> the purpose that the terrorists would use them to commit extrajudicial killings
> and other war crimes. This is not, therefore, a case where a defendant is being
> haled into court under the ATS exclusively for actions that took place on
> foreign soil.

In contrast, there have been five instances in which the 'touch and
concern' language has been used to enable an ATS suit against a US
defendant to survive a post-*Kiobel* challenge to jurisdiction. First, there is
Sexual Minorities Uganda v. Lively[61] which involved a claim against a
US citizen residing in Massachusetts for allegedly aiding and abetting
a claim for persecution amounting to a crime against humanity, based on
a systematic and widespread campaign of persecution against lesbian,
gay, bisexual, transgender and intersex people in Uganda.[62] Judge Ponsor
held that there was jurisdiction to hear the claim under the ATS. Although
the impact of the defendant's conduct was felt in Uganda his actions in
planning and managing a campaign of repression in Uganda had taken
place in the US and were 'analogous to a terrorist designing and
manufacturing a bomb in this country, which he then mails to Uganda
with the intent that it explode there'. The presumption against extra-
territoriality came into play only where a defendant's conduct lacked
sufficient connection to the US. Even under the separate concurrence of
Justice Alito and Justice Thomas which required that the 'domestic

---

[60]　Citing *Saleh v. Titan Corp*, 580 F 3d 1 (DC Cir 2010), *Ali v. Rumsfeld*,
649 F 3d 762 (DC Cir. 2011) and the pre-*Sosa* decision, in *Sanchez-Espinoza v.
Reagan*, 770 F 2d 202 (DC Cir 1985).

[61]　960 F Supp 2d 304 (D Mass 2013).

[62]　Although there was a Circuit split as to the *mens rea* element for aiding
and abetting under international law, the court did not need to resolve the issue as
the plaintiffs had pleaded that the defendant had given purposive assistance to the
Ugandan authorities.

conduct is sufficient to violate an international law norm that satisfies Sosa's requirements of definiteness and acceptance among civilized nations'.[63] There would be jurisdiction here because the amended complaint adequately set out actionable conduct undertaken by the defendant in the US to provide assistance in the campaign of persecution in Uganda.

The second case is *Mwani v. bin Laden*[64] where Judge Facciola held that the presumption against extra-territoriality had been displaced in a claim under the ATS arising out of the bombing of the US embassy in Nairobi by Al Qaida in 1998:

> It is obvious that a case involving an attack on the United States Embassy in Nairobi is tied much more closely to our national interests than a case whose only tie to our nation is a corporate presence here. Ample evidence has been presented for me to conclude that the events at issue in this case were directed at the United States government, with the intention of harming this country and its citizens ... Surely, if any circumstances were to fit the Court's framework of 'touching and concerning the United States with sufficient force,' it would be a terrorist attack that 1) was plotted in part within the United States, and 2) was directed at a United States Embassy and its employees.[65]

The third case *Al Shimari v. CACI Intern, Inc* has seen a reversal of opinion in the Fourth Circuit. Initially, Judge Lee held that a claim against a US defendant corporation arising out of alleged torture and war crimes arising at Abu Ghraib had to be dismissed for lack of subject-matter jurisdiction, as the alleged conduct occurred exclusively on foreign soil.[66] For this purpose Iraq was a territory external to the US and was not subject to the de facto sovereignty of the US during the military occupation of that country. As in *Balintulo* the court held that the presumption against extra-territorial application is only rebuttable by legislative act and not by judicial decision. It was also unclear how 'touch and concern' inquiry would apply to a purely jurisdictional statute such as the ATS. In June 2014 the Fourth Circuit overruled this finding

---

[63] *Kiobel,* note 34 above, 167.

[64] 947 F Supp 2d 1 (DDC 2013), 2013 WL 2325166, at *4. Osama Bin Laden was subsequently dismissed from the suit, due to his death. 302 FRD 22 (DDC 2014).

[65] However, given that this was likely to be the first opinion given after *Kiobel,* Judge Facciola immediately certified this issue for appeal to the Court of Appeals under 28 USC § 1292(b).

[66] 951 F Supp 2d 857 (ED Va 2013). The tort claims were subject to Iraqi law which provided immunity for the defendant.

and held that the claims did sufficiently 'touch and concern' the US.[67] Judge Barbara Keenan found that the case differed from *Kiobel* and *Balintulo* in that: the claim's substantial ties to US territory arose out of performance of a contract executed by a US corporation with the US government in respect of alleged torture at a military facility operated by US government personnel; the employees who allegedly participated in the acts of torture were hired in the US by CACI to fulfil the terms of CACI's contract with the US Department of the Interior; the CACI interrogators were required to obtain security clearances from the US Department of Defense; the additional allegation that CACI's US managers were aware of the alleged misconduct in Iraq and attempted to cover it up and implicitly encouraged it.

In two subsequent decisions, in *Doe v. Nestle USA (Inc)*[68] and *Doe v. Exxon Mobil Corporation*,[69] the district courts have given the plaintiffs leave to amend their pleadings in the light of the Supreme Court's decision in *Kiobel* so as to allege that some of the activity underlying the ATS claim took place in the US. In *Exxon* Judge Lamberth reviewed the cases after *Kiobel* on whether the conduct 'touched and concerned' the US, from which it was clear that corporate presence in the US and incorporation in the US would be insufficient. Some conduct had to have taken place in the US. This was the case in *Al Shimari* and *SMUG* but not in *Balintulo* where all the aiding and abetting took place in South Africa and the claim against the US parent defendants was based on vicarious liability. Plaintiffs alleged that Exxon provided material support to its security personnel but did not specify where the support was planned or authorised or if any of the material or monetary support came from the US and were given leave to amend their pleadings to restate their ATS claims and to allege additional facts showing that the claims sufficiently touched and concerned the US to displace the presumption against extra-territoriality. In the light of the more demanding pleading standards

---

[67]   *Al Shimari v. CACI Premier Technology, Inc*, 758 F 3d 516 (4th Cir 2014). In *In re South African Apartheid Litigation*, Slip Copy, 2014 WL 4290444 (SDNY 2014) Judge Schiendlin distinguished *Al-Shimari* as a case involving much greater contact with the US government, military, citizens and territory. As with *Balintulo* the case involved vicarious liability of US parent corporations in respect of actions committed by their subsidiaries in South Africa all of whose conduct took place abroad.

[68]   ___ F 3d ___, 2014 WL 4358453 (9th Cir 2014).

[69]   ___ F Supp 3d ___, 2014 WL 4746256 (DDC 2014). On 6 July 2015 Judge Lamberth found that the plaintiffs had adequately pled conduct by the US corporate defendant, but not its Indonesian subsidiary, that touched and concerned the US. 2015 WL 5042118 (D.D.C.).

set out in *Iqbal* the plaintiffs will have to particularise the conduct in the US giving rise to liability for aiding and abetting an international crime before discovery. This is likely to prove a demanding burden. The plaintiffs failed to satisfy it in *Chowdhury v. Worldtel Bangladesh Holding, Ltd*,[70] and in *Mujica v. Airscan*[71] the Ninth Circuit declined to give the plaintiffs leave to amend their pleadings as this would be futile, Judge Bybee explaining:

> Defendants filed a supplemental brief in the wake of the *Kiobel* decision urging dismissal of Plaintiffs' ATS claims, and Plaintiffs devoted 15 pages of their reply brief to *Kiobel*'s touch-and-concern test. Plaintiffs admitted in that brief that they likely 'cannot uncover the evidence they need' to allege 'plotting [by Defendants] in the United States without jurisdictional discovery.'[72]

On 30 December 2014 the plaintiffs in *Chiquita* petitioned the Supreme Court for certiorari on the question:

> Whether law of nations violations alleged in an ATS cause of action must occur entirely within U.S. territory, as the Eleventh Circuit held in this case, or whether the ATS permits an action where a substantial nexus to the United States is present, such as U.S. nationality of the defendant and substantial relevant conduct in the United States that furthers human rights violations, as the Ninth, Fourth and Second Circuits have held.

On 20 April 2015 the US Supreme Court denied certiorari in the case.[73] The circuit split, therefore, remains.

One possible alternative outlet for claims based on violations of customary international law is 28 USC § 1331 which gives federal courts jurisdiction over matters arising under the Constitution and federal laws. For 200 years it has been recognised that the domestic law of the US recognises the law of nations.[74] This might suggest that there would be

---

[70]   746 F 3d 42 (2d Cir 2014).

[71]   771 F 3d 580 (9th Cir 2014).

[72]   Ibid., 593. In their reply brief, filed after *Kiobel*, the plaintiffs speculated that some of the conduct forming the basis of the aiding and abetting claim, such as the making of the contract between the two defendants, could have occurred in the US, but this was not an adequate basis on which to allow the claims to proceed.

[73]   ___ S Ct ___, 2015 WL 1757186 (Mem) US 2015.

[74]   In cases such as *The Paquete Habana*, 175 US, 700, 20 S Ct 290, "International law is part of our law, and must be ascertained and administered by the courts of justice of appropriate jurisdiction, as often as questions of right

jurisdiction under this provision for suits for violations of the law of nations. This was the view taken in *Bodner v. Banque Paribas*[75] where it was held that US citizens could sue a French bank in respect of the looting of their possessions in World War Two, which constituted a war crime. In contrast in *Xuncax v. Gramajo*[76] it was held that federal law gave rise to no autonomous right to sue for breaches of customary international law. This is supported by subsequent observations of Justice Souter in *Sosa*:

> Our position does not, as Justice Scalia suggests, imply that every grant of jurisdiction to a federal court carries with it an opportunity to develop common law (so that the grant of federal-question jurisdiction would be equally as good for our purposes as § 1350) ... Section 1350 was enacted on the congressional understanding that courts would exercise jurisdiction by entertaining some common law claims derived from the law of nations; and we know of no reason to think that federal-question jurisdiction was extended subject to any comparable congressional assumption. Further, our holding today is consistent with the division of responsibilities between federal and state courts after *Erie*, ... as a more expansive common law power related to 28 U.S.C. § 1331 might not be.[77]

This analysis makes it unlikely that a cause of action for violations under customary international law could arise under any other grant of jurisdiction to the federal courts than that granted under the ATS.

---

depending upon it are duly presented for their determination", and *Sabbatino*, 376 US, 423, 84 S Ct 923 (1964) '[I]t is, of course, true that United States courts apply international law as a part of our own in appropriate circumstances.' In *Murray v. The Charming Betsy*, 6 US (2 Cranch) 64 (1804), Chief Justice Marshall stated that 'an act of Congress ought never to be construed to violate the law of nations if any other possible construction remains.' In *Serra v. Lappin*, 600 F 3d 1191 (2010) the Ninth Circuit held that the doctrine had no application in the construction of domestic statutes and would be applied canon only where conformity with the law of nations was relevant to considerations of international comity.

[75]   114 F. Supp 2d 117, 127 (EDNY 2000). As US citizens, they could not have recourse to ATCA. Neither, given the nature of the violation of customary international law, could they have recourse to the TVPA.

[76]   886 F Supp 162, 182–4 (Mass DC 1995).

[77]   *Sosa*, note 20 above, 731. Referring to Justice Souter's observation, Judge Clifton in *Serra v. Lappin*, note 74 above, [7] stated that the ATS 'is the only possible vehicle for a claim like Plaintiffs' because no other statute recognizes a general cause of action under the law of nations.'

2. THE 1991 TORTURE VICTIMS PROTECTION ACT

In 1992 Congress extended to individuals of whatever nationality the right hitherto enjoyed only by aliens under the ATS of making civil claims in the federal courts in respect of certain human rights abuses, by enacting the TVPA 1991 which took effect on March 12 1992.[78] Section 1 provides:

> Liability. – An individual who, under actual or apparent authority, or color of law, of any foreign nation –
>
> (1) subjects an individual to torture shall, in a civil action, be liable for damages to that individual; or (2) subjects an individual to extrajudicial killing shall, in a civil action, be liable for damages to the individual's legal representative, or to any person who may be a claimant in an action for wrongful death.

Claims may be made under the statute in respect of aiding and abetting torture.[79] In *Chowdhury v. WorldTel*[80] it was confirmed that the TVPA does have extra-territorial reach and that aliens may sue under it. The 'color of law' requirement is satisfied when an individual acts together with State officials or with significant State aid and in addition a defendant may be held liable for the acts of State officials in committing torture if they have been acting as his agents.

However, the TVPA, although it overlaps with the ATS, contains the following important differences. First, it does not extend to all torts committed in violation of the law of nations but only applies to acts of torture and extra-judicial killings. Secondly, these must occur 'under actual or apparent authority, or color of law, of any foreign nation'. Suits, therefore, would not be possible against US officials as it is unlikely they

---

[78] The TVPA does not have retroactive effect. *Cabello v. Fernández-Larios*, 402 F.3d 1148, 1153–4 (11th Cir. 2005).

[79] The legislative history provides that the TVPA allows suits: Senate Report No. 249, 102d Cong, 1st Sess, at § IV(E) (1991) states that the statute permits suits 'against persons who ordered, abetted, or assisted in the torture'. And that 'anyone with higher authority who authorized, tolerated or knowingly ignored the commission of actionable torts' is liable for them. Courts have concluded that the statute was intended to extend to secondary forms of responsibility such as ordering, aiding and abetting, command responsibility, and conspiracy. *See Chavez v. Carranza*, 559 F 3d 486, 498–9 (6th Cir), *cert. denied*, 558 US 822 (2009); *Cabello v. Fernández-Larios*, note 79 above, 1157–8; *Ford* ex rel. *Estate of Ford v. Garcia*, 289 F 2d 1283, 1286 (11th Cir 2002).

[80] 746 F 3d (2d Cir 2014).

would be acting under the actual or apparent authority, or colour of law, of a foreign nation.[81] Thirdly, the TVPA contains a ten-year limitation period, unlike the ATS which has none (although in *Papa*, it was held that ATS claims should be subject to the same limitation period as claims under TVPA). Fourthly, the TVPA, unlike the ATS, explicitly requires the plaintiff to have exhausted domestic remedies. The burden of proof in establishing this falls on the defendant and in many instances it will be difficult to satisfy, given the likelihood of retaliatory action against a plaintiff who commenced suit against his torturers in the place where he had been tortured. Fifthly, the TVPA gives a right to claim against 'individuals' which the Supreme Court held in *Mohamad v. Palestinian Authority* means natural persons and so precludes claims against corporations.[82] There is a circuit split as to whether a plaintiff may claim under both the TVPA and the ATS.[83]

3. CIVIL CAUSES OF ACTION FOR US NATIONALS IN RESPECT OF TERRORISM

Two statutory provisions provide civil causes of actions for US citizens who are killed or injured in terrorist attacks wherever they occur.[84] The first is under the amended section 1605(a)(7) of title 28 United States

---

[81] The TVPA does not include US government officers or private US persons as possible defendants. *Doe v. Rumsfeld*, 683 F 3d 390, 396 (DC Cir 2012) *Meshal v. Higgenbotham*, 47 F Supp 3d 115 (DDC 2014).

[82] 132 S Ct 1702 (2012). Whether there had previously been a circuit split on this point is unclear. The district courts have taken the view that 'individuals' do not comprise corporations, in *Beanal v. Freeport McMoran, Doe I v. Exxon Mobil Corp*, 393 F Supp 2d 20 (DDC 2005), and. *Bowoto v. Chevron Corp*, 2010 621 F 3d 1116 (9th Cir 2010). The contrary position had been taken in *Sinaltrainal v. Coca Cola*, 256 F Supp 2d 1345 (SD Fla 2003), 1359 and *Estate of Rodriguez v. Drummond*, 256 F Supp 2d 1250 (WD Al 2003), 1266–7.

[83] The Eleventh Circuit has held that both statutes may be invoked. *Aldana v. Del Monte Fresh Produce, N.A., Inc*, 416 F 3d 1242, 1250–51 (11th Cir 2005). *Mujica v. Occidental Petroleum Corp*, 381 F Supp 2d 1164, 1179 n.13 (CD Cal 2005). In contrast, the Seventh Circuit held that for aliens and citizens alike, the TVPA is the sole avenue for relief based on claims of torture or extrajudicial killing. *Enahoro v. Abubakar*, 408 F 3d 877, 884–5 (7th Cir 2005), *cert. denied*, 546 US 1175 (2006).

[84] Terrorism has been held not to involve a violation of the law of nations for ATS claims. *In re Terrorist Attacks on September 11, 2001*, 714 F 3d 659 (2d Cir 2013).

Code[85] under which foreign sovereign immunity was removed for actions against a country that the State Department has listed as a State Sponsor of Terrorism and that either: (1) engaged in a direct act of terror; or (2) provided material support or resources for terrorist acts. Currently four States, Cuba,[86] Syria, Sudan, and Iran are so designated. Five months later Congress adopted what is commonly known as the 'Flatow Amendment', named after Alisa Flatow a 20-year-old US student killed in a suicide bomb attack in Israel in April 1995. This provides that a foreign State or an agent of a State sponsoring terrorism:

> shall be liable to a United States national or the national's legal representative for personal injury or death caused by acts of that [party] for which the courts of the United States may maintain jurisdiction under section 1605(a)(7) of title 28 United States Code [repealed] for money damages ... [including] punitive damages.

The combination of the original exception and the amendment gave plaintiffs both access to federal courts but also a substantive legal right to recover punitive damages.

In 2004, the Court of Appeals for the District of Columbia, in the case of *Cicippio-Puleo v. Islamic Republic of Iran*,[87] ruled that neither section 1605(a)(7) nor the Flatow Amendment established a cause of action against foreign State sponsors of terrorism. Section 1605(a)(7) was 'merely a jurisdiction conferring provision' and the Flatow Amendment only provided a right against individual agents, officers, or employees of the foreign State, but 'not against the foreign state itself'. In response, Congress repealed section 1605(a)(7) and replaced it with section 1605A. The new law's exception to foreign sovereign immunity remains identical to that in the repealed legislation, but the new law expressly provides a federal right of action, access to punitive damages, compensation for special masters appointed to assist the courts in determining damages awards, and enhanced mechanisms for the enforcement of civil judgments.

---

[85] Mandatory Victims Restitution Act of 1996, which was a part of the Anti-Terrorism and Effective Death Penalty Act of 1996. Pub L No 104-132, §221(a)(1)(C), 110 Stat 1214, 1241 (formerly codified at 28 USC § 1605(a)(7)).

[86] On 14 April 2015 President Obama announced his intention to remove Cuba from the list of State sponsors of terrorism.

[87] 353 F 3d 1024, 1032–3 (DC Cir 2004).

The second provision is the civil cause of action for US nationals[88] injured by international terrorism which appears in the Anti-Terrorism Act 1992 (ATA), 18 US Code § 2333 which provides:

> (a) Action and Jurisdiction. – Any national of the United States injured in his or her person, property, or business by reason of an act of international terrorism, or his or her estate, survivors, or heirs, may sue therefor in any appropriate district court of the United States and shall recover threefold the damages he or she sustains and the cost of the suit, including attorney's fees.[89]

'International terrorism' is defined in § 2331(1) as follows.[90] The act must 'involve violent acts or acts dangerous to human life that are a violation of the criminal laws of the United States'.[91] The act must 'appear to be intended – (i) to intimidate or coerce a civilian population; (ii) to influence the policy of a government by intimidation or coercion; or (iii) to affect the conduct of a government by mass destruction, assassination, or kidnapping'.[92] The act must 'occur primarily outside the territorial jurisdiction of the United States'.[93]

There have been a series of claims under the ATA against financial institutions in connection with transfers of money that have ended up in the hands of terrorists. Some courts have found that claims for aiding and abetting terrorism may be made under the ATA.[94] In *Boim v. Holy Land Foundation*[95] the Seventh Circuit, sitting *en banc*, rejected its previous

---

[88] In December 2013 when the Senate took up the National Defense Authorization Act, one of the proposed amendments before it was one that would amend the ATA to permit non-US nationals to sue persons (including corporations) for 'aiding and abetting' acts of terrorism. The amendment which had the potential to turn the ATA into a mini Alien Tort Statute did not go through.

[89] The statute of limitations for ATA claims was initially four years but was extended by Congress on January 3 2013, to ten years, applying to all pending actions under the ATA, along with the implementation of a special limitations period for ATA claims arising from acts of international terrorism that occurred on or after September 11, 2001, allowing plaintiffs to bring those claims until January 2, 2019, or until the expiry of the ten-year limitations period, whichever is longer.

[90] 18 USC § 2331(1) (2006).

[91] Ibid., § 2331(1)(A).

[92] Ibid., § 2331(1)(B).

[93] Ibid., § 2331(1)(C).

[94] *Julin v. Chiqita Brands International Inc*, 690 F Supp 2d 1296 (SD Fla 2010); *Wultz v. Islamic Republic of Iran*, 755 F Supp 2d 1 (DDC 2010).

[95] 549 F 3d 685 (7th Cir 2008).

finding to this effect[96] but held that by a chain of statutory incorporation a donor to a terrorist group could incur primary liability under the ATA by making a donation to a terrorist group that targetted Americans outside the US. The mental element of the tort was knowingly or recklessly contributing to an organisation that engages in terrorist activities, even if it also engages in other non-terrorist activities and the donor did not intend the donation to be used for terrorist purposes. Providing funds to a government that funds terrorist organisations, though, would not necessarily trigger liability.

In *Rothstein v. UBS AG*[97] the claim arose in respect of injuries sustained in Israel by US citizens as a result of terrorist attacks from Hizbollah and Hamas. UBS had transferred US currency to Iran and it was argued that as Iran was a sponsor of the two terrorist organisations, UBS should be liable under the ATA. Section 2333(a) granted a private right of action to a US national injured 'by reason of' an act of international terrorism. This required a plaintiff to show that his injury was proximately caused by the defendant. However, the plaintiffs' injuries were not proximately caused by the transfers of US currency to Iran. It was not alleged that UBS was a participant in the terrorist attacks that injured the plaintiffs, nor that they provided money to Hizbollah or Hamas, nor that US currency UBS transferred to Iran was given to Hizbollah or Hamas, nor that if UBS had not transferred US currency to Iran, Iran would not have funded the attacks in which plaintiffs were injured.[98]

On 22 September 2014 the first trial under the ATA, in *Linde v. Arab Bank plc,* concluded with a jury finding against the defendant bank on 24 counts under the ATA in relation to funds provided to Hamas. Judge Gershon directed the jury that the plaintiffs were not required to show 'but for' causation, nor were they required to trace specific dollars to specific terrorist attacks. On 9 April 2015 Judge Cogan in a post-trial

---

[96] *Boim v. Quranic Literacy Inst,* 291 F 3d 1000, 1012–16 (7th Cir 2002).

[97] 08 F 3d 82 (2d Cir 2013).

[98] *Rothstein* was distinguished shortly afterwards in *Strauss v. Credit Lyonnais, S.A.*, 925 F Supp 2d 414 (EDNY 2013) where the claims arose out of transfers of money to 13 charities acting as fronts for Hamas. The money from the defendant was purportedly going directly to Hamas front-groups, at a time when Hamas carried out the attacks in question, rather than to a government which performs legitimate functions in addition to allegedly funding terrorist organisations.

review[99] held that Judge Gershon had applied the correct test in relation to liability under the ATA.[100]

4. THE TRAFFICKING VICTIMS PROTECTION REAUTHORISATION ACT 2003

The Trafficking Victims Protection Reauthorisation Act 2003 (TVPRA 2003) permits an individual who is a victim of forced labour (18 US Code §1589), peonage, slavery, or involuntary servitude (18 US Code §1590), or sex trafficking (18 US Code §1591) to file a civil action against their traffickers in an appropriate district court and recover damages (actual and punitive) and reasonable attorney fees.[101] The civil action may be filed to supplement any criminal proceedings, or as an alternative to criminal prosecution if they choose not to participate in prosecution. The Act does not indicate a statute of limitations for bringing claims for human trafficking.

---

[99]   Case 1:04-cv-02799-BMC-VVP Document 1241 Filed 04/08/15. Slip Copy, 2015 WL 1565479 EDNY 2015.

[100]   There was, however, no evidence that Hamas had carried out two of the 24 attacks in question.

[101]   The civil remedy was not included in the original Trafficking Victims Protection Act of 2000 which set out criminal sanctions against human traffickers. The Act has subsequently been reauthorised in 2005, 2008 and 2013.

4. The 'law of nations' as a cause of action in the US

In this chapter we shall examine how the US federal courts have determined the cause of action that arises under the ATS. Although *Kiobel* has foreclosed future 'foreign cubed' suits being brought under the ATS, save as regards piracy, the position is still uncertain as regards 'foreign squared' suits against US defendants. Much depends on how one interprets Chief Justice Roberts' reference to suits that 'touch and concern' the US, and decisions post-*Kiobel* are divided as to this. The US analysis of civil liability for violations of customary international law is also of continuing interest for claimants who wish to bring actions on this basis in the courts of other jurisdictions, such as the UK. The US jurisprudence on this new form of civil liability will be approached in seven steps. First, what constitutes the law of nations? Second, how are non-State actors held liable for violations of the law of nations? Third, what is the *actus reus* for criminal liability of non-State actors under international law? Fourth, what is the *mens rea* for criminal liability of non-State actors under international law? Fifth, is the claimant required to exhaust domestic remedies before bringing a claim in a foreign court? Sixth, can a corporation incur civil liability in respect of violations of the law of nations? Seventh, how are issues of vicarious liability and veil piercing dealt with in suits based on a violation of the law of nations?

1. WHAT CONSTITUTES 'THE LAW OF NATIONS'?

A year before *Sosa* the Second Circuit undertook a detailed analysis of what constitutes the law of nations, in *Flores v. Southern Peru Copper Corp.*[1] The plaintiffs claimed that the alleged environmental pollution from emissions from the defendant's copper mine in Peru had led to infractions of their rights to life, health and sustainable development. Judge Haight held such rights to be too ill-defined to be capable of

---

[1]   414 F 3d 233 (2d Cir 2003).

generating norms of customary international law.[2] His decision was then affirmed by the Second Circuit who addressed in some detail the key threshold question of what rules constitute norms of customary international law.

The Second Circuit began by defining customary international law as being 'composed only of those rules that States universally abide by, or accede to, out of a sense of legal obligation and *mutual* concern'. Guidance as to the sources that could evidence a rule of customary international law was to be found in Article 38(1) of the Statute of the International Court of Justice which lists the following sources of customary international law.

(a) international conventions, whether general or particular, establishing rules expressly recognised by the contesting States;
(b) international custom as evidence of a general practice recognised by civilised nations;
(c) the general principles of law recognised by civilised nations;
(d) subject to the provisions of Article 59[3] judicial decisions and the teachings of the most highly qualified publicists of the various nations as subsidiary means for the determination of rules of law.

The Second Circuit noted that treaties, conventions and covenants bound only States that become parties to them by consenting to be bound. However, a treaty could constitute sufficient proof of a norm of customary international law, but only if it had been ratified by an overwhelming majority of States and those States had uniformly and consistently acted in acceptance with its principles. The more States that ratified the treaty, and the greater the relative international influence of those States in international affairs, the greater would be the treaty's evidentiary value. In practice, this meant that a rule that was rejected by the US would almost never attain the status of a rule of customary international law. The evidentiary value also increases if States parties have actually taken official action to enforce the principles set forth in the treaty either internationally or within their own boundaries. Only one of the treaties relied on by the plaintiffs, the 1966 International Covenant on Civil and Political Rights (the ICCPR), had been ratified by the US, although it

---

[2] In an earlier decision, *Amlon Metals v. FMC*, 775 F Supp 668 (SDNY 1991) claims arising out of the export of a contaminated consignment from the UK to the US were held not to involve a violation of the law of nations.

[3] 'The decision of the court has no binding force except between the parties and in respect of that particular case.'

was not self-executing. It contained nothing specific on pollution, while its references to the right to life were insufficiently definite. The other treaties relied on by the plaintiffs were also found to be vague and aspirational and did not profess to govern the conduct of private parties.[4]

This was also the case with non-binding Declarations of the UN General Assembly which were not proper sources of customary international law, being merely aspirational, as they were never intended to be binding on UN Member States.[5] Although *Filartiga* had cited the Universal Declaration of Human Rights (1948) in respect of the right to be free of torture, this was only an initial step in the process by which that right had come to be recognised as a norm of customary international law. The declaration had created an *expectation* of adherence but only evidenced customary international law 'insofar as the expectation is gradually justified by State practice'. In *Filartiga* there had been extensive evidence of the repudiation of the official use of torture by States in their domestic and international practices. Multinational declarations of principle, such as the American Declaration of the Rights and Duties of Man (1948) and the Rio Declaration (1992) were also of no evidential value, being aspirational only and creating no legal obligations on participating States. Decisions of the European Court of Human Rights (ECtHR) also lacked evidential worth as that court was empowered only to interpret rules of an instrument applicable only to its regional States parties and not to create new rules of customary international law. Finally, the views of publicists, which under Article 38 were secondary sources only, were only useful for analysis of what the law was and not for speculations as to what it ought to be.[6]

The call for judicial restraint in *Sosa* as to the recognition of new causes of action based on violations of customary international law might have indicated that such norms be limited to those for which universal criminal jurisdiction exists – the five norms listed in section 404 of the

---

[4] These were: the American Convention on Human Rights (1969); the International Covenant on Economic Social and Cultural Rights (1966); the UN Convention on the Rights of the Child (1989).

[5] The power to make legally binding pronouncements is reserved to the Security Council.

[6] At fn 26 the Second Circuit noted that this term suffers from an anachronism as the nineteenth and early twentieth centuries international law scholars collected international practices in compilations, explications and digests of primary legal materials. Contemporary scholarship is more characterised by normative rather than positive argument, in that it contains speculations as to what the law ought to be as opposed to evidence of what the law is.

Restatement.[7] This is particularly so in the light of Justice Breyer's view that there must be both substantive and procedural consensus on how breaches of specific norms of customary international law should be prosecuted, both criminally and civilly. Notwithstanding the Supreme Court's exhortations, it has been very much 'business as usual' in the federal courts where most of the norms of customary international law recognised before *Sosa* have continued to be recognised as grounding claims under ATS. There has been no limitation of ATS claims to those norms of customary international law which impose universal criminal jurisdiction.

Currently, the district courts have confirmed a cause of action under the ATS in respect of violation of the norms of customary international law prohibiting: torture;[8] extra-judicial killing; arbitrary denationalisation and apartheid by state actors;[9] navigation in violation of the Collision Regulations issued by the International Maritime Organisation.[10] The District Court in *Wiwa* has confirmed that there may be a cause of action for crimes against humanity, notwithstanding that the norm was evidenced by treaties which the US had classified as non-self executing.[11] Although the Eleventh Circuit[12] declined to recognise a cause of action for cruel, inhuman or degrading treatment,[13] in *In re South African Apartheid Litigation* Judge Schiendlin held that it did form the basis of a cause of action under ATS, defining the international norm as a prohibition against 'the intentional infliction of mental or physical suffering,

---

[7] These are: piracy; slave trade; attacks on or hijacking of aircraft; genocide; war crimes; and perhaps terrorism.

[8] However, a claim in respect of torture by detainees at Guantanamo Bay was dismissed in *Rasul v. Myers*, 563 F 3d 527 (CA DC 2009), because 'torture is a foreseeable consequence of the military's detention of suspected enemy combatants'.

[9] *In re South African Apartheid Litigation*, 617 F Supp 2d 228 (SDNY 2009). Judge Schiendlin also rejected the defendants' argument that ATS had no extra-territorial reach.

[10] *Institute of Cetacean Research v. Sea Shepherd Conservation Soc*, 860 F Supp 2d 1216 (WD Wash 2012).

[11] *Wiwa (2009)*, 626 F Supp 2d 377 (SDNY 2009).

[12] *Aldana v. Del Monte Fresh Produce, N.A., Inc*, 416 F 3d 1242, 1247 (11th Cir 2005).

[13] See, too, Morrow J in *Sarei v. Rio Tinto*, 650 F.Supp.2d 1004 (C.D.Cal.2009) defining the norm as 'acts which inflict mental or physical suffering, anguish, humiliation, fear and debasement, which fall short of torture'; the principal difference between torture and CIDT being the intensity of the suffering inflicted.

anguish, humiliation, fear, or debasement against a person in the offend-er's custody or control that nevertheless falls short of torture'.[14]

The most expansive recognition of a norm of customary international law was seen in the majority decision of the Second Circuit in *Abdullahi v Pfizer* – a norm prohibiting non-consensual experimentation by private actors.[15] The claim arose out of drug trials in Nigeria in 1995/96. The norm was primarily evidenced by the Nuremberg Code which evolved to form part of Article7 of the ICCPR which entered into force in 1976 and guaranteed individuals the right to be free of non-consensual medical experimentation by any actors, State or private. On its own the ICCPR would not establish a norm of international law but it served to reaffirm the norm articulated in the Nuremberg Code, as did the fact that this norm had been embedded in domestic US legislation. Agreements that were not self-executing, such as the ICCPR, could still be considered as part of the evidence of the current state of customary international law, even though the adoption of a self-executing treaty might provide the best evidence of a particular country's custom or practice of recognising the norm.

The norm was further evidenced by: the 1964 Declaration of Helsinki adopted by the World Medical Association whose informed consent provisions had been imported into the laws and regulations of at least 84 countries, although the Declaration was not binding; the EU's Clinical Trial Directive which accepted the informed consent provisions of the 1996 version of the Declaration of Helsinki; Article 5 of the 1997 Convention on Human Rights and Medicine, signed by 34 Members of the Council of Europe; the Universal Declaration on Bioethics and Human Rights adopted by UNESCO in 2005. The ICCPR and the 1997 Convention evidenced that States had not only acted independently to outlaw large-scale, non-consensual drug testing but had acted in concert in so doing, thereby showing that they had acted out of a sense of mutual concern. However, it must be doubted whether these sources would evidence such a binding norm applying the analysis of the Second Circuit in *Flores*, given the non-binding and regional nature of these sources, together with the fact that three of them came into existence after the

---

[14]   617 F.Supp.2d 228, 253 (S.D.N.Y.). In *John Roe v. Bridgestone Corporation*, 492 F Supp 2d 988 (SD Indiana 2007), it was held that exploitative working conditions for adult labourers did not constitute a violation of the norm against CIDT.

[15]   562 F 3d 163 (2d Cir 2009). To establish liability for violation of this norm, it would, however, be necessary to establish that the private actor had acted under 'color of law' pursuant to s 1983.

drug trials in Nigeria. That would leave only the Nuremberg Code and the ICCPR.[16]

On the other hand the Second Circuit has rejected a cause of action based on: private racial discrimination and for failure to provide consular notification and access after arrest;[17] for denial of the right to peaceful assembly;[18] for the threatened extrajudicial killing of a US citizen abroad;[19] for terrorism.[20] The Second Circuit has also held that a norm of customary international law cannot be evidenced retrospectively.[21]

2. LIABILITY OF NON-STATE ACTORS FOR VIOLATIONS OF THE LAW OF NATIONS

Most established norms of customary international law only proscribe the conduct of states rather than that of private actors. However, there exists a core of *jus cogens* norms in respect of which non-State actors may incur liability. These are the prohibitions against piracy, slave trading (extending to slavery and use of forced labour), war crimes, and genocide. In *Kadic v. Karadzic* the Second Circuit held that individual participants in the civil war in the former Yugolavia, who were not acting

---

[16]   Judge Wesley, dissenting, dismissed both these sources as evidencing a general norm of international law prohibiting non-consensual medical experimentation. The defendants at Nuremberg were not charged with conducting non-consensual medical experimentation per se, but rather with 'war crimes' when conducted on prisoners of war and 'crimes against humanity' when conducted on civilians imprisoned in concentration camps. The defendants were not private actors. All of them held positions of authority in the Nazi regime and the atrocities were committed in state-administered concentration camps.

[17]   *Mora v. New York*, 524 F.3d 183 (2d Cir.2008).

[18]   *Wiwa (2009)*, 626 F Supp 2d 377 (SDNY 2009).

[19]   *Al-Aulaqi v. Obama*, 727 F Supp 2d 1 (DDC 2010).

[20]   *In re Terrorist Attacks on September 11, 2001* 714 F 3d 659 (2d Cir 2013). However, some terrorist acts may constitute crimes against humanity when: (1) committed an enumerated act as part of a widespread or systematic attack against any civilian population with knowledge of that attack; and (2) as a course of conduct pursuant to or in furtherance of a State or organizational policy of a non-State entity which, although not a part of the legitimate government, has *de facto* control over a defined territory. *Krishanthi v. Rajaratnam*, 2010 WL 3429529 (DNJ).

[21]   *Vietnam Ass'n for Victims of Agent Orange v. Dow Chem. Co*, 517 F 3d 104, 115 (2d Cir 2008).

in a state capacity, could be held directly liable under ATS in respect of violations of such norms.[22]

Since *Sosa* a few ATS claims have been considered by the courts in which the plaintiffs have alleged that a corporation has incurred a direct liability in respect of a breach of one of the non-State actor norms of customary international law.[23] In *Sinaltrainal v. Coca Cola Co* the plaintiffs alleged that the defendant corporation was liable in respect of war crimes, arising out of the murder and torture of trade unionists in Colombia by paramilitary forces, allegedly acting as the defendant's agents, during a period of civil war in Colombia. However, a claim for war crimes could not be advanced because these acts were not committed in the course of the civil war.

> In this case there is no suggestion the plaintiffs' murder and torture was perpetrated because of the ongoing civil war or in the course of civil war clashes. The civil war provided the background for the unfortunate events that unfolded, but the civil war did not precipitate the violence that befell the plaintiffs.[24]

A similar analysis was applied in *Re XE Services* where claims were made by Iraqi nationals and estates of nineteen deceased nationals, alleging death and serious injury at the hands of security guards working for one of 11 business entities hired as contractors for the US government in Iraq.[25] Some nexus had to be shown between the conduct and the armed conflict, with the plaintiffs having to plead that the alleged conduct was perpetrated in the context of, and in association with, the armed conflict.

Claims involving direct liability of a corporation for employing forced labour were considered in *John Roe v. Bridgestone Corporation*.[26] Exploitative working conditions for adult labourers in a Liberian rubber plantation were held not to amount to forced labour. Claims of the adult

---

[22]   70 F 3d. 232 (2d Cir 1995).

[23]   In *Estate of Manook v. Research Triangle Institute, International*, F Supp 2d, 2010 WL 675264; (DDC 2010), State action was held to be required when suing a non-State actor for war crimes. However, State action was held not to be required in such circumstances in *Sinaltrainal v. Coca Cola Co*, 2009 578 F 3d 1252; nor was it required when the plaintiffs alleged the defendants had committed murder and torture in the course of war crimes. The same finding was made in *Adikhari v. Daoud and Partners*, 2009 WL 6067064 (SD Tex); 2010 WL 744237 (SD Tex) as regards claims against non-State actors for private acts of trafficking in forced labour.

[24]   578 F 3d 1252 (11th Cir 2009), [28].

[25]   665 F Supp 2d 569 (ED Va 2009).

[26]   492 F Supp 2d 988 (SD Indiana 2007).

workers were not the same as those involving forced labour in Nazi Germany, Japan, Burma. Being kept on the job by poverty, fear and ignorance was not the same as being kidnapped and deported to labour camps. None of the indicators from the International Labour Organisation's 2005 report on Forced Labour applied here. The threat of dismissal was not a 'menace of a penalty', even in a poor country with 80 to 85 per cent unemployment, nor did the existence of the company's security force amount to coercion. However, the use of child labour could amount to a breach of this norm of customary international law.

However, it seems there can be no primary liability in respect of crimes against humanity. In *Abagninin v AMVAC Chemical Corporation*[27] the Ninth Circuit held that a corporation that manufactured an agricultural pesticide, that was alleged to have caused sterilisation of residents and workers in Ivory Coast on banana and pineapple plantations, could not be directly liable for crimes against humanity. These crimes could only be committed pursuant to a policy by state or state-like organisations.[28]

The more common situation involves an allegation that the non-State actor has assisted State officials in the violation of a norm of customary international law, or that the non-State actor's conduct towards the plaintiff has violated a norm of customary international law that does not engage private actors. There are two ways in which ATS claims can be brought against a non-State actor in such circumstances. The first is by reference to the US principles of 'color of law' to be found in 42 USC section 1983 'Civil action for deprivation of rights',[29] which provides:

> Every person who, under color of any statute, ordinance, regulation, custom, or usage, of any State ... . subjects, or causes to be subjected, any citizen of the United States or other person within the jurisdiction thereof to the deprivation of any rights, privileges, or immunities secured by the Constitution and laws, shall be liable to the party injured in an action at law, suit in equity, or other proper proceeding for redress ... .

---

[27]   545 F 3d 733 (9th Cir 2008).

[28]   However, claims for aiding and abetting such violations by state or state-like organisations can be brought under the ATS. See *Bowoto v. Chevron Corp*, 2006 WL 2455752 (ND Cal.) and *Krishanthi v. Rajaratnam*, note 20 above.

[29]   This was enacted on April 20, 1871 as part of the Civil Rights Act of 1871. One of its primary purposes was to provide a civil remedy against the abuses that were being committed in the southern states, especially by the Ku Klux Klan.

If section 1983 is engaged the effect is that though the defendant, or its agents, may have committed the tort, the finding of state involvement in the tort will enable an ATS claim to be brought against a non-State actor for a violation of customary international law. In *Gallagher v. Neil Young Freedom Concert*[30] the Tenth Circuit identified four principles from previous Supreme Court decisions relating to the state action doctrine. First, the Court has considered 'whether there is a sufficiently close nexus between the State and the challenged action of the regulated entity so that the action of the latter may be fairly treated as that of the State itself'.[31] Second the Court has also inquired whether the state has 'so far insinuated itself into a position of interdependence'[32] with the private party, that there is a 'symbiotic relationship' between them.[33] In addition, the Court has held that if a private party is 'a willful participant in joint activity with the State or its agents', then State action is present.[34] Finally, the Court has ruled that a private entity that exercises 'powers traditionally exclusively reserved to the State' is engaged in State action.[35] The more common situation in ATS proceedings is what Sarah Joseph has described as 'reverse state action' where the wrongs have been committed by the foreign State and the plaintiff seeks to link the defendant to those violations.[36] This engages a fifth alternative test, that of 'proximate cause'. In 2000 in *Doe v. Unocal*[37] where the alleged violations of international law had been committed by the Burmese Military, Judge Lew applied this test and held that on the evidence there was no proof of State action under either test.[38]

---

[30]   49 F 3d 1442 (10th Circuit 1995).

[31]   *Jackson v. Metropolitan Edison Co*, 419 US 345, 349, (1974).

[32]   *Burton v. Wilmington Parking Authority*, 365 US 715, 725, (1961).

[33]   *Moose Lodge No. 107 v. Irvis*, 407 US 163, 175, (1972).

[34]   *Adickes v. S H Kress & Co*, 398 US 144, 152, (1970) (quoting *United States v. Price*, 383 US 787, 794, (1966)).

[35]   *Jackson*, note 31 above, 454.

[36]   Sarah Joseph, 'Corporations and Transnational Human Rights Litigation.' Hart Publishing (2004), 35.

[37]   110 F Supp 2d 1294 (CD Cal 2000). The proximate cause test required proof that Unocal had exercised control over the Burmese government's decision to use forced labour on the pipeline project. or that it conspired with the government of Burma. Findings of State action were made in *Wiwa v. Royal Dutch Petroleum Co*, No. 96 Civ. 8386, 2002 WL 319887, at *7–9 (S.D.N.Y. Feb. 28, 2002) and in *Sarei v. Rio Tinto lc*, 221 F Supp 2d 1116 (CD Cal 2002).

[38]   The former required proof that Unocal had "participated in or influenced" the use of forced labour by the Burmese state. The proximate cause test required proof that Unocal had exercised control over the Burmese government's decision

The tenor of the majority judgments in *Sosa* would indicate that causes of action under the ATS should be determined exclusively by reference to customary international law. Accordingly, the US domestic 'color of law' jurisprudence under section 1983 should no longer play any role in determining whether a cause of action under ATS lies against a private actor. This was the view adopted in *Doe I v. Exxon Mobil Corp*[39] in which Judge Oberdorfer stated that 'Grafting s.1983 color of law analysis onto international law claims would be an end-run around the accepted principle that most violations of international law can be committed only by states ... Recognising acts under color of law would dramatically expand the extraterritorial reach of the statute.' A similar finding was made in *Bowoto v. Chevron Corp.*[40] The plaintiffs had provided no international law authority to support the view that a defendant acting under 'color of law' could be found liable for the violation of a norm of international law. Accordingly, section 1983 jurisprudence could not be said to constitute a well-developed norm of customary international law. However, there continues to be a divergence of judicial views on this issue and many courts have continued to apply the 'color of law' jurisprudence to ATS claims.[41]

The second approach, that adopted by the majority of the Ninth Circuit in *Doe v. Unocal*, has been to have recourse to principles of international criminal law regarding aiding and abetting.[42] Referring to *Kadic v. Karadzic*[43] the majority held that non-State actors could be held directly liable as regards violations of a limited category of core *jus cogens* norms of customary international law, including the prohibition against slave trading.[44] The majority then went on to hold that these norms extended to *secondary* liability so that a corporation could be held liable under the

---

to use forced labour on the pipeline project. or that it conspired with the government of Burma

[39]	393 F Supp 2d 20 (DDC 2005).

[40]	*Bowoto v. Chevron Corp*, note 28 above.

[41]	*Aldana v. Del Monte Fresh Produce, N.A., Inc*, 416 F 3d 1242, 1247 (11th Cir 2005); *Chavez v. Carranza*, 413 F Supp 2d 891, 899 (WD Tenn 2005); *Doe v. Saravia*, 348 F Supp 2d 1112, 1150 (E D Cal 2004); *Estate of Manook v. Research Triangle Institute, International*, 759 F Supp 2d 674 (EDNC 2010); (DDC 2010); *Abdullahi v. Pfizer*, 562 F 3d 163 (2d Cir 2009).

[42]	*Doe v. Unocal*, 395 F 3d 932, (2002).

[43]	*Kadic v. Karadzic*, 70 F 3d 232. (2d Cir 1995).

[44]	In *Talisman (2003)*, 244 F Supp 2d 289 (SDNY 2003) Judge Schwarz stated that private actor liability exists in respect of *all* violations of *jus cogens* norms. This, however, is inconsistent with *Kadic* as well as with the finding in *Wiwa* that State action was required in respect of the human rights violations in

ATS as an accomplice to such a violation committed by a State, in the instant case the norm against forced labour that was derived from the norm against slave trading. The claim arose out of Unocal's participation as a joint venturer in the Yadana pipeline project in Burma in the 1990s. The pipeline was to run eastbound through Burma's Tenasserim region, a rural area in the southern portion of Burma that is subject to insurgent activity. Accordingly, the Burmese military increased its presence in the pipeline region to provide security for the project. The plaintiffs were Tenasserim villagers who alleged that the Burmese military had committed the following human rights violations against them in connection with the project: forcing the plaintiffs and others, under threat of violence, to work on these projects and to serve as porters for the military for days at a time; forcibly relocating entire villages for the benefit of the pipeline project; the commission of numerous acts of violence, torture and rape in connection with the forced labour and forced relocations.

The majority of the Ninth Circuit held that the plaintiffs' allegations, if substantiated at trial, would show that the use of forced labour constituted a violation by the Burmese military of the norm of customary international law prohibiting slavery. This was a norm for which a non-State actor could be held liable. It was, therefore, possible for Unocal to be held liable for aiding and abetting the use of forced labour by the Burmese military. They could not, however, be held liable in respect of aiding and abetting torture, or rape, as these did not engage norms of customary international law which impose liability on non-State actors. They could, however, be held liable for aiding and abetting torture and rape that occurred in the course of forced labour. The law to be applied was that which had been developed in decisions of international criminal tribunals such as in International Criminal Tribunal for Former Yugoslavia (ICTY) *Prosecutor v. Furundzija.*[45]

Judge Reinhardt, however, concluded that the issue of secondary liability in an ATS claim fell to be determined under principles of domestic federal tort law. The decision was vacated in February 2003 and an *en banc* rehearing reordered, primarily to clarify whether international law or federal tort law was the applicable law for an ATS claim.[46] The hearing took place in June 2004 and on 17 June was prorogued pending

---

question, which included violations of *jus cogens* norms such as the prohibition on torture.

[45]   Case No. IT-95-17/1, Trial Chamber Judgment, ¶ 155 (Dec. 10, 1998).

[46]   The effect of vacating the decision is that it has no precedential effect and may not be cited on the Ninth Circuit.

the result of the Supreme Court's decision in *Sosa*. In December 2004, the day before the rehearing was due to start, the claims were settled.

This divergence of judicial opinion on the question of whether aiding and abetting liability in ATS claims should be determined by federal law or international law has been reflected in US academic writings. In 'International Human Rights Litigation in U.S. Courts' it has been argued that federal law should apply[47] and that questions of modes of liability are ancillary rather than conduct regulating norms.[48] In contrast, Professor Chimène I. Keitner has argued that the 'ancillary question' approach makes sense for matters of practice and procedure, but not for accomplice liability standards. She notes that:

> Determining whether or not the norm in question regulates conduct offers a principled method for differentiating between substantive and ancillary matters. Defining ancillary questions as those that do not regulate conduct provides a coherent basis for distinguishing issues that are governed by international law from those that are governed by federal common law. Because the prohibition on aiding and abetting wrongdoing regulates conduct, it is governed by international law under the ATS framework.[49]

Two decisions in the Second Circuit have adopted the latter view that the question of aiding and abetting liability under the ATS is to be determined by reference to customary international law. The first was in 2009 in *In re South African Apartheid Litigation* when the case was remitted to the district court for determination of whether a cause of action lay against the corporate defendants under the ATS.[50] Judge Schiendlin held that the question of accomplice liability was to be determined by reference to customary international law, reasoning that:

---

[47] Beth Stephens, Judith Chomsky, Jennifer Green, Paul Hoffman, and Michael Ratner (2d ed. 2008), 319.

[48] Ibid., 37. The authors contend that rules relating to mode of liability are not 'conduct-regulating' norms.

[49] 'Conceptualizing Complicity in Alien Tort Cases' 60 *Hastings L J* 61 (2008), 78, Keitner adopts the terminology of a 'conduct-regulating norm' from Professor Casto 'The New Federal Common Law of Tort Remedies for Violations of International Law', 37 *Rutgers L J* 635, 643 (2006).

[50] *In re South African Apartheid Litigation*, note 9 above. Previously the Second Circuit had split on this issue with the majority finding that secondary liability was governed by international law and Judge Hall applying federal common law principles, *Khulumani v. Barclay Nat. Bank Ltd*, 504 F 3d 254 (2d Cir 2007).

Although cases in this Circuit have only required consultation of the law of nations concerning the existence of substantive offences, the language and logic of *Sosa* require that this Court turn to customary international law to ascertain the contours of secondary liability as well.

Aiding and abetting claims created liability for a distinct form of conduct and as the ATS was merely a jurisdictional vehicle for the enforcement of universal norms, that liability must stem from international sources. Judge Schiendlin observed: 'Ideally, the outcome of an ATS case should not differ from the result that would be reached under analogous jurisdictional provisions in nations such as Belgium, Canada or Spain.'[51] This approach was subsequently adopted by the Second Circuit in *Presbyterian Church of Sudan v. Talisman Energy, Inc,* (*Talisman*) in which it confirmed that the issue of secondary liability under the ATS fell to be determined under customary international law.[52] However, the position of other circuits on this issue is divided. In the Ninth Circuit in *Bowoto v. Chevron* Judge Illston applied customary international law on aiding and abetting,[53] whereas in *Cabello v. Fernandez-Larios*, the Eleventh Circuit applied domestic law to this issue, and also to a conspiracy claim.[54]

Another way of linking a non-State actor to a wrong committed by State officials is by alleging a conspiracy involving the non-State actor and the perpetrators of the wrong. Under international criminal law the analogue of conspiracy is participation in a 'joint criminal enterprise' which had been recognised by the ICTY in *Prosecutor v. Tadic*.[55] In *Talisman*, the Second Circuit, without deciding whether such a crime could form the basis of a claim under the ATS, pointed out that an essential element of a joint criminal enterprise was 'a criminal intention to participate in a common criminal design' which would impose the same burden on the plaintiffs as regards *mens rea* as was the case with their aiding and abetting claims.[56]

---

[51] Ibid., 256.

[52] 582 F 3d 244 (2d Cir 2009).

[53] See, too, the decision of the District Court in *Abecassis v. Wyatt*, 2010 WL 1286871 (SD Tex) to the effect that secondary liability is determined by principles of customary international law.

[54] 402 F 3d 1148, 1157–8 (11th Cir 2005).

[55] Case No.: -94-1-A 15 July 1999 at para 220.

[56] Note 52, at 260.

3. THE EXTENT OF THE INTERNATIONAL LAW NORM RELATING TO AIDING AND ABETTING

The ATS jurisprudence on the identification of a norm of customary international law that encompasses aiding and abetting has proceeded on the basis that non-State actors will incur civil liability for violations of the laws of nations in circumstances in which they would incur criminal liability. This assumption was challenged by Judge Sprizzo in *In re: South African Apartheid Litigation*[57] in which he held that sources relating to criminal responsibility for aiding and abetting under international criminal law could not establish a norm of international law imposing civil liability on aiders and abetters. Judge Sprizzo was also 'mindful of the collateral consequences and possible foreign relations repercussions that would result from allowing courts in this country to hear civil suits for the aiding and abetting of violations of international norms across the globe'. His finding was reversed in the Second Circuit where all three judges held that liability for aiding and abetting could be alleged in an ATS claim, although there was disagreement as to whether this was to be determined in accordance with principles of US tort law or by reference to the principles of international criminal law. Judge Katzman, applying norms of international criminal law, held the past reliance on criminal law norms was entirely appropriate given that international law did not maintain a hermetic seal between criminal and civil law.[58] He referred to Justice Breyer's concurrence in *Sosa* where he stated '[T]he criminal courts of many nations combine civil and criminal proceedings, allowing those injured by criminal conduct to be represented, and to recover damages, in the criminal proceeding itself.'[59]

Having established the existence of a norm of customary international law imposing *civil* liability on aiders and abetters, the next issue is defining the extent of that norm. One view is that this secondary liability attaches only in respect of those norms for which a non-State actor could be held *directly* liable. This was the view taken by the majority of the Ninth Circuit in *Unocal* and also by Judge Illston in *Bowoto v Chevron Corp* in 2006.[60] She held that the international law norms invoked by the

---

[57]   346 F Supp.2d 538 (SDNY 2004).

[58]   *Khulumani v. Barclay Nat. Bank Ltd*, note 14 above, fn 5, 270.

[59]   Sosa, 542 US, 762–3, 124 S Ct 2739. Moreover, the ICTY has recognised the propriety of civil remedies for violations of international criminal law in certain circumstances, noting for example that a torture victim might 'bring a civil suit for damage in a foreign court'. *Prosecutor v. Furundzija*, note 45 above.

[60]   *Bowoto v. Chevron Corp*, note 28 above.

plaintiff (the prohibition of torture, and of extra judicial killing) placed no direct liability on a private party so it would be inappropriate to allow liability to be imposed on a private party for aiding and abetting a breach of such a norm. However, in 2007 Judge Illston reversed her previous finding and accepted that it had been based on the faulty premise that if a party could not be liable as principal it could not be liable as aider and abetter.[61] However, this was not the case under civil common law[62] and neither was it the case under customary international law. Consequently, civil liability for aiding and abetting could arise under the ATS in respect of any norm of customary international law that was sufficiently established under the criteria set out by the Supreme Court in *Sosa*.

It is, however, the case that all the cases involving aiding and abetting before international criminal tribunals have involved those norms for which an individual person could incur criminal liability as a principal. It is difficult to see, though, how there can be criminal liability for aiding and abetting a violation of a norm of customary international law, when the breach of that norm will not lead to the imposition of criminal liability under international law on any individual as perpetrator of that breach. For example, in *In re South African Apartheid Litigation*[63] the norms prohibiting apartheid and arbitrary denationalisation by State actors were sufficiently established under customary international law to form the basis of an ATS claim based on aiding and abetting, even though the norms did not cover the conduct of non-State actors.[64] However, if a norm is not one in respect of which customary international law has imposed criminal liability on State actors who violate it, then it is hard to see how the conduct of the accessory 'borrows the criminality of the act committed by the principal perpetrator of the criminal enterprise'. It is submitted that the criminal liability of an

---

[61]   *Bowoto v. Chevron Corp*, 2007 WL 2349341 (ND Cal 2007), August 14, 2007.

[62]   The Restatement (Second) of Torts § 876, and *Talbot v. Janson*, 3 US (3 Dall) 133, 156–8, 1 L Ed 540, 3 Dall 133 (1795) (seriatim opinion of Paterson, J) (holding a French citizen civilly liable for aiding a US citizen to unlawfully capture a Dutch ship); ibid., 167–8 (seriatim opinion of Iredell, J) (similar); 1 Op. Att'y Gen 57, 59 (1795) (describing [ATS] jurisdiction and noting that those who commit[ ], aid[ ], or abet [ ] hostilities have render[ed] themselves liable to punishment under the laws of nations); Act of April 30, 1790, ch. 9 § 10, 1 Stat. 114 (criminalising aiding and abetting piracy).

[63]   Note 50 above.

[64]   The plaintiffs had also argued that the defendants were directly liable for breach of this norm but Judge Schiendlin held that there was no norm prohibiting racial discrimination by private actors.

accessory depends on there being someone who is capable of incurring criminal liability as a principal under customary international law, although the principal need not be a non-State actor. A non-State actor would, therefore, be capable of being held criminally liable for aiding and abetting torture, a norm, which by definition can only be violated by a State actor.

4. THE CONTENT OF THE INTERNATIONAL LAW NORM ON AIDING AND ABETTING

Having established that there are norms of customary international law relating to aiding and abetting and that these are capable of reaching corporate defendants in civil claims under the ATS, we now turn to the substance of the norm of customary international law by which criminal liability can be imposed on accomplices to violations of international law. As regards the elements of the *actus reus* of criminal liability for aiding and abetting under international law, the federal courts have turned to two sources of customary international law; the Nuremberg trials, and the decisions of the ICTY and ICTR. As regards the *mens rea* requirements they have considered a third source, the Rome Statute establishing the International Criminal Court (ICC) (which contains a definition of *mens rea* for international criminal liability of accessories, but is silent as regards *actus reus*).

A. *Actus Reus*

The *actus reus* for aiding and abetting under international criminal law was defined by the ICTY Tribunal in *Prosecutor v. Furundzija*, as 'practical assistance, encouragement, or moral support which has a *substantial effect* on the perpetration of the crime'.[65] This definition has been adopted in ATS cases, although in *Unocal (2002)* the majority of the Ninth Circuit expressed doubts as to the reference to 'encouragement or moral support'.[66] In *Talisman*[67] Judge Cote adopted the definition propounded by the Appeals Chamber of the ICTY in *Prosecutor v.*

---

[65]   Note 45 above.

[66]   395 F 3d 932 (2002). However, the full *Furundzija* definition of the *actus reus* requirement has been applied in *Bowoto v. Chevron Corp*, note 28 above and in *In re South African Apartheid Litigation*, note 9 above.

[67]   453 F Supp 2d 633 (SDNY 2006).

Vasiljevic[68] that the accused must have carried out 'acts *specifically directed* to assist, encourage or lend moral support to the perpetration of a certain specific crime [emphasis added]'. Judge Cote thought that the inclusion of the words 'specifically directed' may have been designed to address the issue of whether assistance must be 'direct'.

Two decisions of international criminal tribunals in 2013 have led to different formulations as regards the *actus reus* of aiding and abetting. In *Prosecutor v. Charles Ghankay Taylor* it was held, "[T]he *actus reus* of aiding and abetting liability is established by assistance that has a substantial effect on the crimes, not the particular manner in which such assistance is provided."[69] In contrast in *Prosecutor v. Perisic*, it was held that 'specific direction remains an element of the *actus reus* of aiding and abetting', while noting that 'specific direction may be addressed implicitly in the context of analysing substantial contribution'.[70] In *Doe I v. Nestle USA, Inc*,[71] the Ninth Circuit granted the plaintiffs leave to amend their complaint in light of this recent authority regarding the *actus reus* standard for aiding and abetting.[72] The Ninth Circuit later held that *actus reus* required substantial assistance, but passed the issue of whether it must be 'specifically directed' to the district court to determine in the light of the conflicting international criminal law cases in *Perisic* and *Taylor*.[73] On 23 January 2014 the discrepancy between these decisions was resolved in *Prosecutor v. Nikola Šainović*[74] in which the Appeals Chamber of the ICTY concluded that 'specific direction' is not an element of aiding and abetting liability.

In *In re South African Apartheid Litigation*[75] Judge Schiendlin, adopting the *Furundzija* standard, started her analysis by noting that merely doing business in a State which was committing violations of customary international law would not be sufficient to constitute the *actus reus* of aiding and abetting. The claims arose out of the business relationships between the South African government during the apartheid period and

---

[68]   *Prosecutor v. Vasiljevic*, Case No. IT-98-32-A, Judgment, 102(i) (App. Chamber, Feb. 25, 2004).

[69]   Case No SCSL–03–01–A Judgment, at ¶ 475 (SCSL Sept. 26, 2013).

[70]   Case No. IT–04–81–A Judgment, at ¶ 36 & n. 97 (ICTY Feb. 28, 2013).

[71]   738 F 3d 1048.

[72]   A similar order was made by Court of Appeals for the District of Columbia in *Doe v. Exxon Mobil Corp*, 527, Fed Appx 7. (CADC July 26 2013).

[73]   ___ F 3d___, 2014 WL 4358453 (9th Cir 2014).

[74]   ICTY, Judgment (Appeals Chamber) (Case No IT-05-87-A), 23 January 2014

[75]   Note 9 above.

various corporations; automotive corporations who had provided vehicles to the security forces; computer corporations who had provided hardware and software that had been used to effect the denationalisation of black South Africans; banking corporations who had lent money to the South African defence force and had adopted racially discriminatory employment practices. In determining whether or not the alleged assistance had had a 'substantial effect' on the commission of the crime, guidance could be obtained from a comparison of the two decisions in *The Ministries Case* at Nuremberg. In one, Rasche who had supplied loans to the SS was found not guilty,[76] while in the other Tesch had who supplied poison gas to death camps was found guilty. The two cases could be distinguished by reference to the quality of the assistance provided to the primary violator.[77] Accordingly, some specific link was required between the state's violation of customary international law and the corporation's assistance of that violation. The facts alleged by the plaintiffs against the automotive defendants disclosed just such a direct link through the sale of specialised military vehicles to the South African Government, as well as components of the 'Casspir' and 'Buffer' vehicles that were allegedly used by the internal security forces to patrol the townships. Similarly a very direct link with violations of the norms against arbitrary denationalisation and apartheid by a State actor would be established by the sale of computers to the governments of South Africa and of the bantustans for use in the registration of individuals, leading to their being stripped of their South African citizenship, and segregated in particular areas of South Africa. In contrast, the *actus reus* of aiding and abetting apartheid and CIDT was not made out against Barclays. Their employment practices in systematically denying employment opportunities on the basis of race were aligned with the geographic segregation already established by the South African government and involved acquiescence in, rather than the provision of essential support for, apartheid. Nor would the *actus reus* of aiding and abetting any of the violations of customary international law alleged against the apartheid regime in South Africa be established by the banks' provision of loans and purchase of South African defence forces bonds. To supply a violator of the law of nations with funds – even funds that could not have been obtained but for those loans – was not sufficiently connected to the primary violation.

---

[76] *United States v. Von Weizsacker (The Ministries Case)*, in 14 Trials of War Criminals Before the Nuremberg Military Tribunals, 622, 851–2 (1950).

[77] *Trial of Bruno Tesch and Two Others (The Zyklon B Case)*, in 1 Law Reports of Trials of War Criminals 93–103. (1947).

B. *Mens Rea*

The three sources of international law relied on by the federal courts have given conflicting indications as to whether the *mens rea* of aiding and abetting under international law requires intentional assistance or whether knowing assistance will suffice. The first source, the Nuremberg jurisprudence, contains decisions in which either knowledge or intent has been required to establish the culpability of the party providing assistance to the violation of a norm of customary international law. In the *Zyklon B* case, decided by a British military court in Hamburg, the owner of Tesch and Stabenow and a senior official, Weinbacher, were hanged on the basis that they accepted and processed orders for Zyklon B which were then shipped directly to the SS concentration camps where they were then used to exterminate allied nationals. Their knowledge of the intended use of the product coupled with its substantial assistance in war crimes made them liable as aiders and abetters.[78] In contrast in *US v. von Weizsaecker (the Ministries case)* Karl Rasche, Chairman of Dresdner Bank, was charged with lending money to SS enterprises which he knew were making use of forced labour.[79] He was acquitted but another banker, Emil Puhl, was found guilty as an accessory to crimes against humanity in that he knowingly participated in the disposal of gold, including gold teeth and crowns, and valuables taken from Holocaust victims.[80]

The second source, the decisions of the ICTY and ICTR, leans towards a knowledge standard.[81] This has recently been confirmed in *Prosecutor v. Nikola Šainović*[82] where the Appeals Chamber of the ICTY held that the *mens rea* standard required the accused to be aware of the essential elements of the specific crime committed, including the mental state of the perpetrators. The third source is the 1998 Rome Statute establishing the International Criminal Court. Article 25(3)(c) provides that a person 'shall be criminally responsible and liable for punishment for a crime' if that person '[f]or *the purpose* of facilitating the commission of such a crime, aids, abets or otherwise assists in its commission or its attempted

---

[78] Ibid.

[79] *The Ministries Case* note 76 above, 622, 851–2.

[80] Ibid., 621–2, 868.

[81] In *Prosecutor v. Furundzija*, note 45 above, knowledge was held to be the basis of the *mens rea* of aiding and abetting.

[82] Note 74 above.

commission, including providing the means for its commission' (emphasis added).[83] However, Article 25(3) does not exist in isolation, and has to be read in conjunction with Article 30. Paragraph 1 provides, 'Unless otherwise provided, a person shall be criminally responsible and liable for punishment for a crime within the jurisdiction of the Court only if the material elements are committed with intent and knowledge.' Paragraph 2 then provides that a person has intent where: '(a) In relation to conduct, that person means to engage in the conduct; [and] (b) In relation to a consequence, that person means to cause that consequence *or is aware* that it will occur in the ordinary course of events' (emphasis added).

The courts of the Second Circuit have differed in their identification of the *mens rea* for aiding and abetting under customary international law. The key question is whether it is necessary that the accomplice intended to further the primary violation of the law of nations or whether mere knowledge would suffice. In 2007 in *Khulumani v Barclay Nat. Bank Ltd* the Second Circuit split on this issue.[84] Judge Hall applied federal law which applied a knowledge test in civil claims against aiders and abetters. Judge Katzman and Judge Korman both held that intention was required under customary international law, although Judge Korman held that aiding and abetting claims could not be brought against corporations. Judge Katzman's judgment is particularly significant as it forms the basis for the subsequent decision of the Second Circuit in *Presbyterian Church of Sudan v. Talisman Energy* on this issue.[85] He held that Article 25(3)(c) of the Rome Statute constituted authoritative guidance on the international law standard for *mens rea* in criminal proceedings against aiders and abetters, 'because, unlike other sources of international legislation, it

---

[83]   Article 25(d), however, deals with aiding and abetting the commission of a crime by a *group of persons* by providing for the criminal responsibility of a person who:

> In any other way contributes to the commission or attempted commission of such a crime by a group of persons acting with a common purpose. Such contribution shall be intentional and shall either:
> (i) Be made with the aim of furthering the criminal activity or criminal purpose of the group, where such activity or purpose involves the commission of a crime within the jurisdiction of the Court; or
> (ii) Be made in the knowledge of the intention of the group to commit the crime ...

[84]   Note 14 above.
[85]   Note 52 above.

articulates the *mens rea* required for aiding and abetting liability'.[86] He recognised that the Rome Statute had yet to be considered by the ICC and that 'its precise contours and the extent to which it may differ from customary international law thus remain somewhat uncertain'. The Rome Statute's *mens rea* standard was consistent with the application of accomplice liability under other sources of customary international law, in particular the *Ministries* case at Nuremberg in which the tribunal declined to impose criminal liability on the banker, Rasche, in respect of making a loan to the SS. The matter was remitted to the district court for reconsideration by Judge Schiendlin in *In re South African Apartheid Litigation*.[87] She noted that the vast majority of international legal materials specified knowledge and, after examining the Nuremberg decisions, concluded that the *Rasche* case was not authority for requiring intent as the basis of the decision was that there was no *actus reus*. She then turned to the Rome Statute and concluded that this was not intended to eliminate rights existing under the law of nations. Where the Rome Statute *explicitly* deviates from the law of nations, it could fairly be assumed that those rules are unique to the ICC, rather than a rejection of customary international law. In the absence of an explicit deviation in the Rome Statute with regard to aiding and abetting liability, Article 25(c) could reasonably be interpreted to conform to pre-Rome Statute customary international law.[88]

Judge Schiendlin also pointed out that a secondary purpose could be inferred from knowledge of the likely consequences of an act.

> This logic is particularly prominent in the case of a person or corporation who provides the means by which a crime in violation of the law of nations is carried out, as the primary purpose profit is furthered by the success of an ongoing crime. Thus it may reasonably be inferred that an arms dealer

---

[86] Ibid., 276. The Statute had been signed by 139 countries and ratified by 105, including most of the mature democracies of the world and could therefore be taken 'by and large … as constituting an authoritative expression of the legal views of a great number of States'. The US failure to ratify the statute was not due to any concerns about its provisions on aiding and abetting.

[87] Note 9 above.

[88] Article 10 of the Rome Statute, which provides 'Nothing in this Part shall be interpreted as limiting or prejudicing in any way existing or developing rules of international law for purposes other than this Statute' would appear to support this view. However, this article appears in Part Two of the Statute, 'Jurisdiction, Admissibility and Applicable Law', whereas art 25 appears in Part Three 'General Principles of Criminal Law'.

providing weapons to perpetrators of a genocide tacitly supports the genocide, as it creates demand for that increases profit.

Article 30(2) of the Rome Statute also had to be taken into account.[89] Judge Schiendlin reasoned that even assuming that Article 25(c) carried an intent requirement, the context of the Rome Statute 'intent' did not require that an aider or abettor share the primary actor's purpose. Rather it meant that the *actions* must be taken intentionally, and not under duress. However, Article 30(2) provided for a knowledge requirement for the *mens rea* requirement relating to the outcome – rather than the act.

> Under the Rome Statute – and under customary international law – there was no difference between amorality and immorality. One who substantially assisted a violator of the law of nations was equally liable if he or she desires the crime to occur or if he or she knows it will occur and simply does not care.[90]

This analysis is supported by the pre-trial decision in *Prosecutor v. Lubanga* in which the ICC stated that the volitional element in Article 30(2):

> also encompasses other forms of the concept of *dolus* which have already been resorted to by the jurisprudence of the *ad hoc* tribunals, that is: i. situations in which the suspect, without having the concrete intent to bring about the objective elements of the crime, is aware that such elements will be the necessary outcome of his or her actions or omissions (also known as *dolus directus* of the second degree); and ii. situations in which the suspect (a) is aware of the risk that the objective elements of the crime may result from his or her actions or omissions, and (b) accepts such an outcome by reconciling himself or herself with it or consenting to it (also known as *dolus eventualis*).' In the second situation, where the risk of bringing about the objective elements of the crime is substantial, the suspect's acceptance can be inferred from: 'i. the awareness by the suspect of the substantial likelihood that his or her actions or omissions would result in the realisation of the objective elements of the crime; and ii. the decision by the suspect to carry out his or her actions or omissions despite such awareness.[91]

---

[89] This provides that a person has intent where: '(a) In relation to conduct, that person means to engage in the conduct; [and] (b) In relation to a consequence, that person means to cause that consequence *or is aware* that it will occur in the ordinary course of events'(emphasis added).

[90] *South African Litigation,* note 9 above, 262.

[91] *Prosecutor v. Thomas Lubanga Dyilo*, Case No. ICC/01/04–01/06, Pre–Trial Chamber Decision on the Confirmation of Charges (Jan. 29, 2007), paras 351-353.

If, however, the risk of bringing about the objective elements of the crime is low, the suspect must have 'clearly or expressly accepted the idea that such objective elements may result from his or her actions'.

Subsequently in October 2009 in *Talisman*[92] the Second Circuit decided that the *mens rea* of aiding and abetting under customary international law required intention rather than knowledge decision, adopting Judge Katzman's analysis put forward in *Khulumani* in 2007. The Second Circuit had heard argument in January 2009 before Judge Schiendlin's decision on this issue. The Second Circuit's analysis of this issue is somewhat brief and, unlike that engaged in by Judge Schiendlin in *In re South African Apartheid Litigation*, fails to take account of Article 30(2) of the Rome Statute, or of the fact that the decision in *US v. Von Weizsaecker* was based on the absence of the *actus reus* of aiding and abetting.

The decision has subsequently been trenchantly criticised by David Scheffer who, as US Ambassador at Large for War Crimes Issues between 1997 and 2001, was involved in the negotiations for the Rome Statute.[93] Scheffer and Kaeb point out that the wording 'purpose' was reached as a compromise between proponents of 'intent' and 'knowledge' and that Article 25(3)(c) was not intended to be a statement of customary international law. They also argue that the adoption of a purpose standard for *mens rea* destroys the distinction between aiders and abetters and co-perpetrators who incur primary liability as participants in a joint criminal enterprise in which they share the intent of the principal perpetrator. Instead, the *mens rea* requirement for aiding and abetting in the Rome Statute is to be found in Article 30(2)(b), namely '[i]n relation to a consequence, that person means to cause that consequence or is aware that it will occur in the ordinary course of events', and is not to be limited to the first prong of this formulation. Rather the compromise phrase 'purpose' in Article 25(3)(c) 'stated the de minimus and obvious point, namely, that an aider and abetter purposely acts in a manner that has the consequence of facilitating the commission of a crime, but one

---

[92]   582 F 3d 244 (2d Cir 2009).

[93]   'The Five Levels of CSR Compliance. The Resiliency of Corporate Liability under the Alien Tort Statute and the Case for a Counterattack Strategy in Compliance Theory,' David Scheffer and Caroline Kaeb. North Western University School of Law, Public Policy Roundtable – The Alien Tort Statute and US Enforcement of Foreign Judgments. Thursday, April 29th, 2010 – Friday, April 30, 2010. <http://www.law.northwestern.edu/searlecenter/uploads/Scheffer_Kaeb_CSR.pdf> (accessed 18 July 2010).

must look to Article 30(2)(b) for guidance on how to frame the intent of the aider or abettor with respect to that consequence'.[94]

The position of other circuits on this question is mixed. In *Sarei v. Rio Tinto* the Ninth Circuit was prepared to assume that the *mens rea* for aiding and abetting under international criminal law was purposive assistance, without deciding the issue.[95] In *Aziz v. Alcolac* the Fourth Circuit held that purposive assistance was required[96] as did the District Court in Maryland in *Du Daobin v. Cisco Systems Inc.*[97] In contrast in *Doe v. Exxon Corporation* the majority of the Court of Appeals for District of Columbia held that customary international law on aiding and abetting was to be found in the decisions of the ICTY and ICTR and that, in any event, the Rome Statute contemplated a *mens rea* requirement based on knowledge rather than intention.[98] In *Doe v. Nestle* when the case returned to the Ninth Circuit in 2014 the majority made no finding as to whether the *mens rea* requirement was knowledge or purpose, holding that there was sufficient purpose. The plaintiffs' allegations satisfied the more stringent purpose standard by suggesting that a myopic focus on profit over human welfare drove the defendants to act with the purpose of obtaining the cheapest cocoa possible, even if it meant facilitating child slavery. Judge Rawlinson was of the view that purposive assistance was required.[99]

The position in international criminal tribunals was, until recently, equally mixed with two decisions in 2013 going different ways: *Prosecutor v. Perišić*[100] where the ICTY held that it had to be established that the

---

[94]   Ibid., 29.

[95]   *Sarei v. Rio Tinto, plc*, 671 F 3d 736 (9th Cir 2011).

[96]   658 F 3d 388 (4th Cir 2011).

[97]   Case 8:11-cv-01538-PJM. 24 February 2014.

[98]   *Doe v. Exxon Mobil Corp*, 654 F 3d 11, (DC Cir 2011). Judge Rogers pointed to art 25(3)(d) which provides liability for an individual who, 'contributes to the commission or attempted commission of such a crime by a group of persons acting with a common purpose' where such contribution is 'intentional' and either 'made with the aim of furthering the criminal activity or criminal purpose of the group' or 'made in the knowledge of the intention of the group to commit the crime'; to art 30 which provides that 'a person has intent where … [i]n relation to a consequence, that person means to cause that consequence or is aware that it will occur in the ordinary course of events'; and to the decision in. *Prosecutor v. Thomas Lubanga Dyilo*, note 91 above, which applied a 'knowledge' standard under art 25(3)(a) to international law violations by a co-perpetrator.

[99]   766 F.3d 1013 (9th Cir 2014).

[100]   IT-04-81-A (Int'l Crim. Trib. for the Former Yugoslavia Feb. 28, 2013).

defendant's assistance was "specifically directed" to aiding the commission of the offence; *Prosecutor v. Taylor*[101] where the SCSL Appeals Chamber held that the *mens rea* of aiding and abetting was knowledge. However, in *Prosecutor v. Nikola Šainović*[102] the Appeals Chamber of the ICTY held that the *mens rea* standard required the accused to be aware of the essential elements of the specific crime committed, including the mental state of the perpetrators.

5. MUST THE PLAINTIFF EXHAUST DOMESTIC REMEDIES?

In *Sarei v Rio Tinto plc.* an en banc panel of the Ninth Circuit considered Justice Souter's suggestion in *Sosa* that ATS suits might be subject to a requirement of prior exhaustion of remedies.[103] The suit involved claims by inhabitants of Bougainville who had suffered during the civil war and resulting blockade of the Island by Papua New Guinea, prompted by protests against Rio Tinto's operation of its giant Panguna mine. The claim was brought against Rio Tinto and the allegation was that it had been complicit in various violations of customary international law by the Papua New Guinea Defence Force. The Ninth Circuit remanded the action for the limited purpose of ascertaining whether, as an initial, prudential matter, exhaustion of domestic remedies should be required. Judge McKeown concluded that 'in ATS cases where the United States "nexus" is weak, courts should carefully consider the question of exhaustion of domestic remedies, particularly – but not exclusively – with respect to claims that do not involve matters of "universal concern"'. When the case was remitted to the district court to Judge Morrow she found that the question of exhaustion did not need to be considered as regards claims involving matters of universal concern, such as the claims for crimes against humanity, war crimes, and racial discrimination.[104] However, the traditional two-step exhaustion analysis[105] would be applied to the other ATS claims for violation of the rights to health, life, and

---

[101]   SCSL-03-01-A (10766-11114) (Special Court for Sierra Leone Sept. 26, 2013).

[102]   Note 74 above.

[103]   550 F 3d 822 (9th Cir 2008).

[104]   650 F Supp 2d 1004 (CD Cal 2009).

[105]   The analysis requires determining whether local remedies exist as the first step and then, as a second step, determining whether they are ineffective, unobtainable, unduly prolonged, inadequate, or otherwise futile to pursue.

security of the person; cruel, inhuman, and degrading treatment; international environmental violations; and a consistent pattern of gross human rights violations. The plaintiffs decided to abandon these claims.[106]

6. CORPORATE LIABILITY UNDER THE LAW OF NATIONS

It has been argued that the ATS does not cover claims against corporations because corporations cannot incur obligations under customary international law. The essence of such arguments is that civil liability of non-State actors under customary international law will be imposed in circumstances when criminal liability would be imposed on them, either primarily or secondarily, for violation of a norm of customary international law. Therefore, if a corporation is incapable of incurring criminal liability under customary international law, it must follow that it is also incapable of incurring a civil liability under the ATS for violation of the law of nations. These arguments were dismissed by Judge Schwarz in 2003 in *Talisman* in which he held that ATS claims could be brought against corporations,[107] and again by Judge Cote when the issue was reconsidered in 2005.[108] Until 2010 only Judge Korman's minority judgment in *Khulumani* in 2007[109] supported the view that corporations could not be the subject of claims under the ATS. In neither of the cases against corporations that proceeded to trial, *Bowoto v. Chevron* and *Romero v. Drummond*,[110] did the defendants raise the issue that a

---

[106]   Judge Morrow's decisions as regards the claims for crimes against humanity, war crimes, and racial discrimination was upheld by the Ninth Circuit, 671 F 3d 736 (9th Cir 2011). The Seventh Circuit declined to apply an exhaustion analysis in *Flomo v. Firestone* 643 F 3d 1013 (7th Cir. 2011).

[107]   *Talisman* note 44 above.

[108]   *Presbyterian Church of Sudan v. Talisman Energy, Inc*, 374 F Supp 2d 331 (SDNY 2005).

[109]   *Khulumani v. Barclay Nat. Bank Ltd* 504 F 3d 254 (2d Cir 2007).

[110]   *See* Business and Human Rights Resource Center, *Case Profile Drummond Law Suit (re Columbia)*, http://www.businesshumanrights.org/Categories/Lawlawsuits/Lawsuitsregulatoryaction/LawsuitsSelectedcases/Drummondlawsuitre Colombia (last visited 24 Sept. 2013) and BOWOTO V. CHEVRON TRIAL BLOG, (Dec. 1, 2008, 3.12 PM), *Verdict: Chevron Found Not Guilty*, http://bowotov chevron.wordpress.com/2008/12/01/chevron-not-liableon- all-claims/ <accessed 24 Sept 2013>.

corporation could not incur civil liability under customary international law.[111]

However, the Second Circuit's position on this issue changed drastically with its majority decision in *Kiobel v Royal Dutch Petroleum Co* on 21 September 2010.[112] The same court as had decided *Talisman* in 2009 now considered the issue of whether the ATS reached corporate defendants.[113] The majority, whose opinion was given by Judge Cabranes, held that it did not. Judge Cabranes reviewed the development of international law as it applied to individuals from the starting point of the Nuremberg trials which made explicit what had previously been implicit the proposition that individuals could incur liability for committing international crimes. However, at Nuremberg this principle had been expressly confined to natural persons. Although the tribunals had the authority to declare an organisation to be criminal, this was with a view towards facilitating the imposition of liability on the individual members of the organisation. The tribunals had no jurisdiction to impose criminal liability on the organisation itself. All subsequent international criminal tribunals from the ICTY and ICTR to the ICC had possessed jurisdiction over natural persons, but not over legal persons.[114] The Rome Statute which created the International Criminal Court provided for jurisdiction over 'natural persons' and French proposals for bringing in corporations and other juridical person had been rejected.[115] The ATS tort jurisdiction extended to those individuals who had committed international crimes and it, therefore, followed, that it could not extend to corporations, although individual perpetrators in a corporation could still incur liability. International law and not domestic law determined the reach of the ATS. International law determined both the 'what' – the norm that was broken

---

[111]   In both cases the jury found for the defendant.

[112]   621 F 3d 111, (2d Cir 2010). Shortly before the decision, the district court in California in *Doe v. Nestle*, 748 F Supp. 2d 1057 (CD Cal 2010) No. CV 05-5133, slip op. at 120–60 (CD Cal Sept.8, 2010) had held that ATS claims could not be pursued against corporations.

[113]   This was a decision as regards jurisdiction, rather than as regards merits. This was significant because it allowed the Second Circuit to raise the issue *sua sponte*. The issue of the liability of corporate defendants under the ATS had not been considered by the district court judge, nor raised by the defendant.

[114]   Unlike the Nuremberg tribunals, these subsequent tribunals had not been given jurisdiction to declare organisations to be criminal.

[115]   A similar proposal, advanced by Australia, had been rejected when the Committee on International Legal Jurisdiction, under the auspices of the ILC, released its report on this issue in 1953 UN GAOR, 9th Sess, Supp No 12, UN Doc. A/2645 (1954).

– and the 'who' – the persons liable for breach of that norm.[116] For this reason, the norm for aiding and abetting was to be found in international law, rather than in domestic law.[117] Footnote 20 of Justice Souter's opinion in *Sosa* also mandated that the courts use international law to determine the subjects of international law. Judge Schwarz's judgment in *Talisman* in 2003 was flawed in that it over-valued treaties imposing liabilities on corporations as evidencing a norm that corporations were the subjects of customary international law. A limited number of treaties on specialised questions neither codified an existing, general rule of customary international law, nor crystalised an emerging norm of customary international law.

In contrast, Judge Leval, dissenting, looked to customary international law to determine the norms imposing liability, including those relating to aiding and abetting, and then to domestic law to supply the remedy for breach. The second stage determined who could be liable and as corporations were subject to civil liability under US domestic law, they could also be liable under the ATS. Judge Leval pointed to two opinions of US attorney generals, in 1795 and 1907, in which the view had been expressed that corporations could incur liability for breaches of customary international law, and could also advance claims for wrongs done to them under customary international law.[118] Judge Leval was of the view that the majority had misunderstood how the law of nations functions:

> Civil liability *under the ATS* for violation of the law of nations is not awarded because of a perception that international law commands civil liability throughout the world. It is awarded in U.S. courts because the law of nations has outlawed certain conduct, leaving it to each State to resolve questions of civil liability, and the United States has chosen through the ATS to impose civil liability. The majority's ruling defeats the objective of international law

---

[116]   *Kiobel*, note 112 above, 117–23, 127–41.

[117]   If the norm on aiding and abetting had to be derived from domestic law, plaintiffs would face the problem of the Supreme Court's decision in *Central Bank of Denver v. First Interstate Bank*, 511 US 164 (1994) that aiding and abetting liability under a statute will not be implied.

[118]   In 1795, the attorney general opined that a British corporation could pursue a civil action under the ATS for injury caused to it in violation of international law by American citizens who, in concert with a French fleet, had attacked a settlement managed by the corporation in Sierra Leone in violation of international law. *See* 1 Op. Att'y Gen. 57 (1795). In 1907, the attorney general opined that an American corporation could be held liable under the ATS to Mexican nationals if the defendant's 'diversion of the water [of the Rio Grande] was an injury to substantial rights of citizens of Mexico under the principles of international law or by treaty'. 26 Op. Att'y Gen. 252, 253 (1907).

to allow each nation to formulate its own approach to the enforcement of international law.[119]

However, Judge Leval agreed that the case should be dismissed, because the plaintiffs had failed to show evidence that the corporation had acted with the purpose of assisting the State actors' violations of customary international law.[120]

A circuit split on this issue has recently opened up with contrary decisions in three other Circuits. In *Doe v. Exxon* the majority of the Court of Appeals for District of Columbia held that the norms of conduct in an ATS suit were derived from customary international law, including those relating to aiding and abetting, but not the norms of attribution, which fell under domestic law. Customary international law identified the prohibitions on conduct whereas the "technical accoutrements" to the ATS cause of action, such as corporate liability and agency law, derived from federal common law. In *Flomo v. Firestone Natural Rubber Co, LLC,* the Seventh Circuit held that there was a norm of customary international law by which corporations could be held civilly liable in respect of their primary or secondary involvement in violations of *jus cogens* norms of customary international law.[121] Judge Posner held that the factual premise underlying the majority's decision in *Kiobel* was incorrect and that at Nuremberg two measures had specifically provided sanctions against organisations: Council Law No. 2, 'Providing for the Termination and Liquidation of the Nazi Organizations';[122] and Control Council Law No. 9, 'Providing for the Seizure of Property Owned by IG Farbenindustrie and the Control Thereof', under which the seizure of all IG Farben's assets was ordered with a direction that some of them be made 'available for reparations'.[123] Judge Posner noted, '[a]nd suppose no corporation *had* ever been punished for violating customary international law. There is always a first time for litigation to enforce a norm; there has to be. There were no multinational prosecutions for aggression and crimes against humanity before the Nuremberg Tribunal was created.'[124] Thirdly, there is the decision of the Ninth Circuit in *Sarei v. Rio*

---

[119]   *Kiobel*, note 112 above, 175.
[120]   Ibid., 189–93.
[121]   *Flomo* note 106 above.
[122]   Oct. 10, 1945, reprinted in 1 *Enactments and Approved Papers of the Control Council and Coordinating Committee* 131 (1945) available at www. loc.gov/rr/frd/Military_Law/enactments-home.html.
[123]   Nov. 30, 1945, ibid., 225.
[124]   *Flomo*, note 106 above, 1017.

Tinto plc, in which it was held that corporations could incur liability as aiders and abetters of violations of customary international law.[125] Judge Schroeder noted:

> We, however, believe the proper inquiry is not whether there is a specific precedent so holding, but whether international law extends its prohibitions to the perpetrators in question. After *Sosa* we must look to congressional intent when the ATS was enacted. Congress then could hardly have fathomed the array of international institutions that impose liability on states and non-state actors alike in modern times. That an international tribunal has not yet held a corporation criminally liable does not mean that an international tribunal could not or would not hold a corporation criminally liable under customary international law.[126]

Judge Schroeder held neither the language nor the legislative history of the ATS suggested that corporate liability was excluded and that only liability of natural persons was intended.[127] Footnote 20 of *Sosa*:

> [e]xpressly frames the relevant international-law inquiry to be the scope of liability of private actors for a violation of the 'given norm,' i.e. an international-law inquiry specific to each cause of action asserted ... The proper inquiry, therefore, should consider separately each violation of international law alleged and which actors may violate it.[128]

With regard to genocide, the International Court of Justice's (ICJ) decision in *Bosnia and Herzegovina*,[129] made it explicitly clear that a State may be responsible for genocide committed by groups or persons whose actions are attributable to States.

> This clarity about collective responsibility implies that organizational actors such as corporations or paramilitary groups may commit genocide. Given the universal nature of the prohibition, if an actor is capable of committing genocide, that actor can necessarily be held liable for violating the *jus cogens* prohibition on genocide.[130]

---

[125]   671 F 3d 736, (9th Cir 2011).

[126]   Ibid., at 760–1. On 22 April 2013, the US Supreme Court granted the defendant's petition for a writ of certiorari and the Ninth Circuit's judgment was vacated, and the case remanded to the US Court of Appeals for the Ninth Circuit for further consideration in light of *Kiobel,* 133 S Ct 1995 (2013).

[127]   *Sarei,* note 95 above, [8].

[128]   Ibid., [9].

[129]   *Bosnia and Herzogovina v. Serbia and Montenegro,* Judgment of the International Court of Justice of 26 February 2007, para [167].

[130]   *Sarei,* note 95 above, [22].

A similar conclusion was reached as regards war crimes. The text of Common Article III of the 1949 Fourth Geneva Convention binds 'each Party to the conflict'. Because parties to a non-international conflict must by definition include at least one non-State actor, entity, or group, the provision could not reasonably be interpreted to be limited to States.[131]

The issue was due to be resolved by the Supreme Court who in 2011 granted a writ of certiorari in *Kiobel* to determine the issue of 'whether corporations are immune from tort liability for violations of the law of nations such as torture, extrajudicial executions or genocide [or]may instead be sued in the same manner as any other private party defendant under the ATS for such egregious violations'.[132] However, after oral argument in February 2012, the Supreme Court directed the parties to file supplemental briefs addressing an additional question: 'Whether and under what circumstances the [ATS] allows courts to recognize a cause of action for violations of the law of nations occurring within the territory of a sovereign other than the United States.' The Supreme Court heard oral argument on this issue in October 2012 and on 17 April 2013 unanimously upheld the Second Circuit's dismissal of the complaint.[133] Its judgment was based entirely on its answer to the second question. Accordingly, this issue remains unresolved and is likely to remain so given that the effect of the Supreme Court's decision on the extra-territorial reach of the ATS is likely to call a halt on future ATS suits.

Where does this leave suits against corporations under the ATS? Clearly, these will no longer be possible in the Second Circuit, unless there is a contrary decision from the Supreme Court. However, in other circuits ATS claims against corporations have proceeded to trial in *Bowoto v. Chevron* and *Romero v. Drummond*, although in neither case did the defendants raise the issue that a corporation could not incur civil liability under customary international law.[134] Furthermore, as Cassel has observed, a finding that corporations are not subject to liability under

---

[131] Ibid., [27].

[132] 132 S Ct 472 (2011) granting petition for writ of certiorari. In 2012 the Supreme Court held that claims under the Torture Victims Protection Act 1991 could only be advanced against natural persons, *Mohamad v. Palestinian Authority*, 132 S Ct 1702 (2012).

[133] *Kiobel v. Royal Dutch Petroleum Co*, 133 S Ct 1659 (2013).

[134] In both cases the jury found for the defendant. The Eleventh Circuit in *Romero v. Drummond Co, Inc*, 552 F 3d 1303, 1316 (11th Cir 2008) has held that corporations can incur liability under the ATS. In *Re XE Services*, 665 F Supp 2d 569 (ED Virginia Alexandria Division) Judge Ellis held that claims alleging direct liability of a corporation for breaches of customary international law were cognisable under ATS.

customary international law would not necessarily get them off the hook in ATS suits.

> If the Court exempted corporations from liability, and stopped there, without reaching the question of or defining standards for aiding and abetting by *other* ATS defendants, then corporate executives would be left holding the bag of uncertainties. However, assuming that corporations indemnify their executives from such liability, the corporations would have to pick up their bags. In defending their executives in court, they would face the still unanswered questions about the source and scope of aiding and abetting liability. Only the financial stakes would be lower, since juries are not likely to award damages against corporate executives as large as against the corporations themselves.[135]

Indeed, in *Kiobel* Judge Cabranes specifically mentioned that this possible avenue of suit remained possible under the ATS.[136]

Since the Supreme Court's decision in *Kiobel* the issue of corporate liability under the ATS which the Supreme Court did not address has resurfaced in the Second Circuit. On February 10 2014, the Second Circuit issued a decision in *Chowdhury v. Worldtel Bangladesh Holding, Ltd*,[137] dismissing an ATS claim against a defendant corporation on the grounds that the alleged conduct took place entirely in Bangladesh. Judge Cabranes, the author of the majority opinion, and the author of the majority decision in *Kiobel* in 2010 also noted[138] that a second obstacle to the suit was the fact that the defendant was a corporation. Judge Pooler in her concurrence noted that these views were dicta only.[139] In *Licci ex*

---

[135]   Doug Cassel, 'Corporate Aiding and Abetting of Human Rights Violations: Confusion in the Courts,' 6(2) *North Western Journal of International Law* 304, 321–2 (2008).

[136]   Liability of a corporation may not, however, necessarily translate into a liability on the part of its officers. The finding of knowledge in the ATS proceedings against Unocal was based on the knowledge of Unocal directors, Imle and Beach. However, in the parallel tort proceedings before the Superior Court of California in the *Unocal* litigation, Judge Chaney dismissed the negligence claims against these individuals in the absence of any evidence that the activity of the Myanmar military was under their control and that they had negligently failed to take action to avoid the harm.

[137]   746 F 3d 42 (2d Cir 2014).

[138]   Ibid., fn 6.

[139]   Ibid., fn 2. Judge Pooler further noted that '[a]t least one sister circuit has determined that, by not passing on the question of corporate liability and by making reference to "mere corporate presence" in its opinion, the Supreme Court established definitively the possibility of corporate liability under the ATS'.

rel. Licci v. Lebanese Canadian Bank,[140] the Second Circuit held open the possibility that corporate liability under the ATS might still be possible following the Supreme Court's decision in *Kiobel*, Judge Sack stating:

> Because the question of subject matter jurisdiction was not briefed on appeal, because the Supreme Court's opinion did not directly address the question of corporate liability under the ATS, and in light of the other claims brought by the plaintiffs, we now think it best for the district court to address this issue in the first instance.

In April 2014 Judge Schiendlin picked up the ball in *In Re South African Apartheid Litigation* and held that corporate liability under the ATS was still possible.[141] She reasoned that:

> The Supreme Court's opinions in *Kiobel II* and *Daimler* directly undermine the central holding of *Kiobel I* – that corporations cannot be held liable for claims brought under the ATS. The opinions explicitly recognize that corporate presence alone is insufficient to overcome the presumption against extraterritoriality or to permit a court to exercise personal jurisdiction over a defendant in an ATS case, respectively. By necessity, that recognition implies that corporate presence plus additional factors can suffice under either holding.[142]

On the basis of *Chowdhury* and the fact that in *Licci* the Second Circuit had remanded the question of corporate liability because the issue had not been briefed on appeal, rather than immediately resolving the issue without further briefing, she regarded the question as an open one. She adopted the minority opinion of Judge Leval in *Kiobel*, that international law determined whether the alleged conduct violates a definite and universal international norm necessary to sustain an ATS action after *Sosa*. However, federal common law governed the issue of who could be liable for a violation of a norm of customary international law which was

---

140   732 F 3d 161 (2d Cir 2013).
141   15 F.Supp.3d 454 (SDNY 2014).
142   The Ninth Circuit in *Doe I v. Nestle U.S.A, Inc*, 738 F 3d 1048, 1049 (9th Cir 2013) were also of the view that dicta in *Kiobel II* suggest that corporations may be liable under ATS so long as the presumption against extraterritorial application is overcome.

an issue as to the determination of the means of enforcement for that violation rather than of the substantive obligations established by the norm.[143]

7. TERTIARY LIABILITY OF PARENT CORPORATIONS

A finding of vicarious liability through agency, or a piercing of the corporate veil of the subsidiary, will be crucial to the success of a claim against a parent corporation in respect of violations of customary international law committed by a subsidiary, either directly or as an aider and abetter. In *Bowoto v Chevron* the plaintiffs filed a motion for a new trial, following the jury's verdict in favour of the defendant, and argued that the jury's verdict must be set aside because there was no evidence contradicting plaintiffs' claims that they were shot, beaten and tortured without justification. Judge Illston denied the motion, stating: 'Moreover, jurors could have believed that plaintiffs were injured but might still have decided defendants were not liable if the jury was not persuaded by plaintiffs' evidence of secondary and tertiary liability.'[144]

Courts applying international law as the cause of action in ATS cases have had recourse to domestic law on this topic, in the absence of clear standards under international law. In *In re South African Apartheid Litigation*[145] Schiendlin held that although the ATS requires the application of customary international law whenever possible, it was necessary to rely on federal common law in limited instances in order to fill gaps.[146] Vicarious liability was clearly established under customary international law, obviating any concerns regarding universality. Command responsibility, the military analogue to holding a principal liable for the acts of an agent, was firmly established by the Nuremberg Tribunals. However, as the international law of agency had not developed precise standards in the civil context federal common law principles concerning agency would be applied. Shortly after giving judgment,

---

[143]   A consequence of this finding was that purposive assistance was required for aiding and abetting, as opposed to knowing assistance which Judge Schiendlin had previously found determined liability under international criminal law.

[144]   *Bowoto v. Chevron* 2009 WL 593872 (ND Cal), 3, 9 March 2009.

[145]   Note 9 above.

[146]   See, too, *Sarei v. Rio Tinto*, 487 F 3d 1193 (9th Cir 2007) in which domestic US law was applied to the issue of vicarious liability of a parent corporation for the defaults of a subsidiary.

Judge Schiendlin revisited this issue in dealing with the defendants' motion for reconsideration. She reiterated that vicarious liability was universally accepted as a component of customary international law, as evidenced by the principle of command responsibility.[147]

However, she recognised that the contours of vicarious civil liability had not been defined with the 'definite content' required for recognition of a cause of action under *Sosa*. This did not require that courts exercising ATS jurisdiction to decline to impose vicarious liability. Vicarious liability was not a cause of action but a principle for the distribution of civil liability for an independent tort.

> Although both prohibitory norms and liability-distributing rules influence incentives, the former bars conduct while the latter merely allocates responsibility. Thus a prohibitory norm contains a distinct moral element of universal condemnation, and liability-distributing rules do not, as liability stems not from the use of an agent alone but from the use of an agent to accomplish an unlawful end.[148]

Therefore the court was entitled to resort to federal common law to establish principles of vicarious liability, which were the means of domestic enforcement against those who violate internationally recognised torts.[149]

---

[147] Citing Control Council Law No 10, art II, reprinted in Telford Taylor, *Final Report to the Secretary of the Army on the Nuremberg War Crimes Trials Under Control Council Law No. 10*, at 251 (1949). Steve Ratner, 'Corporations and Human Rights: A Theory of Legal Responsibility', 111 Yale L.J. 443, 504–6 (2001) has argued that the war crimes theory of command responsibility provides a plausible way of developing customary international law on this issue.

[148] *South African Litigation*, note 9 above, 301–2.

[149] In *Wiwa* at fn 10 Judge Kimba Wood stated that she found Judge Schiendlin's approach to this issue persuasive, although she found that questions of vicarious liability were not relevant to the issue of whether a federal court had jurisdiction under the ATS. She noted that in *Adbullahi* the Second Circuit had *concluded* its jurisdictional analysis on establishing the existence of a norm of customary international law prohibiting the kind of tortious conduct alleged. Only then did it consider whether the corporate defendant could be held liable for violating that norm.

5. Tort claims against transnational corporations in the US

Since the Bhopal gas explosion of 4/5 December 1984 a substantial number of tort claims have been brought before the US courts against US parent corporations in respect of the overseas activities of their subsidiaries. Claims may be filed in state courts, or in the federal district courts under the diversity jurisdiction set out in Art. III of the US Constitution. The Bhopal gas explosion resulted in claims being filed against Union Carbide in the Southern District of New York,[1] and since then tort claims have been filed before the same court in respect of oil pollution in the Amazon basin,[2] and in respect of pollution caused by mining operations in Peru,[3] and in various States in respect of personal injuries allegedly sustained by workers on banana plantations who handled the pesticide DBCP. Some human rights claims have also been brought as tort claims in parallel with ATS claims in the district courts or in state courts. However, only a handful have come to trial. A tort claim brought in parallel with an ATS claim was heard in the District Court in California in 2008 where the jury found for the defendant.[4] A tort claim brought before the state court in California in the DBCP litigation initially resulted in an award of damages for the Nicaraguan plaintiffs which was subsequently overturned following findings of fraud on the part of the plaintiffs' lawyers.[5] Most of the other claims have been dismissed on the grounds of *forum non conveniens*, or on applications for summary judgment for failure to show cause.

---

[1] *In re: Union Carbide Corp Gas Plant Disaster*, F Supp 842 (SDNY 1986). Aff'd. 809 F 2d. 195 (2d Cir 1987).

[2] *Aguinda v. Texaco, Inc*, 142 F Supp 2d 534, (SDNY 2001). Aff'd 303 F 3d 470 (2d Cir 2002).

[3] *Flores v. SPCC*, 253 F Supp 2d 510 (SDNY 2002). Aff'd 343 F 3d 140 (2d Cir 2003).

[4] Bowoto v. Chevron Trial Blog, (Dec. 1, 2008, 3.12 pm), *Verdict: Chevron Found Not Guilty*, http://bowotovchevron.wordpress.com/2008/12/01/chevron-not-liableon- all-claims/ <accessed 26 April 2015>.

[5] *Mejia v. Dole*, Case No.BD40049; Judgment available at *online.wsj.com/public/resources/.../WSJ-Dole_Chaney_ruling.pdf* <accessed 8 April 2015>.

Such transnational tort claims involve a determination of the applicable law of the tort, and also of how a parent corporation can be made liable for torts committed by its overseas subsidiary, an issue which also applies to suits under the ATS in respect of torts committed in violation of the law of nations. The chapter will conclude with considering how the type of international law claims that have been brought against US transnational corporations (TNCs) under the ATS might be recast as tort claims brought either in the district courts under diversity jurisdiction or in state courts.

1. APPLICABLE LAW

There are seven conflicts of law approaches currently used in US states.[6] First, the traditional approach, which applies the law of the State where the alleged tort is completed; ten US states currently use this approach. Second, the most significant contacts rule. This applies the local law of the State which has the most significant contacts with the occurrence and the parties, the most significant factors being the parties' domicile and the location of the tort; three US states currently use this approach. Third, the Restatement approach which applies Restatement (Second) of Conflict of Laws section 145;[7] 24 US states currently use this approach. Fourth, the governmental interests analysis. This requires the court to evaluate the governmental policies underlying the applicable laws and determine which jurisdiction's policy would be more advanced by the

---

[6] The information on US conflicts of law rules is taken from Symeon C. Symeonides 'Choice of Law in the American Courts in 2013: Twenty-Seventh Annual Survey'. 62 *Am. J. Comp. L.* 223, (2014). At section VI in Table 2 Symeonides sets out the conflict rules applied in each state.

[7] This provides:

(1) A court, subject to constitutional restrictions, will follow a statutory directive of its own state on choice of law.
(2) When there is no such directive, the factors relevant to the choice of the applicable rule of law include (a) the needs of the interstate and international systems, (b) the relevant policies of the forum, (c) the relevant policies of other interested states and the relative interests of those states in the determination of the particular issue, (d) the protection of justified expectations, (e) the basic policies underlying the particular field of law, (f) certainty, predictability and uniformity of result, and (g) ease in the determination and application of the law to be applied.

application of its law to the facts of the case under review;[8] two US states, California and District of Columbia, currently use this approach. Fifth, the law of the forum which is used by Kentucky and Michigan. The law of the forum will be applied unless its connection to the dispute is too remote, as will be the case with 'foreign cubed' suits, involving foreign plaintiffs suing foreign defendants in respect of events that took place outside the jurisdiction; in which case the law with the greatest governmental interest in the dispute would be applied. Sixth, the combined modern approach which blends elements of the various approaches and is currently used by six US states, including New York. Seventh, the 'better law' approach which involves evaluating which of the competing State laws is empirically better and applying that law (usually the law of the forum) and is currently used by five US states. Each of these analyses will lead to the application of the law of the forum or the law where the wrong occurred or the law of the place in which the corporate defendant is incorporated. With issues of piercing the corporate veil, the relevant law will be either that of the forum, the place of incorporation, or the place where the wrong occurred.

Although nearly every State will have some form of tort law, there will be differences in national laws on recoverable damages, limitation of actions, causation, piercing the corporate veil, attribution of knowledge to companies. Accordingly, an important element in any transnational tort case is determining which State's law is to be applied.[9] This can be illustrated by *Caci v. Al Shimari*[10] where a US company was hired to provide interrogation services at Abu Ghraib prison in Iraq where it was alleged that it directed and participated in illegal conduct, including torture. In June 2013 Judge Lee held that, applying the choice of law rules of Ohio, the tort claims were subject to Iraqi law, which provided

---

[8]   This involves a three-step analysis. First, the court examines the substantive law of each jurisdiction to determine whether the laws differ as applied to the relevant transaction. Secondly, if the laws do differ, the court determines whether a true conflict exists in that each of the relevant jurisdictions has an interest in having its law applied. If only one jurisdiction has a legitimate interest in the application of its rule of decision, there is a false conflict and the law of the interested jurisdiction is applied. Third, if more than one jurisdiction has a legitimate interest, the courts seek to identify and apply the law of the State whose interest would be the more impaired if its law were not applied.

[9]   For an analysis of the likely application of these choice of law to tort based human rights cases see Roger Alford, 'Human Rights after Kiobel: Choice of Law and the Rise of Transnational Tort Litigation,' 63 *Emory Law Journal* 1089,1145 (2014).

[10]   951 F Supp 2d 857 (ED Va 2013).

immunity for the defendant for acts related to its contract with coalition forces in Iraq or performed in connection with military combat operations. However, in some cases US judges have refused to apply a foreign law mandated by the State's choice of law rules, on grounds of public policy. In the state law claims before the Superior Court of California in *Doe v. Unocal*, Judge Chaney found that public policy mandated that the law of Burma, where the torts had occurred, could not be applied as it did not recognise claims based on forced labour.[11]

2. PARENT CORPORATION LIABILITY: ALTER EGO, AGENCY, ENTERPRISE LIABILITY, DIRECT LIABILITY

A major problem facing the plaintiffs in the US, whether in a tort claim or an ATS claim, will be that of finding a way to make a parent company liable in respect of the negligence of its subsidiary. Shareholder liability is limited to the amount of unpaid share capital, a principle that applies equally to corporate groups where a parent company holds the majority, or even the totality, of shares in a subsidiary. This is the case notwithstanding that the principle was established before the emergence of corporate groups. Indeed, Blumberg has pointed out that in the US the principles of limited liability were established at a time when, in most states, corporations were actually prohibited from owning shares in other corporations.[12] However, US federal common law provides three possible avenues of derivative liability by which the faults of the subsidiary can be attributed to the parent.

The issue of veil piercing may also fall to be dealt with under state law and there is no clear decision as to whether state law or federal common law is to be applied in ATS cases.[13] The issue was raised in *Bowoto* where Judge Illston applied federal common law, observing:

---

[11] Unreported decision of 31 July 2003.

[12] P. Blumberg, *The Multinational Challenge to Corporation Law* (1993) Oxford University Press.

[13] The Supreme Court declined to give guidance on the issue when considering indirect liability under the Comprehensive Environmental Response, Compensation, and Liability Act of 1980 (CERCLA) in *US v. Bestfoods*, 524 US 51, 63 n9, (1998), noting the 'significant disagreement among courts and commentators over whether, in enforcing CERCLA's indirect liability, courts should borrow state law, or instead apply a federal common law of veil piercing'.

Where the causes of action in the complaint are federal in nature, application of federal law will better effectuate the purposes of those statutes. Finally, state and federal precedent on this issue do not appear to diverge in any way meaningful to the adjudication of this case. For these reasons, this Court will apply such federal law as it can find.[14]

Federal common law has been applied by the Ninth Circuit in *Doe v. Unocal*[15] and by Judge Schiendlin in *In Re South African Apartheid Litigation*.[16]

In contrast, state conflicts of law principles were applied by Judge Cote in *Presbyterian Church of Sudan v. Talisman Energy* in 2006[17] which illustrates the complexity of ascertaining applicable law to this issue with the law of five different States, Canada, New York, England, Mauritius, the Netherlands, all in play at some stage in the analysis which involved tracing a complex chain of attribution through multiple levels of subsidiaries between the parent corporation and the corporation that aided and abetted the violation of the law of nations. The ATS claim was made against a Canadian parent corporation, Talisman, in respect of aiding and abetting international crimes committed by the Sudanese government in the civil war in Southern Sudan. Talisman itself had no presence in Sudan. A second level subsidiary was a participant in an oil exploration consortium organised through a company Greater Nile Petrolcum Operating Company Ltd (GNPOC) in which the participants were shareholders. The claim as initially presented was that Talisman itself had aided and abetted those crimes. Judge Cote found against the plaintiffs and then denied their application to amend their case so that Talisman could be found liable for wrongs committed by GNPOC. However, she then reviewed the area of secondary liability, applying the conflicts of law of the forum, New York, under which the piercing of the corporate veil fell to be determined under the law of the place of incorporation of the company whose veil is to be pierced. GNPOC, the company created to exploit the oil resources in Southern Sudan, was incorporated under the law of Mauritius. To link Talisman with GNPOC the corporate veil of GNPOC would have to be pierced under the law of Mauritius, as would the corporate veils of the chain of the Netherlands and English subsidiary

---

[14] *Bowoto v. Chevron*, 312 F Supp 2d 1229 (ND Cal 2004), 1237.

[15] *Doe v. Unocal*, 395 F 3d 932 (2002).

[16] *In re South African Apartheid Litigation*, 617 F Supp 2d 228 (SDNY 2009).

[17] 453 F Supp 2d 633 (SDNY 2006).

companies leading down to the Talisman subsidiary that was a share-holder in GNPOC. On the facts this would point to the application of the laws of Mauritius, Netherlands and England respectively, none of which would permit the piercing of the veil of the corporation in question.[18] As regards the allegation that the subsidiaries had acted as agents of the parent, New York's rules on conflicts of laws for tort pointed to Sudan as the *lex loci delicti* and domicile of most plaintiffs or to Canada as domicile of Talisman, with a presumption in favour of the former.[19]

A. Alter ego

The corporate veil will be disregarded when the subsidiary is held to have been the 'alter ego' in which case parent and subsidiary will be treated as one. In *Seymour v. Hull & Moreland Engineering*,[20] the federal test for piercing the corporate veil on this ground was said to involve three general factors:

> the amount of respect given to the separate identity of the corporation by its shareholders, the degree of injustice visited on the litigants by recognition of the corporate entity, and the fraudulent intent of the incorporators. Federal decisions naturally draw upon state law for guidance in this field.[21]

As regards the first factor, officers of a parent corporation may be involved in the supervision of a subsidiary corporation without incurring liability for the parent corporation provided they act within the bounds of corporate formalities. In *US v. Bestfoods*[22] the Supreme Court considered that 'monitoring of the subsidiary's performance, supervision of the subsidiary's finance and capital budget and articulation of general policies and procedures' all constituted examples of appropriate parental involvement as well as holding that liability would not be imposed on a

---

[18]   The plaintiffs also argued the participants in the Sudanese oil exploration consortium constituted a joint venture, as had been found to exist in *Doe v. Unocal*. The first step in deciding a potential choice of law issue under New York law was to determine whether there is an actual conflict between the laws of the two jurisdictions involved. However, GNPOC or the activities of the Consortium Partners did not qualify as a joint venture under the law of Mauritius, or of New York.

[19]   *Neumeier v. Kuehner*, 31 NY 2d 121 (1972).

[20]   *Seymour v. Hull & Moreland Engineering*, 605 F 2d. 1105, 1111 (9th Cir 1979).

[21]   The third factor, however, is not universally accepted as state law.

[22]   *US v. Bestfoods*, 524 US, 69, 118 S Ct 1876.

parent merely because its directors also served as directors of the subsidiary. As regards the second factor, the inability of the subsidiary to meet its liabilities will not be enough to trigger a finding of alter ego.

It has, therefore, proved very difficult to establish derivative liability on this ground. This is illustrated by *Bowoto v. Chevron*.[23] Chevron Nigeria Ltd (CNL) operated a joint venture with the Nigerian National Petroleum Company, the Nigerian State oil company. The case arose out of claims that CNL had recruited the Nigerian military and police to fire at protesters on an oil platform and to open fire on a village from Chevron helicopters, flown by Chevron pilots, as well as using Chevron sea trucks to transport the military to a village where they then fired on the inhabitants.[24] The sole issue at this stage of the proceedings was the extent of a parent corporation's responsibility for the acts of its subsidiaries. The defendants were both Chevron Texaco Corporation (CVX)[25] and its wholly owned subsidiary, Chevron Overseas Petroleum, Inc. (COPI).[26]

Judge Illston held that the alter ego theory did not apply on the facts alleged by the plaintiffs. The plaintiff could not show that the subsidiary was a mere instrumentality of the parent. The mere fact that officers of a parent corporation were involved in the supervision of a subsidiary corporation was not sufficient to attribute liability to the parent corporation, actions in that capacity being attributable to the parent corporation. Nor had the plaintiffs been able to produce any evidence to show that observing the corporate form would achieve an inequitable result. Their inability to recover their losses was not a sufficient inequity to justify overlooking the corporate form.

B. Agency

Secondly, where the parent corporation may be held liable where the subsidiary is found to have acted as its agent in respect of the particular

---

[23] *Bowoto v. Chevron*, note 14 above.

[24] The first incident occurred on May 28, 1998 when a number of Nigerians staged a protest on Chevron's Parabe oil platform. The Nigerian military and police opened fire at the protestors, killing two of them. This was followed by two further incidents which occurred on January 4, 1999 in which it was alleged that a helicopter flown by Chevron pilots and transporting Nigerian military and/or police had overflown the community of Opia and opened fire on the villagers, killing one person and injuring others and had then flown on to the Ikenyan community where similar abuses were allegedly committed.

[25] Formerly, the Chevron Corporation.

[26] Subsequently, Chevron Texaco Overseas Petroleum, Inc. (CTOP).

action giving rise to the claim. Unlike the 'alter ego' theory, a finding of agency does not detract from the separate corporate personalities of the parent and subsidiary. The Restatement 2d of Agency 14 M states:

> ... a subsidiary may become an agent for the corporation which controls it, or the corporation may become the agent of the subsidiary. In some situations, a court may find that the subsidiary has no real existence or assets, that its formal existence is to cloak a fraud or other illegal conduct. As in a similar situation in which an individual is the offender, it may be found that the parent company is the real party to a transaction conducted by the illusory subsidiary and responsible for its transactions as a principal.

Unlike liability under the alter ego or veil-piercing test, agency liability does not require the court to disregard the corporate form.[27]

In *Bowoto v. Chevron* Judge Illston set out the factors that would support a finding of derivative liability based on agency. First, there must exist a close relationship or domination between the parent and subsidiary, and moreover there must also be a finding that the injury allegedly inflicted by the subsidiary, for which the parent is being held liable, was within the scope of the subsidiary's authority as an agent. Judge Illston held that on the facts alleged by the plaintiffs this required was satisfied:

> Here, defendant functioned as a multi-national corporation in which CNL played a significant role. Defendant had much more than the usual degree of control over CNL's operations, and particularly in setting security policy. The revolving door of managers and directors at the highest levels between CNL and defendants is dramatic evidence of the close relationship that was shared and can be viewed as further evidence of an agency relationship.[28]

Significantly, this high level of control was particularly apparent in the area of security. The defendants and CNL had regular communications regarding security measures before and after the attacks with an extraordinarily high volume of phone calls between defendants' personnel in the US and CNL on May 27, 1998, the first day of the occupation of the Parabe platform.

A second factor was that CNL had engaged in activities in Nigeria that, but for its presence there, the US defendants would have had to undertake themselves. Apart from the very close relation between parent

---

[27] The distinction between veil-piercing and agency theories of liability is noted in the Restatement (Second) of Agency, Appendix S 14M, Reporter's Notes at 68 (1958).

[28] *Bowoto*, note 14 above, 1245.

and subsidiary as evidenced above, there was the fact that the CVX annual report portrayed defendants as part of an integrated operation with CNL whose oil operations represented 20 per cent of COPI's earnings.[29] Taken together, the evidence could support a finding of agency which directly related to the plaintiffs' causes of action, which alleged that defendants were significantly involved in security matters and benefitted directly from CNL's oil production, which was made possible, or at least protected by the military's wrongful use of force to quell local unrest. The plaintiffs also contended that defendants and CNL increased their revenues both through the military's response to Nigerian unrest and through their cover-up in the US of the events after they occurred.

C. Single Economic Entity

Thirdly, in limited circumstances the corporate veil may be pierced when the courts find that parent and subsidiary have acted as a single economic entity, the so-called theory of enterprise liability. In *The Amoco Cadiz*[30] Judge McGarr held that Standard Oil was responsible for the tortious acts of two of its wholly owned subsidiaries which had resulted in an oil spill from a tanker. These were Transport, the nominal owner of the vessel, and AIOC who exercised complete control over its operation, maintenance and repair, as well as over the selection and training of its crew. The basis of Standard's liability for the defaults of these two subsidiary companies was that it exercised such control over its subsidiaries that those entities would be considered to be mere instrumentalities of Standard.[31] These findings were not challenged when the case was subsequently appealed. However, the decision goes against the whole tenor of US decisions on veil piercing, and, furthermore, is imprecise as to exactly which facts will justify a finding that the subsidiary was a mere instrumentality. In *Bowoto v. Chevron Corp*, in which *The Amoco*

---

[29] In particular, the annual report described CVX as, 'an international company that, through its subsidiaries and affiliates engages in fully integrated petroleum operations, chemical operations and coalmining in the United States and approximately 90 countries'.

[30] *The Amoco Cadiz*, [1984] 2 Lloyd's Rep 304 esp, 338, F, 43–46. *Aff'd* 954 F 2d 2179 (7th Cir 1992).

[31] Judge McGarr also found that Standard was also personally liable because it had initially been involved in and controlled the designing, construction, operation and management of the vessel which it had treated as its own.

Cadiz was not cited, Illston J declined to apply an integrated enterprise theory to the issue of veil piercing.[32]

D. Direct Liability

Apart from piercing the corporate veil, the parent might also be held liable in respect of its own primary breach of duty, rather than vicariously in respect of the breach of its subsidiary. As is the case with English law, this question involves uncharted areas of tort law, particularly as regards the question of whether a parent company will ever owe supervisory duties in relation to the activities of a foreign subsidiary.

The general principles were reviewed by the Supreme Court in *US v. Bestfoods* in 1998.[33] Proceedings were brought under section 107(a)(2) of the Comprehensive Environmental Response, Compensation, and Liability Act of 1980 (CERCLA) against, CPC International Inc, the parent corporation of the defunct Ott Chemical Co (Ott II), for the costs of cleaning up industrial waste generated by Ott II's chemical plant. Section 107(a)(2) authorises suits against, among others, 'any person who at the time of disposal of any hazardous substance owned or operated any facility'. The question arose as to whether Ott II's parent corporation could be viewed as an 'operator' under CERCLA. The district court held that this would be the case where it had exerted power or influence over its subsidiary, by actively participating in, and exercising control over, the subsidiary's business during a period of hazardous waste disposal. CPC were therefore held liable because they had selected Ott II's board of directors and populated its executive ranks with CPC officials, and another CPC official had played a significant role in shaping Ott II's environmental compliance policy. The sixth circuit reversed the decision on the grounds that a parent company could only be held directly liable under section 107(a)(2) if it actually operated its subsidiary's facility in the stead of the subsidiary, or alongside it, as a joint venturer.[34] A parent corporation's liability for operating a facility ostensibly operated by its subsidiary depended on whether the degree to which the parent controls the subsidiary and the extent and manner of its involvement with the facility amounted to an abuse of the corporate form sufficient to warrant piercing the corporate veil.

---

[32] Such a theory had been applied in specific statutory contexts, principally those relating to the liability of employers, but it could not be imported without examination into different contexts involving the issue of veil piercing.

[33] 524 U.S. 51, 118 S.Ct. 1876.

[34] F.3d 572 (6th Cir. 1997).

The Supreme Court, for whom Justice Souter gave judgment, rejected the direct liability analysis of the district court, which had mistakenly focused on the relationship between parent and subsidiary, and premised liability on little more than CPC's ownership of Ott II and its majority control over Ott II's board of directors. The issue of direct liability by the parent had to be kept distinct from its possible derivative liability for its subsidiary's operation of the facility. Instead, the analysis should have focused on the relationship between CPC and the facility itself, i.e., on whether CPC 'operated' the facility, as evidenced by its direct participation in the facility's activities. The sixth circuit, however, had been unduly restrictive in limiting direct liability under CERCLA to a parent's sole or joint venture operation. The parent could also 'operate' a facility when joint officers or directors conducted the affairs of the facility on behalf of the parent, or agents of the parent, with no position in the subsidiary, managed or directed activities at the subsidiary's facility. Norms of corporate behaviour were crucial reference points for: (a) determining whether a dual officer or director had served the parent in conducting operations at the facility; and (b) for distinguishing a parental officer's oversight of a subsidiary from his control over the operation of the subsidiary's facility. The district court's opinion had identified both an agent who had played a conspicuous part in dealing with the toxic risks emanating from the plant's operation, and some evidence that these activities were eccentric under accepted norms of parental oversight of a subsidiary's facility. Accordingly, the case was referred to the lower courts for re-evaluation and resolution.

It is significant that the Supreme Court's approach focuses on positive involvement by the parent in the activity of the subsidiary that goes beyond established norms of corporate behaviour. Where the problem is parental inactivity then it is very unlikely that any duty of care will come into existence. Radu Mares has argued that responsibility to oversee the activities of a subsidiary company should be based on the concept of a specific type of vulnerability of those affected by the subsidiary's activities, in having no remedies when risks materialise:

> Such vulnerability comes precisely from regulatory gaps and the ineffective remedies right holders have at their disposal. These are the 'governance gaps' that Ruggie refers to in his writings. So the situation creating problems for the core company is not the risk of harm but the risk of *unremedied* harm in affiliate operations. Where right holders systematically lack institutional channels to contest human rights abuses and poor working conditions, this is

disabling and highly problematic from a human rights perspective. Vulnerability is a key concept in justifying a responsibility to act imposed on the core company.[35]

However, it is unlikely that the courts will find that there is any duty of supervision on the part of a corporation in respect of its subsidiary's activities. The issue arose when claims arising out of the operation of the Bhopal plant, that were unrelated to the 1984 gas explosion, came back before Judge Keenan in 2012 in *Sahu v. Union Carbide (Sahu I)*.[36] These were tort claims for personal injuries allegedly caused by exposure to soil and drinking water polluted by hazardous wastes at the Bhopal pesticide plant. Judge Keenan dismissed the claim on the merits, but noted that he could have dismissed it on grounds of *forum non conveniens*, as he had done in 1986 with the claims arising out of the gas explosion. The plaintiffs alleged that Union Carbide were directly responsible for the plaintiff's injuries in that they:

> participated in the creation of the pollution by approving the back-integration of the Bhopal Plant, designing the Bhopal Plant's waste disposal systems, transferring technology to UCIL, by its knowledge of water pollution risks, and by its 'intimate participation' in environmental remediation efforts 'designed the faulty waste disposal systems installed at the Bhopal plant'; and transferred manufacturing technology to UCIL.

Judge Keenan rejected all these allegations and found that Union Carbide were not directly responsible for the plaintiffs' injuries, basing his findings on those he had made in the *forum non conveniens* dismissal of the 1986 gas explosion case,[37] where he found that 'UCIL may have consulted UCC about its plans early on, but UCIL was the ultimate decision maker, so primary responsibility for the design and construction of the waste disposal system at the Bhopal Plant rested with UCIL.' Judge Keenan found that there was no evidence that any technology provided by UCC 'itself was polluting' or 'caused pollution, in and of

---

[35] R. Mares (ed.), *The UN Guiding Principles on Business and Human Rights – Foundations and Implementation*, Martinus Nijhoff Publishers (Leiden, Boston 2012), 169–92,180.

[36] WL 2422757 (S.D.N.Y.2012). The case had previously come before Judge Keenan in 2006 and had been dismissed on procedural grounds.

[37] In the gas explosion *forum non conveniens* dismissal in 1986 Judge Keenan found that Union Carbide's participation in the design, construction and operation of the plant was limited. Any involvement it may have had in plant operations had ended long before the accident.

itself' and that 'that the evidence demonstrates that the allegedly unproven and improper technology used at the Bhopal Plant was selected and/or developed by UCIL, not Union Carbide'. Although Union Carbide recognised potential waste disposal issues that did not give rise to liability and furthermore it had made its subsidiary fully aware of these issues. He also rejected any claim to pierce the corporate veil of the corporations. The subsidiary was always adequately capitalised and was an independent going concern. The subsidiary had 'discretion which is completely inconsistent with plaintiffs' theory of absolute control' and there was no evidence of domination by Union Carbide.

The case, however, has still not finished. In 2007 a further case in *Sahu II* was filed alleging property damage which was stayed pending the appeal in *Sahu I*, and was dismissed in July 2014.[38] Judge Keenan rejected the evidence of two waste disposal experts to the effect that the pollution was caused by Union Carbide's manufacturing design and 'high risk' waste management strategy, as well as the declaration of the project manager for the construction of the plant, L.J. Couvaras, that he was employed by Union Carbide when he oversaw and approved all design and construction of the plant in India. An appeal was lodged in November 2014.[39]

E. Supply Chains

Where corporations' overseas operations are conducted contractually through suppliers and licensees, it becomes even more difficult to attribute liability to the domestic corporation's overall behaviour and policies of subcontractors and suppliers throughout the supply chain. As noted in 2001 by Steven R. Ratner:

> A corporate entity may operate through joint ventures with other businesses, contractors, and subcontractors; and it may rely upon obtaining inputs from certain suppliers and selling outputs to certain buyers, each creating a variety of economic ties. In some cases, these links originate in contracts establishing long-term relationships; in others, the economic interactions result from the economic importance of the corporation to the supplier or purchaser. A theory of corporate duties must take these relationships into account through some guidelines regarding attribution.[40]

---

[38]   WL 3765556 (S.D.N.Y.,2014).

[39]   ww.earthrights.org/legal/sahu-v-union-carbide <accessed 17 September 2015>.

[40]   Ratner, 'Corporations and Human Rights: A Theory of Legal Responsibility,' 111 *Yale Law Journal* 443, 519 (2001).

Ratner argued that such a theory should be based on the concept of control,[41] although acknowledging the difficulties of applying such a theory to relationships outside the corporate group paradigm. Two subsequent decisions show that it is virtually impossible for a corporation to be held liable for defaults of its licensees and contractual parties.

First, in *Sinaltrainal v. The Coca-Cola Company*[42] the plaintiffs alleged that Coca-Cola USA should be held liable for the actions of Coca-Cola Colombia and of the local Colombian licensors whom it was alleged had conspired with paramilitaries to murder union activists. The plaintiffs claimed that Coca-Cola Colombia and Bebidas were either the alter ego of or the agent of Coca-Cola USA because of its control over their day-to-day activities. The plaintiffs relied on the bottler's agreement with Bebidas. However, it established that neither Coca-Cola USA nor Coca-Cola Colombia had a duty to monitor, enforce or control labour policies at the Bebidas bottling plant. The agreement only permitted Coca-Cola USA to require Bebidas, as a Coca-Cola bottler, to meet certain standards necessary to protect Coca-Cola's product in the marketplace (i.e., use of the trademark, packaging, quality control, etc.). Therefore, Coca-Cola USA did not have the total control necessary to establish that the Colombian licensees were their alter egos or agents.

Second, in *Doe v. Wal-Mart Stores Inc*[43] a contractual code of conduct in Wal-Mart's contracts with its suppliers was held not to give rise to any duty of care on the part of Wal-Mart towards employees of its foreign suppliers. Claims were made against Wal-Mart by employees of foreign companies who supplied goods to it in connection with their working conditions. The claim was based on a code of conduct in Wal-Mart's supply contracts as to the labour standards which suppliers had to meet and Wal-Mart reserved the right to inspect the suppliers and to cancel contracts if contractual breaches were revealed. The Ninth Circuit rejected the claim. The plaintiffs were not third-party beneficiaries of the supply contracts and Wal-Mart was not a joint employer as it exercised minimal or no control over the plaintiffs' day-to-day work in the suppliers' factories. No duty of care in tort arose as Wal-Mart had given no undertaking to protect and was under no duty to exercise reasonable care in monitoring its suppliers for compliance with the labour code.

---

[41] Adopting the arguments set out in 1990 by Hugh Collins, 'Ascription of Legal Responsibility to Groups in Complex Patterns of Economic Integration,' 53 *Modern Law Review* 731 (1990) in which he urged a revision of common law principles of liability with respect to integrated economic enterprises.

[42]   256 F Supp 2d 1345 (SD Florida 2003).

[43]   572 F 3d 677 (9th Cir 2009).

Wal-Mart had a contractual right to inspect, but not a duty and any breaches were purely gratuitous.[44]

3. TORT CLAIMS FOR HUMAN RIGHTS VIOLATIONS

Following *Kiobel*, future human rights claims against US TNCs are likely to be brought in tort either in the district courts if there is diversity, or in state courts.[45] There has been vigorous academic speculation about life after *Kiobel* and Professor Roger Alford has identified various advantages to bringing human rights claims as tort claims before state courts: there are no presumptions limiting the extra-territorial application of state tort laws; every state will have some form of tort law analogue to the common law torts of negligence, nuisance, trespass to the person; it will be easier to establish liability under domestic or foreign tort law principles than by reference to international criminal law; there will be no uncertainty regarding corporate liability as every national system of tort law recognises that corporations can be liable in tort; claims pursued in state courts will avoid the heightened pleading standards now applied in federal courts; claims pursued in state courts are less likely to be dismissed for *forum non conveniens* as state court standards tend to be less stringent.[46]

---

[44] A corporation may, however, incur a contractual liability in respect of the code it imposes on its suppliers. In July 2012 Adidas was sued by the trustees of the University of Wisconsin for breach of a contract to supply sportswear to them, under which Adidas agreed to enter into and operate a Standard Retail Product Licensing Agreement incorporating labour codes of conduct. The pleadings alleged that Adidas was contractually obliged to pay severance pay due to workers employed by its Indonesian supplier PT Kizone following the factory's closure in 2011. Adidas argued that the contract did not require it to provide for unpaid benefits due from its contractor, but in April 2013 it announced that it would pay severance pay to 2,700 former employees of PT Kizone and the suit was withdrawn. http://news.wisc.edu/21841 <accessed 17 September 2015>.

[45] It is possible that claims for violations of international law may also be brought in state courts on the grounds that state common law has historically incorporated customary international law. In the district courts such an argument is precluded by the denial of a general common law in *Erie Railroad Co v. Tompkins*, 304 US 64, 58 S Ct 817 (1938).

[46] Alford, 'Human Rights after Kiobel: Choice of Law and the Rise of Transnational Tort Litigation,' 63 *Emory Law Journal* 1089,1161 (2014). See, too, Donald Earl Childress III, 'The Alien Tort Statute, Federalism, and the Next Wave of Transnational Litigation,' 100 *Georgia Law Journal* 709 (2012).

In three ATS cases, *Doe v. Unocal*; *Bowoto v. Chevron*; and *Doe v. Exxon*, tort claims were brought in parallel with the ATS claims. All three claims arose out of the ATS paradigm of claims for violations of customary international law committed by government security forces providing security on an overseas oil project of a subsidiary of a US corporation. The claims were made against the parent corporation which involves the following attributional links, assuming the allegations against the security providers were made out. First, the subsidiary must be found responsible for the acts of the government security forces. Under the ATS the claim will be pled on the basis that the subsidiary aided and abetted the commission of a crime against humanity by the security forces. Secondly, the faults of the subsidiary must be linked to the parent which involves a process of piercing the corporate veil, or a finding that the subsidiary acted as the agent of the parent.

In *Doe v. Unocal* tort claims were brought in the Superior Court of California.[47] The first stage involved finding whether a reasonable trier of fact could conclude that Unocal's subsidiaries who were participants in the Yadana gas pipeline project could be held responsible for the forced labour allegedly imposed by the Burmese military who were providing security for the project. Judge Chaney applying the conflict of laws rules of California ended up applying the law of California. She found that Unocal could not be found liable on the basis of its own actions for the three potential heads of liability advanced by the plaintiffs: as a co-tortfeasor in aiding and abetting, intentional torts, negligence.[48] The first potential head of liability would be for aiding and abetting. This required knowledge that a tort had been, or was to be, committed, coupled with acts done with the intent of facilitating the commission of that tort.[49] Unocal's day-to-day involvement with the military in the

---

[47]   Case Nos: BC 237 980 and BC 237 679.

[48]   Case Nos: BC 237 980; and BC 237 679 Ruling on Defendants' Motion for Summary Judgment, or in the Alternative, Summary Adjudication on Each of Plaintiffs' Tort Claims. 6 July 2002. Available at http://www.earthrights.org/legal/doe-v-unocal <accessed 14th April 2015>.

[49]   In contrast, the international criminal law standard applied by the majority of the Ninth Circuit in the ATS claim only required substantial assistance with knowledge, rather than purpose. The Ninth Circuit found that the plaintiffs' evidence was sufficient that a reasonable trier of fact could conclude that Unocal had aided and abetted forced labour by the Burmese military. Judge Reinhardt, who applied federal tort law, held that the plaintiffs might also have a viable claim against Unocal under the common law theory of recklessness or reckless disregard based on the allegation that they had suffered harm due to Unocal's disregard of the risk of unreasonable harm to the plaintiffs caused by their

management of the pipeline project did not show it had acted with the intent of facilitating the commission of the Burmese military's torts. In addition the substantial assistance required as the *actus reus* of aiding and abetting was not made out.[50] It had been alleged that Unocal had provided maps to the military, and was aware that other participants in the Yadana project, Total and Total Myanmar Exploration & Production, were providing food, trucks, a bulldozer and possibly payment to the military for security, but this conduct did not make a significant contribution to the plaintiffs' injuries. Nor had Unocal's negotiations for and entry into the project had such an effect, as Total would have proceeded with the project in any event, even without Unocal.[51] Unocal's participation in the project would have been unlikely to affect the operation of the pipeline.[52] Even if Unocal had protested to the Burmese government, and threatened to withdraw its investment, or had actually carried out such a threat the military's abuses would still have continued. Unocal had not been responsible for hiring the military. It was Total who were responsible for pipeline security.

The second potential head of claim was in respect of five intentional tort causes of action: battery; assault; false imprisonment; intentional infliction of emotional distress; and conversion. However, although there was a triable issue of fact on the *mens rea* element of the torts, given evidence which suggested that Unocal knew that forced labor was being utilised and that the joint venturers benefitted from the practice, the claims faltered on the *actus reus* of the torts. The Burmese military, and not Unocal, was the actor as to the intentional tort causes of action.

Thirdly, the claims were brought in negligence but foundered on the lack of a duty of care owed by Unocal to the plaintiffs. A person owed no duty to control the conduct of a third person to prevent him from causing physical harm to another, in the absence of a special relationship between the defendant and the plaintiff or the person whose conduct needed to be controlled. Unocal did not have the ability to control the Burmese military. However, there might also have been a duty of care not to place another person in a situation in which the other person was exposed to an

---

decision to use the military for pipeline security, a risk of which they were, or should have been, aware.

[50]   In contrast the majority in the Ninth Circuit Court subsequently found that Unocal's involvement did amount to substantial assistance in that, without it, the military's abuses would probably not have occurred in the same way.

[51]   This factual analysis derives from the findings in *Doe v. Unocal Corp.* (9th Cir. 2001) 248 F 3d 915, 925.

[52]   *Unocal. Doe v. Unocal Corp*, 67 F Supp 2d 1140, 1147 (CD Cal 1999).

unreasonable risk of harm through the reasonably foreseeable conduct of a third person. Where the defendant had made the plaintiffs' position worse and has created a foreseeable risk of harm from the third person, then a duty of care to prevent foreseeable harm would arise from conduct which contributed to, increased or changed the risk of harm that would otherwise have existed. While there was a possibility that Unocal's investment perpetuated the risk, there was no evidence that Unocal's investment placed plaintiffs in a risky situation or *created* a risk of harm from the Burmese military. Accordingly, the negligence claims were dismissed.[53]

However, Judge Chaney allowed the claims to proceed on the basis of a plausible claim that Unocal, as a participant in the joint venture, was vicariously liable for the acts of the joint venturers' agents, the Burmese military. She held that the military could not be regarded as the alter ego of MOGE, the Myanmar state entity that was one of the joint venturers in the gas exploration project. It could, however, be regarded as the agent of the joint venturers. A principal would be liable for the intentional torts of his agent committed within the scope of the employment, which depended whether the principal could have foreseen the wrongdoing of the agent. An agency relationship might be precluded if the joint venture lacked the legal right to control the military's activities. If this were the case, then the military would have acted as an independent contractor which the joint venture had directed to accomplish certain tasks, including security and the preparation of roads and helipads. The joint venture would incur liability because it should have recognised that the methods adopted by the military were likely to cause harm, given the military's well-known human rights' record.

The second stage of the enquiry focused on the link between the parent corporation and its two subsidiary corporations.[54] Judge Chaney again applied the law of California to this issue.[55] She rejected Myanmar law as

---

[53]   Judge Chaney also dismissed the parallel negligence claims against Unocal directors, Imle and Beach in the absence of any evidence that the activity of the Myanmar military was under their control and that they had negligently failed to take action to avoid the harm.

[54]   Ruling on Unocal's motion for judgment. 14 September 2004. Available at http://www.earthrights.org/legal/doe-v-unocal <accessed 14th April 2015>.

[55]   31 July 2003. She also rejected the application of the law of Bermuda, where the Unocal subsidiaries had been re-incorporated, because although the subsidiaries had been incorporated in Bermuda they were 'exempt' corporations which meant they could not do business in Bermuda and consequently Bermuda had a diminished interest in regulating the conduct of such entities. A copy of the

being radically indeterminate and therefore assumed it to be not out of harmony with Californian law, which she proceeded to apply. She also found that Myanmar law barred tort claims based on allegations of forced labour, and its application would have been contrary to public policy. She concluded: 'Application of this rule is not unfair in this case. Prior to its involvement in the pipeline project, Unocal had specific knowledge that the use of forced labor was likely, and nevertheless chose to proceed.' Although Judge Chaney found that the Unocal subsidiaries could not be regarded as the alter egos of the parent corporation,[56] this did not rule out a finding that the subsidiaries may have acted as agents for the parent corporation. The main factual sub-issue in the alter ego analysis was the degree of control exercised by the parent over the subsidiary. This would need to be re-examined because a lesser degree of control would suffice to establish a finding of agency.[57]

Similar analyses have been adopted in two other tort claims brought in parallel with claims under the ATS. In *Bowoto v. Chevron* Judge Illston, applying California's conflict of law rules, found that the tort claims would be decided under the law of California. Triable issues had been raised as regards the plaintiffs claims for: aiding and abetting, where liability depended on proof the defendant had actual knowledge of the

---

decision is not available, but a summary is available on the website of the Center for Constitutional Rights. http://ccrjustice.org/newsroom/press-releases/ccr-wins-significant-legal-motion-unocal-case <accessed 14 April 2015>.

[56]   17 November 2003. A copy of the decision is not available, but the decision is referred to in Ruling on Unocal's motion for judgment. 14 September 2004. She found that although there was some commingling of funds among the defendants and their subsidiaries, the subsidiaries controlled their own assets and the corporate formalities had been observed. Unocal had not exercised inappropriate control over the subsidiaries' daily operations through the companies' sharing of officers, directors, employees and offices. The subsidiaries were adequately capitalised and none was a shell, nor was ownership concealed. Appropriate arm's length relationships had been maintained between parents and subsidiaries.

[57]   This is in contrast to the subsequent analysis of this issue by the Ninth Circuit in the ATS case where the majority concluded that there was evidence that would allow a reasonable factfinder to conclude that the Unocal Pipeline Corp and the Unocal Offshore Co were alter egos of Unocal, namely: their under-capitalisation; the direct involvement in and direction of their business by Unocal President Imle, Unocal CEO Beach, and other Unocal officers and employees. An alter ego finding would lead to a finding that Unocal was directly, rather than vicariously, liable for aiding and abetting forced labour.

specific primary wrong the defendant substantially assisted;[58] conspiracy which required knowledge of a plan to engage in the specific wrongful conduct at issue, and agreement to participate in that plan; vicarious liability by way of agency for the actions of the Nigerian security forces. In *Doe v. Exxon Corporation*[59] in the District of Columbia, Judge Oberdorfer, having decided that the state law tort claims were to be determined by the law of the forum[60] found that there were triable issues: that Exxon Mobil Oil Indonesia (EMOI), Exxon's Indonesian subsidiary, had hired Indonesian soldiers to provide security, knowing that they had been committing human rights abuses, which would be sufficient to establish liability on the basis that the soldiers acted as independent contractors engaged in an inherently dangerous activity – the provision of security in a country afflicted by civil war; that EMOI acted as Exxon's agent with regard to the military security for the huge Arun gas field, by reason of evidence that Exxon Mobil exerted significant control over EMOI's security, particularly through Exxon Mobil's Global Security division.

---

[58] *Casey v. US Bank Nat'l Ass'n*, 127 Cal App. 4th 1138, 1145 (Cal Ct app 2005). This contrasts with Judge Chaney's previous finding in *Unocal* that intentional assistance was required.

[59] 573 F Supp 2d 16 (DDC 2008).

[60] Judge Oberdorfer's choice of law analysis was subsequently overruled when the District of Columbia Circuit Court found that Indonesian law was the applicable law. 654 F 3d 11, 15, 57 (DC Cir 2011).

6. Tort claims against transnational corporations in the UK

Over the last 20 years London solicitors, Leigh Day, have taken on a number of cases involving pollution, industrial injury, human rights abuses by transnational corporations (TNCs) which have occurred in developing countries.[1] These cases have seen the development of tort law as a means of obtaining compensation and deterring bad practice by impacting on reputation. There are four hurdles to surmount in bringing such claims before the courts of the UK. First, there is the need to establish jurisdiction. Second, there is the need to find a way round the separate corporate personality of the English parent company and its foreign subsidiary. Third, there is the need to establish the applicable law governing the tort claim. Fourth, there is the need to be able to fund the litigation.

1. ESTABLISHING JURISDICTION

In the UK jurisdiction is based on the Brussels Regulation (EC) No. 44/2001 and on the common law rules. For legal proceedings instituted on or after 10 January 2015, the applicable law is now to be found in Regulation (EU) No. 1215/2012 on jurisdiction and recognition and enforcement of judgments in civil and commercial matters (recast) (the Judgments Regulation). As well as introducing some substantive changes

---

[1]   In November 2014 a human rights claim against an English multinational, BP, was brought by solicitors Deighton Pierce Glynn who sent a letter before claim to BP and other associated companies claiming damages on behalf of a Colombian trade unionist, Gilberto Torres, who was kidnapped by paramilitaries and imprisoned in a pit for 42 days. Torres claims BP recklessly hired the paramilitaries thugs to protect its Colombian pipeline from left-wing guerrillas, and has previously brought proceedings in the US under the Alien Tort Statute, which were discontinued in January 2014 following the Supreme Court's decision in *Kiobel*. Further details available at http://business-humanrights.org/pt/node/120847 <accessed 7 April 2015>.

to the Brussels regime, there has been a consequential renumbering of existing provisions.

Article 2 (now Article 4) of the Brussels Regulation requires the court to exercise jurisdiction over a defendant domiciled within the jurisdiction.[2] Where the defendant is a corporation, Article 60.1 (now Article 63.1) provides that a company 'or other legal person or association of natural or legal persons' is domiciled 'at the place where it has its: (a) statutory seat, or (b) central administration, or (c) principal place of business'. For the purposes of the UK and Ireland, 'statutory seat' is defined by Article 60.2 (now Article 63.2) as:

> the registered office or, where there is no such office anywhere, the place of incorporation or, where there is no such office anywhere, the place of incorporation or, where there is no such place anywhere, the place under the law of which the formation took place.

Therefore, a company incorporated in a part of the UK but which has no other connection with the UK would be domiciled in the UK for the purposes of Article 2. So, too, would a company which was not incorporated in the UK but which was effectively run from the UK.[3] In *Young v. Anglo-American*[4] the Court of Appeal held that 'central administration' meant the place where a company carries out functions and not where others carry out functions that affect it. Accordingly, a South African subsidiary company which carried out the entirety of its business in South Africa could not be shown to have its central administration in the UK on the grounds that its UK parent corporation made the big decisions affecting the group.

Where there are multiple defendants domiciled in different Member States, Article 6.1 (now Article 8.1) provides that each defendant may be sued in the courts of the State in which any one of them is domiciled.

---

[2]   As an alternative to suing a defendant in its place of domicile, art 5.3 (now art 7.3) of the Brussels Regulation gives the plaintiff the option of proceeding in the courts of another Member State 'in matters relating to tort, delict or quasi-delict, in the courts for the place where the harmful event occurred or may occur'.

[3]   Service of an overseas company with a branch in England and Wales is governed by s 694A (inserted with effect from 1 January 1993) and s 695 of the Companies Act 1985. Alternatively, Civil Procedure Rule (CPR) 6.2(2) permits service under CPR 6.5(6). Unlike s 694A, this provision does not require that the service of process be 'in respect of the carrying on of the business of the [English] branch'.

[4]   [2014] EWCA Civ 1130.

Thus, in *Motto & Ors v. Trafigura*,[5] a claim in negligence for damages from exposure to toxic waste dumped in Africa was brought in the English court against Trafigura Ltd., the UK-domiciled charterer, and also against its parent company Trafigura Beheer BV, domiciled in the Netherlands.

Until 2005 the UK courts applied the doctrine of *forum non conveniens* when jurisdiction was established under Article 2 and there was an alternative forum in a non-Member State. This was the battleground in the early Leigh Day cases. The general principles to be applied in applications to stay on this ground were set out in *The Spiliada*.[6] If another forum is more appropriate for the hearing of the action a stay will be granted, unless, to do so, would cause injustice to the plaintiff.[7] The second limb of *Spiliada* has enabled plaintiffs to see off *forum non conveniens* challenges in several actions brought against an English parent corporation, involving allegations of personal injuries suffered as a result of unsafe working conditions adopted by the foreign subsidiary.[8]

However, in 2005 the scope of the doctrine was drastically reduced by the decision of the European Court of Justice in *Owusu v. Jackson*[9] to the effect that a defendant that is sued in its place of domicile, pursuant to Article 2 of the Brussels Regulation, is not entitled to have those proceedings stayed, even where the alternative forum is outside the EC.[10] Actions against UK parent companies will, therefore, fall within Article 2 of the Brussels Regulation and will no longer be subject to being stayed on the grounds of *forum non conveniens*. However, there may be some cases where the claimant seeks to proceed against a company that falls outside Article 2. Where the defendant is not domiciled in a jurisdiction subject to the Brussels Regulation, Article 4 of the Regulation preserves the domestic rules regarding jurisdiction, including *forum non conveniens*. Unless the defendant can be served in accordance with the provisions relating to service of overseas companies, the claimant will

---

[5]   [2011] EWHC 90206.

[6]   *Spiliada Maritime Corp v. Cansulex*, [1987] AC 460.

[7]   'Public interest' considerations of the sort applied in the US under the *Gilbert* test, have no place to play in the analysis of *forum non conveniens* under English law. *Lubbe v. Cape plc (No. 2)*, [2000] 1 WLR 1545 (HL).

[8]   *Ngcobo v. Thor Chemicals Ltd*, The Times, Nov 10 1995, CA; *Sithole v. Thor Chemicals Ltd*, 2000 WL 1421183 (CA); *Connelly v. RTZ Corporation plc and Ritz Overseas Ltd*, [1998] AC 854, HL; *Lubbe v. Cape plc (No. 2)*, note 6 above.

[9]   Case C-281/02, [2005] ECR I-1383.

[10]   Thus overruling the Court of Appeal's decision on this point in *Re Harrods (Buenos Aires)*, [1992] Ch 72, CA.

need to obtain leave to serve it out of the jurisdiction. This could happen, for example, where a claimant wishes to sue a foreign corporation, which might be the subsidiary of an English parent, in respect of alleged complicity in human rights abuses by agencies of a foreign government. The matter is governed by CPR 6.36. The claimant will have to bring itself within the provisions relating to tort under Practice Direction 6B para 3.1 (9).[11] The most likely way they can do this is if they have relocated to the UK where they have suffered subsequent mental illness consequent upon the original human rights violations they suffered in the foreign jurisdiction.[12] The court will exercise its discretion on grounds similar to those applied with *forum non conveniens* but with the burden of proof falling on the claimant not the defendant.

Therefore, where an action is brought against a company domiciled in the UK the courts of the UK must accept jurisdiction, even if the claim relates to events outside the jurisdiction.[13] Unlike the position in the US and in Canada and Australia,[14] the UK courts will be unable to stay such proceedings on grounds of *forum non conveniens*.

---

[11]   If the claim is brought against a UK parent corporation, the claimant may seek leave to serve its foreign subsidiary out of the jurisdiction under CPR 6.20(3) as a 'necessary or proper party'.

[12]   This was the basis on which leave to serve out of the jurisdiction was granted in *Al-Adsani v. Govt of Kuwait* (1995) 100 ILR 465,; The Times, 29 March 1996.

[13]   As in *Guerrero v. Monterrico Metals plc*, [2009] EWHC 2475 (QB) where a UK parent company was sued in tort in respect of the alleged complicity of its Peruvian subsidiary in violent police suppression in Peru of environmental protests against the activities of the subsidiary. A freezing order was obtained over the parent corporation's assets. The trial was scheduled to start in October 2011 but the case settled in July 2011.

[14]   In other common law jurisdictions, the doctrine of *forum non conveniens* has been successfully invoked in cases involving environmental tort claims against a domestic parent company of a transnational corporation. In Canada in *Recherches Internationales Quebec v. Cambior Inc*, [1998] QJ No 2554, 14 August 1998 the proceedings were stayed on this ground due to the fact that the preponderance of evidence was located in Guyana where the damage occurred. In Australia, however, it is considerably more difficult to stay on this ground due to the decision of the High Court of Australia in *Voth v. Manildra Flour Mill*, (1990) 171 CLR 538 (HCA) that the doctrine will operate only if it is established that Australia is a 'clearly inappropriate' jurisdiction for the litigation. The decision may explain the fact that in *Dagi v. B H P (No 2)*, [1997] 1 VR 428 a claim arising out of pollution caused by the collapse of a tailings dam in a copper mine in Papua New Guinea, the defendants did not seek to dismiss the Australian proceedings on this ground.

A change has been made under the Recast Regulation by which Member State courts now have a granted discretion to stay proceedings in favour of non-Member State courts. Article 33 applies where the two sets of proceedings involve the same cause of action involving, and Article 34 where the proceedings are related. The discretion is exercisable only if all the following criteria are satisfied: proceedings in the non-Member State court must have been started first; the non-Member State judgment is capable of recognition and enforcement in the Member State; and the Member State court considers that a stay is necessary for the proper administration of justice. The Member State court may also lift any stay at any time if it is satisfied that the non-Member State proceedings are stayed or discontinued or will not be concluded in a reasonable time, or if the Member State court considers that the continuation of its proceedings is necessary for the proper administration of justice.

This may lead to potential defendants jumping the gun when alerted to possible litigation before the courts of the Member State in which the parent corporation is based, by commencing proceedings for a declaration of non-liability in the host jurisdiction. This happened in *Kesabo v. African Barrick Gold plc* where the defendant was aware that it was about to be sued in respect of deaths and injuries caused to workers at a mine it operated in Tanzania because of violence allegedly perpetrated by its private security agents and/or the police.[15] Leigh Day initially issued a claim form alleging, inter alia, that Barrick Gold were vicariously liable, but prior to its service Barrick Gold brought proceedings before the courts in Tanzania for a declaration that they were not vicariously liable for the actions of the security firm and the Tanzanian police. Eventually an amended claim form was served with the claimants pleading on the basis of Barrick Gold's direct liability in tort. The claimants successfully obtained an anti-suit injunction restraining the Tanzanian proceedings and were awarded their costs. In future, under Article 33 of the Recast Regulation the defendant to the UK proceedings in such circumstances would be able to ask the court to exercise its discretion to stay those proceedings on the grounds that it had already commenced proceedings involving the same cause of action in a non-Member State.

Where the company is incorporated in a foreign country which is not an EU or Lugano Member State and has a place of business in England that is not its central administration/statutory seat/principal place of business the High Court would have jurisdiction over the company based

---

[15] [2013] EWHC 4045 (QB).

on its traditional rules only. In the UK, the common law basis for asserting jurisdiction is through service of proceedings. Service could be through CPR 6.9 which provides that service of proceedings on a foreign company may be made at 'any place in the jurisdiction where the corporation carries on its activities, or at any place of business of the company within the jurisdiction' or, as regards a company registered as an overseas company, pursuant to section 1139 of the Companies Act 2006. In addition, with the leave of the court, a claim form may be served on a party outside the jurisdiction under CPR 6.36.[16] It is, therefore, quite possible for jurisdiction to be established in a 'foreign cubed' case, although the proceedings are liable to be stayed on the basis of *forum non conveniens*. This will not always be the case for a stay will be denied where the claimant can establish that there would be substantial injustice in being required to proceed in the alternative forum.[17]

Apart from *forum non conveniens* there are two other grounds on which the UK courts may decline jurisdiction. The first is the doctrine of Act of State which applies when a claim calls into question the activity of a foreign state in its own territory. Act of State could be raised in an ATS-type suit in which the UK company is sought to be held liable as a joint tortfeasor with public authorities in another State. It is, however, subject to a public policy exception in cases of violations of international law and human rights. In *Belhaj v. Straw*[18] the Court of Appeal held that

---

[16]   Practice Direction 6(b) para 3(1) contains two provisions relevant to tort claims. First, under heading 3 where:

A claim is made against a person ('the defendant') on whom the claim form has been or will be served (otherwise than in reliance on this paragraph) and –
(a)   there is between the claimant and the defendant a real issue which it is reasonable for the court to try; and
(b)   the claimant wishes to serve the claim form on another person who is a necessary or proper party to that claim.

Second, under heading 9 where: 'A claim is made in tort where (a) damage was sustained within the jurisdiction; or (b) the damage sustained resulted from an act committed within the jurisdiction.'

[17]   An example is provided by *The Vishva Ajay*, [1989] 2 Lloyd's Rep 558 (QB) which involved a collision in an Indian port and a claim made against the Indian owners of the colliding vessel. Service had been effected by the arrest of a sister ship and the English proceedings. Although India was the appropriate forum the court refused to stay the English proceedings following evidence that a trial in India would be delayed for many years, making the evidence of witnesses involved less reliable.

[18]   [2014] EWCA Civ 1394, 30 October 2014.

the doctrine did not bar claims against a former UK government minister and UK civil servants in relation to assistance allegedly given to the extraordinary rendition by the US of suspected terrorists to interrogation centres in China and Thailand. An essential feature of the claims was that the conduct of the agents of foreign States had been unlawful and accordingly the doctrine was engaged. However, the public policy exception[19] applied as the allegations involved serious breaches of international law, such as torture. As regards the US the doctrine did not apply as none of the acts of US agents occurred within the territory of the US. An appeal is due to be heard by the UK Supreme Court in November 2015.

The second ground for declining jurisdiction is that of sovereign immunity. Section 1 of the State Immunity Act 1978 provides that, 'A State is immune from juridiction from the jurisdiction of the courts of the United Kingdom except as provided in the following provisions of this Part.'[20] Notwithstanding the fact that torture is recognised as a *jus cogens* norm of customary international law,[21] and that the 1984 UN Convention against Torture and Other Cruel, Inhuman and Degrading Punishment, expressly grants universal criminal jurisdiction against torturers, the

---

[19]   The basis of the public policy exception was set out in dicta of Lord Cross in *Oppenheimer v. Cattermole (Inspector of Taxes)*, [1976] AC 249, 278 in relation to recognition of a Nazi law of 1941 removing citizenship and property from German Jews who had left Germany:

> But what we are concerned with here is legislation which takes away without compensation from a section of the citizen body singled out on racial grounds all their property on which the state passing the legislation can lay its hands and, in addition, deprives them of their citizenship. To my mind a law of this sort constitutes so grave an infringement of human rights that the courts of this country ought to refuse to recognise it as a law at all.

In *Kuwait Airways Corp v. Iraqi Airways Co (No 5)*, [2002] UKHL 19; [2002] 2 AC 883, the House of Lords, by a 3–2 majority, applied the exception so as to disapply an Iraqi law after Iraq's invasion of Kuwait which dissolved Kuwait Airways and transferred its assets to Iraqi Airways. See, Adeline Chong, 'Transnational Public Policy in Civil and Commercial Matters,' 128 *LQR* 88 (2012).

[20]   Such as the exception under s 3 in respect of commercial transactions entered into by a State, and the exception under s 5 in respect of claims against a State in respect of death or personal injury, or damage to or loss of tangible property, caused by an act or omission in the UK.

[21]   This is a rule of customary international law that has received sufficiently widespread acceptance as to be binding even on those States that do not accept it.

Court of Appeal in *Al Adsani v. Government of Kuwait*[22] held that the 1978 Act precluded a civil suit being brought against a foreign State for breach of this norm. The decision was subsequently upheld by a majority decision of the European Court of Human Rights (ECtHR).[23] In *Jones v. Government of Saudi Arabia*[24] the House of Lords held that this was also the position when a claim was made against an agent of the foreign State in respect of torture, a position subsequently confirmed by the ECtHR when it held that granting immunity from jurisdiction to State officials in civil proceedings with respect to torture was not a violation of Article 6 ECHR.[25] Immunity may not be claimed where a claim is not made against a State or its agent but indirectly impleads the State as where the claim against the defendant is based on its involvement with actions by a foreign State or its agent.[26]

2. CORPORATE VEIL

The second problem in bringing claims against TNCs is the doctrine of the corporate veil. How can a UK parent company be held liable in tort in respect of the activities of its foreign subsidiary?[27] The claimant will need to establish a link between the subsidiary and the parent that will enable the liability of the former to be attributed to the latter. There are two ways in which the parent company can be linked with the activities of its foreign-based subsidiary. The first is to make the parent liable for the defaults of its subsidiary by piercing the corporate veil of the subsidiary or by finding that the subsidiary was acting as the parent's agent. The second is to find the parent primarily liable for a breach of a primary duty of care owed by it towards the claimants.

---

[22]   (1995) 100 ILR 465; The Times 29 March 1996.

[23]   *Al Adsani v. UK,* (2002) 34 EHRR 11.

[24]   [2006] UKHL 26; [2006] 2 WLR 1424.

[25]   *Case of Jones and Others v. United Kingdom*, App nos. 34356/06 and 40528/06 (ECtHR, 14 January 2014).

[26]   *Belhaj v. Straw*, [2014] EWCA Civ 1394, 30 October 2014.

[27]   Scotland has a separate legal system based on civil law. An action against a Scottish parent company would be in delict, rather than in tort. Similar principles govern liability, or *culpa*, in delict to those applicable in tort in England, Wales and Northern Ireland.

A. Vicarious Liability: 'Piercing the Veil'

Since *Salomon v. Salomon*[28] the English courts have upheld the principle
that a company is a legal entity distinct from that of its shareholders.
Shareholder liability is limited to the amount of unpaid share capital. The
principle applies equally to corporate groups where a parent company
holds the majority, or even the totality, of shares in a subsidiary. This is
the case notwithstanding that the principle was established before the
emergence of corporate groups.[29] There are, however, limited situations
in which the courts will ignore this artificial personality and trace back to
the underlying economic reality as far as justice requires. This process of
'piercing the corporate veil' is used by the courts only in exceptional
circumstances and to date there have been no decisions in which an
English court has used it in a tort case.[30] A parent company may also be
found liable for the acts of its subsidiary where the latter has acted as its
agent.

However, under English law, absent clear evidence of a fraudulent use
of the corporate form, the courts will continue to respect the separate
legal identities of corporate defendants. Moreover, the category of fraud
is very narrowly defined. It is limited to the use of corporate personality
to avoid existing contractual obligations[31] and does not apply where the
corporate form is used to minimise the incidence of future liabilities. Any
doubt on this issue was removed by the decision of the Court of Appeal
in *Adams v. Cape Industries plc*.[32] The case involved an attempt to

---

[28]   [1897] AC 22.

[29]   P. Blumberg, *The Multinational Challenge to Corporation Law* (1993)
Oxford University Press.

[30]   For a more general discussion of this topic see L. Gallagher and P. Ziegler,
'Lifting the Corporate Veil in the Pursuit of Justice'. (1990) *JBL* 292. In *DHN
Estates v. Tower Hamlets LBC* [1976] 1 WLR 852, the Court of Appeal gave as
one of their reasons for allowing the loss suffered by the parent to be included
when assessing compensation due to the landowner subsidiary, the fact that the
companies formed a 'single economic unit'. The decision was subsequently
distinguished on the grounds that it involved a wholly owned subsidiary.
Woolfson v. Strathclyde Regional Council, [1978] 38 P&CR 521, and was again
distinguished, almost to vanishing point, in *Adams v. Cape Industries plc*, [1990]
Ch 433, on the grounds that it involved the wording of a specific statute and set
down no general principle of law.

[31]   [1962] 1 WLR 832 where a vendor sought to avoid a sale of his house to
the plaintiff by transferring it to a company incorporated for the purpose of
purchasing the house.

[32]   [1990] Ch 433 CA.

enforce in England a default judgment obtained in Texas against Cape, an English-based multinational corporation involved in the asbestos industry, and Capasco, its English-based marketing subsidiary. Cape had supplied asbestos from its South African mining subsidiary, Egnep, to US customers via its wholly owned Illinois subsidiary, the North American Asbestos Company (NAAC). Workers at an asbestos factory in Texas suffered illness as a result of their exposure to the asbestos. They sued various parties, including Cape, Capasco, NAAC and Egnep. The first batch of litigation, the *Tyler 1 cases*, was settled for US$20m of which the Cape group contributed US$5.2m.

By the time the second batch of litigation, the *Tyler 2 cases*, began, Cape avoided its mistake in the *Tyler 1* proceedings in voluntarily submitting to the court's jurisdiction. Instead, it took no part in the *Tyler 2* proceedings and was content to suffer judgment in default against it. Cape knew that obtaining a judgment was only half the story; enforcing it would be another matter altogether. To frustrate the ultimate enforcement of any Texas judgment against it, Cape had to eliminate its presence in the jurisdiction at the time the *Tyler 2* actions commenced. Its absence from the jurisdiction at this time would subsequently enable it to argue that the general principles of private international law precluded the enforcement of any such judgment in any country, such as the UK, which lacked reciprocal arrangements with the US for the enforcement of judgments.

In order to eliminate its 'presence' from Texas, Cape put NAAC into liquidation and conducted its business through a new company, CPC, set up with Cape money but which had no formal corporate link with Cape. The only way the *Tyler 2* claimants could hope to enforce their judgment in England was by proving that, first through NAAC, and then through CPC, Cape had been present in the jurisdiction. In this they were to prove unsuccessful. The Court of Appeal refused to pierce the corporate veil of either company on the grounds of fraud. There was no fraud if a group of companies chose to use the doctrine of separate corporate personality in such a way as to minimise its group exposure to future liabilities. What is striking is that these future liabilities were not just some distant hypothesis. The success of the *Tyler 1* actions showed that these future liabilities were a very real present factor and it was this which caused Cape to reorganise in the US. It is but a small step from prohibiting the use of corporate personality to avoid subsisting contractual obligations to prohibiting its use to avoid tort suits which you know are about to materialise. Nonetheless, the Court of Appeal refused to take this small step and its decision confirms the latitude the English courts have allowed to corporations in their use of the corporate form as a tool of claims-evasion.

The plaintiffs were also unsuccessful in their attempt to show that Cape, CPC and, to a lesser extent NAAC, had been acting as agents for Cape. Neither company had ever had the power to enter contracts on behalf of Cape, nor had they ever purported to do so. In the words of Buckley LJ in *Okura & Co Ltd v. Forsbacka Jernverks Aktiebolag*, Cape would have been operating 'through' NAAC and CPC but not 'by' them.[33] They could not, therefore, be acting as Cape's agents. After *Adams v. Cape Industries plc*, therefore, the English courts will only disregard the corporate form where it is used to avoid existing legal obligations, or where one company has the power to contract on behalf of another, thereby justifying a finding of agency.[34]

The position regarding veil piercing was confirmed by the Supreme Court in *Prest v. Petrodel*.[35] Lord Sumsion, with whom Lord Mance and Lord Clarke agreed stated that under English law there existed limited circumstances in which the law treats the use of a company as a means of evading the law as dishonest and therefore susceptible to losing the benefit of the corporate form. The court may be justified in piercing the corporate veil if a company's separate legal personality is being abused for the purpose of some relevant wrongdoing. Two principles operated, the 'concealment' principle and the 'evasion' principle.[36] The concealment principle is that the interposition of a company or perhaps several companies so as to conceal the identity of the real actors will not deter the courts from identifying them, assuming that their identity is legally relevant. The evasion principle is that:

> the court may disregard the corporate veil if there is a legal right against the person in control of it which exists independently of the company's involvement, and a company is interposed so that the separate legal personality of the company will defeat the right or frustrate its enforcement.

However, it is not an abuse to cause a legal liability to be incurred by the company in the first place, nor to rely on the fact that a liability is not the controller's because it is the company's.

---

[33] *Okura & Co Ltd v. Forsbacka Jernverks Aktiebolag*, [1914] 1 KB 715, 721.

[34] In *VTB Capital plc v. Nutritek International Corp*, [2013] UKSC 5; [2013] 2 AC 337 a few months earlier Lord Neuberger had doubted whether there was any legal principle under which the corporate veil could be pierced.

[35] [2013] UKSC 34; [2013] 2 AC 415.

[36] [28].

B. Direct Liability

If the parent company is not vicariously liable for the defaults of its subsidiary, it might still incur liability in respect of a duty of care owed to the plaintiff arising out of its own act. The claims against TNCs brought before the English courts by Leigh Day have all been pleaded on the basis of the parent's primary liability. The first two involved allegations that the duty was created by the active involvement of the parent in the harmful activities of its subsidiary.[37] In *Ngcobo v. Thor Chemicals Ltd*[38] and *Sithole v. Thor Chemicals Ltd*[39] claims were made by South African plaintiffs in respect of injuries they had sustained while working for the defendant's subsidiary company in Natal. The English parent company had been engaged in the manufacture and reprocessing of mercury-based chemicals in England but following sustained criticism of its operations by the Health and Safety Executive it relocated these processes to Natal where it established a plant run by a wholly owned subsidiary. The chairman of the parent company was employed by the subsidiary company to design and set up the new plant. The plaintiffs alleged that the South African company dealt with the problem of mercury contamination by testing the blood and urine of their workers and temporarily laying off those with excessive levels of mercury until such time as those levels had reduced. In 1994 two actions on behalf of 20 workers were begun against the parent company and its chairman, by now the only director.[40]

The second claim, *Connelly v. RTZ Corporation plc and Ritz Overseas Ltd*[41] was advanced on the basis of the following allegations: that RTZ,

---

[37]   This was also the basis on which the Australian court in *CSR Ltd v. Wren*, (1997) 44 NSWLR 463 found that a parent company, whose employees were used by the subsidiary company to direct the way in which its operations were conducted, owed a duty of care to the employees of its subsidiary. In contrast in *James Hardie & Co Pty Ltd v. Hall*, (1998) 43 NSWLR 554, there had been no such active involvement in the subsidiary's operations by its parent. The parent's power to control its subsidiary was held to be insufficient to create a duty of care on the parent in relation to the subsidiary's employees.

[38]   The Times, Nov 10 1995, CA.

[39]   2000 WL 1421183 (CA). An application was made under s 423 of the Insolvency Act to reverse transfers made by a company after proceedings had been brought against it.

[40]   The actions were settled out of court in April 1997 for £1.3 million. A third action was brought in 1998 on behalf of another 21 workers which settled out of court in October 2000 for £270,000 plus legal costs.

[41]   [1998] AC 854, HL.

the parent company, had devised the policy on health, safety and the environment adopted by Rossing Uranium Ltd (RUL), its subsidiary in Namibia or had advised RUL as to the contents of the policy. Further, it alleged that employee/s of RTZ had implemented the policy and supervised health, safety and/or environmental protection at the mine operated by RUL at which the plaintiff worked.[42]

In contrast, the third case, *Lubbe v. Cape Plc (No 2)*,[43] was pleaded on the basis of a duty to supervise arising out of a combination of knowledge of a defect in the operations of a subsidiary and the ability to rectify it. The plaintiffs' claim was reformulated as follows:

> Whether a parent company which is proved to exercise de facto control over the operations of a (foreign) subsidiary and which knows, through its directors, that those operations involve risks to the health of workers employed by the subsidiary and/or persons in the vicinity of its factory or other business premises, owes a duty of care to those workers and/or other persons in relation to the control which it exercises over and the advice which it gives to the subsidiary company?[44]

The manner in which the claim was formulated was not challenged either by the defendant or by the courts in the *forum non conveniens* proceedings. In the House of Lords, Lord Bingham of Cornhill noted that in this connection one of the issues that would have to be considered the defendant's responsibility as a parent company for ensuring the observance of proper standards of health and safety by its overseas subsidiaries. His Lordship observed that:

> Resolution of this issue will be likely to involve an inquiry into what part the defendant played in controlling the operations of the group, what its directors and employees knew or ought to have known, what action was taken and not taken, whether the defendant owed a duty of care to employees of group companies overseas and whether, if so, that duty was broken. Much of the evidence material to this inquiry would, in the ordinary way be documentary and much of it would be found in the offices of the parent company, including minutes of meetings, reports by directors and employees on visits overseas and correspondence.[45]

---

[42] These issues of substantive liability were never to be determined as Mr Connelly's claim against the English parent company was subsequently held to have been made out of time.

[43] *Lubbe v. Cape plc (No. 2)*, note 7 above.

[44] Ibid., 1555.

[45] [2000] 2 Lloyd's Rep 383, 390.

In 2012 in *David Brian Chandler v. Cape plc (Chandler)*[46] the Court of Appeal held that a parent company could be liable to employees of a subsidiary on the basis of breach of a duty of care owed to them. Wyn Williams J at first instance had held that a parent company was liable to the employee of its subsidiary on the basis of the common law concept of assumption of responsibility. The claimant contracted asbestosis during a short period of employment in the 1960s with Cape's subsidiary, Cape Products. The claimant worked out of doors loading bricks produced by a brick-manufacturing arm of Cape Products. Asbestos was produced on the same site in a factory with open sides, and dust from that factory migrated into the area where the claimant worked. Wyn Williams J held that there had been 'a systemic failure of which [Cape] was well aware'. Cape were held directly, rather than vicariously liable. Cape employed a scientific officer and a medical officer who together were responsible, for health and safety issues relating to all the employees within the Cape group of companies. The evidence showed that it was Cape, not the individual subsidiary companies, which dictated policy in relation to health and safety issues insofar as its core business impacted upon health and safety. The subsidiaries played a role in implementing that policy but Cape retained overall responsibility.

The Court of Appeal upheld the decision. In *Smith v. Littlewoods Ltd* Lord Goff had stated that there was in general no duty to prevent third parties causing damage to another.[47] However, there would be an exception to this principle where there was 'a relationship between the parties which gives rise to an imposition or assumption of responsibility' on the part of the defendant.[48] By the late 1950s it was clear to Cape that exposure to asbestos brought with it very significant risk of very damaging and life-threatening illness. Cape was fully aware of the 'systemic failure' which resulted from the escape of dust from a factory with no sides. Cape therefore knew that the Uxbridge asbestos business was carried on in a way which risked the health and safety of others at Uxbridge, most particularly the employees engaged in the brick-making business. Cape's state of knowledge about the Cowley Works, and its

---

[46]   [2012] EWCA Civ 525.

[47]   [1987] AC 241, 270.

[48]   p. 272 D. It has twice been held that it is arguable that a parent company may owe a duty of care to employees of subsidiaries: see *Connelly v. Rio Tinto Zinc Corporation* and *Ngcobo v. Thor Chemicals Holdings Ltd*, January 1996, per Maurice Kay J, unreported.

superior knowledge about the nature and management of asbestos risks, made it appropriate to find that they had assumed a duty of care either to advise Cape Products on what steps it had to take in the light of knowledge then available to provide those employees with a safe system of work or to ensure that those steps were taken.

The claimant's injury was the result of that breach of duty. Cape had failed to advise on precautionary measures even though it was doing research and that research had not established (nor could it establish) that the asbestosis and related diseases were not caused by asbestos dust. Four elements indicated that a parent company would incur responsibility for the health and safety of its subsidiary's employees. First, the businesses of the parent and subsidiary were in a relevant respect the same. Second, the parent had, or ought to have had, superior knowledge on some relevant aspect of health and safety in the particular industry. Third, the subsidiary's system of work was unsafe as the parent company knew, or ought to have known. Fourth, the parent knew or ought to have foreseen that the subsidiary or its employees would rely on its using that superior knowledge for the employees' protection. As regards this final element, it was not necessary to show that the parent had been in the practice of intervening in the subsidiary's health and safety policies. The court would look at the relationship between the companies more widely and may find the fourth element is established where the evidence shows that the parent has a practice of intervening in the trading operations of the subsidiary, for example production and funding issues.

An allegation of direct liability of a parent company was also raised in *Guerrero v. Monterrico*, an overseas tort claim based on corporate complicity in human rights violations by local police. The claimants claimed damages from the parent corporation, Monterrico, and its subsidiary, Rio Blanco, for the personal injuries allegedly inflicted on them by police officers during the protest against the development of the Rio Blanco mine in Peru. The claimants contended that officers of the two companies ought to have intervened so as to have prevented the abuse of their human rights and/or were otherwise responsible for the injuries which they suffered. It was undisputed that during the course of the protest there had been brutality and abuse on the part of the police towards the protesters and that a number of them had been detained. As regards the parent company, the claimants put their case as regards the basis of its liability in the following way, under both English and

Peruvian law.[49] First, the direct participation of its personnel in the running of the mine generally and specifically in the events particularised above. Second, the parent had retained specific responsibility for risk management in respect of the operation and management of the subsidiary. Third, the parent exercised effective control over the subsidiary's management. Fourth, the two companies operated in fact as one body. The liability of both companies for omissions was said to arise in the context of their knowledge as to the risk of violence to which environmental protestors could be exposed both generally within the extractive industry in Peru and specifically in respect of the Rio Blanco mining project.

Gloster J considered the case in the context of an application for a freezing order which required her to consider whether the claimants had made out a good arguable case. She said that she was 'just about satisfied that the Claimants have demonstrated that they have surmounted the hurdle of demonstrating a good arguable case for the purposes of supporting a freezing injunction'. She went on to say:

> 27. The alleged facts as to Monterrico's responsibility and participation in the alleged brutality against the protesters would appear to be sufficient to found a cause of action. On any basis the facts are keenly disputed to such an extent that it is impossible for me to resolve them in any meaningful way on an interim application. Despite Mr. Phillips' persuasive arguments to the contrary, the evidence in relation to the participation, or part played, by Monterrico's employees or officers, whether actually at the mining site or behind the scenes, is not so clear cut in my judgment as to exonerate the company conclusively from any legal responsibility for the brutality which it appears occurred as a result of the conduct of the police. On the contrary, although the allegations are unclear, and unspecific, the Fedepaz complaint alleges participation on the part of Rio Blanco/Monterrico employees. Any detailed arguments based on the absence of legal liability, or responsibility on Monterrico's part for the acts of the police, or in relation to limitation issues or issues of foreign law, should, in my judgment, be the subject of a focused Part 24 application rather than deployed in broad brush arguments in defence to an application for a freezing injunction.

---

[49] The claimants contended that, in accordance with the provisions of Part III of the Private International Law (Miscellaneous Provisions) Act 1995, the applicable law in relation to the parent corporation was English law, insofar as its liability arose 'out of responsibility for risk management'; but might be either English law or Peruvian law in respect of the 'remaining basis' of its liability.

In Canada a similar direct liability analysis has been applied in *Choc v. Hudbay Minerals Inc.*[50] It was alleged that security personnel working for subsidiaries of a Canadian milling company, Hudbay Minerals, committed human rights abuses, such as: a shooting; a killing; and gang rapes committed in the vicinity of a proposed open-pit nickel mining operation located in eastern Guatemala. The claim was brought by indigenous Mayan Q'eqchi' from El Estor in Guatemala. Carole J. Brown J in the Ontario Superior Court of Justice denied the defendant's motion to strike out. She allowed the claim to proceed on the basis that the subsidiary had acted as the agent of the parent company and on the basis of the parent company owing a direct duty of care to the plaintiffs. The plaintiffs' pleadings showed numerous expectations and representations on the part of Hudbay/Skye and the plaintiffs, such as public representations by Hudbay concerning its relationship with local communities and its commitment to respecting human rights, which would have led to expectations on the part of the plaintiffs.

> There were also a number of interests engaged, such as Hudbay/Skye's interest in developing the Fenix project, which required a 'relationship with the broader community, whose efficient functioning and support are critical to the long-term success of the company in Guatemala', according to Hudbay's President and CEO. The plaintiffs' interests were clearly engaged when, according to the pleadings, the defendants initiated a mining project near the plaintiffs and requested that they be forcibly evicted.[51]

However, a direct duty on the part of the parent towards employees of its subsidiary will not invariably arise. In *Thompson v. Renwick Group Ltd*,[52] another claim for injury resulting from an employee's contact with asbestos, the parent company was a holding company and had no business other than holding shares. The co-ordination between the subsidiaries did not show that the parent company had assumed control so as to assume a duty of care to employees of those subsidiaries. Neither was the parent liable because it had appointed a manager to the subsidiary pursuant to its power as a shareholder. The special factors that had led to the imposition of a duty of care by the parent in *Chandler* were not present here. The parent was not in a position that its expertise meant that it was better placed to protect the employees of its subsidiary from injury and that the subsidiary would rely on that superior knowledge.

---

[50]   2013 Carswell Ont 10514.
[51]   Ibid., [69].
[52]   [2014] EWCA Civ 635, 13 May 2014.

Chandler has also been considered in the Dutch litigation against Shell and its Nigerian subsidiary in respect of oil pollution from 'bunkering', illegal tapping of oil pipelines, in Goi and Oruma.[53] The Dutch court applied Nigerian law as the law of the place where the damage occurred. Nigerian tort law is based on English law and the Dutch court then considered whether the principle of direct liability set out in *Chandler v. Cape plc* could be relied on to establish a direct liability of the Shell UK and Dutch parent companies in relation to the activities of their Nigerian subsidiary. The court found that *Chandler* involved special circumstances and could not be equated with the situation between Shell and its subsidiary.

> The District Court finds that the special relation or proximity between a parent company and the employees of its subsidiary that operates in the same country cannot be unreservedly equated with the proximity between the parent company of an international group of oil companies and the people living in the vicinity of oil pipelines and oil facilities of its (sub-) subsidiaries in other countries. The District Court is of the opinion that this latter relationship is not nearly as close, so that the requirement of proximity will be fulfilled less readily. The duty of care of a parent company in respect of the employees of a subsidiary that operates in the same country further only comprises a relatively limited group of people, whereas a possible duty of care of a parent company of an international group of oil companies in respect of the people living in the vicinity of oil pipelines and oil facilities of (sub-) subsidiaries would create a duty of care in respect of a virtually unlimited group of people in many countries. The District Court believes that in the case at issue, it is far less quickly fair, just and reasonable than it was in *Chandler v Cape* to assume that such a duty of care on the part of the parent companies of the Shell Group exists.[54]

In *Chandler v. Cape*, the subsidiary itself directly inflicted damage on its employees by allowing them to work in an unhealthy work environment, but in the Shell litigation the parent companies could at best be blamed for failing to ensure that their sub-subsidiary prevented and limited any damage caused to local people as a result of sabotage of the pipelines through bunkering. The businesses of the parent companies SPDC were not essentially the same because:

---

[53] Details of the Dutch litigation including English language versions of the judgments of 30 January 2013 are available at < https://milieudefensie.nl/english/shell/courtcase/documents> (accessed 7 April 2015). *Ogoru v. Royal Dutch Shell*, C/09/330891 / HA ZA 09-0579 and *Ogoru v. Shell Petroleum NV*, C/09/365498 HA ZA 10-1677.

[54] 4.36.

The parent companies formulate general policy lines from The Hague and/or London and are involved in worldwide strategy and risk management, whereas SPDC is involved in the production of oil in Nigeria. It is further not clear why the parent companies should have more knowledge of the specific risks of the industry in which SPDC operates in Nigeria than SPDC itself; thus, it is also unclear why people living in the vicinity like Oguru and Efanga allegedly relied on the fact that the parent companies of the Shell Group would use this superior specific know-how, if any, to protect the local community near Oruma.[55]

3. CHOICE OF LAW

Under the conflicts of law rules developed at common law, a tort that took place within the jurisdiction would be governed by English law.[56] Where there was a claim before the English courts involving a tort that took place outside the jurisdiction, the requirement of 'double actionability' had to be satisfied,[57] viz it must be actionable as a tort according to English law, and actionable (but not necessarily in tort) according to the law of the foreign country where it was done. In *Boys v. Chaplin*,[58] the House of Lords held that, in certain situations, the tort need not be actionable under the law of the *lex loci delicti*. Although the precise *ratio* of the case is elusive, Lord Wilberforce's views that the courts should apply the law of the country that had the 'most significant connection' with the tort has been followed in subsequent cases.[59] In *Thor*; *Connelly*; and *Lubbe* the plaintiffs argued that English law should apply on the basis that the tort by the parent company was committed in England.

For torts committed after 11 May 1996, until the coming into force of the Rome II Regulation on 11 January 2009, the position was governed by the provisions of the Private International Law (Miscellaneous Provisions) Act 1995. Section 11(1) provides a general rule that the applicable law is the law of the country in which the events constituting the tort or delict in question occur. With trans-national torts, where elements of these events occur in different countries, s.11(2) provides

---

[55] 4.38.

[56] *Metall und Rohstoff v. Donaldson Lufkin & Jenrette Inc*, [1990] 1 QB 391.

[57] See *Phillips v. Eyre* [1870] LR 6 QB 1.

[58] [1971] AC 356.

[59] For example, *Coupland v. Arabian Gulf Petroleum Co*, [1983] 3 All ER 226, CA. In *Red Sea Insurance Co Ltd v. Bouygues SA*, [1994] 3 All ER 749 the Privy Council went further and applied Lord Wilberforce's test, applying the law of the *lex loci delicti*, which was most closely connected with the tort, even though the tort would not have been actionable under the *lex loci fori*.

that the applicable law under the general rule is to be taken to be: (a) for personal injury and death claims, the law of the country where the individual was when he sustained the injury; (b) for property damage claims, the law of the country where the property was when it was damaged; and (c) in any other case, the law of the country in which the most significant element or elements of those events occurred.

A claim against a foreign subsidiary arose in *The Bodo Community v. Shell Petroleum Development Company of Nigeria Ltd*[60] which involved substantial land-based oil pollution in Nigeria was brought before the High Court and both parties accepted that Nigerian law applied.[61] In June 2014 preliminary questions of law came before Ackenden J as to whether the Nigerian Oil Pipelines Act 1990 excluded common law claims and provided the exclusive means of claiming compensation for oil pollution. Ackenden J held that as a matter of Nigerian law the Act did have this effect and that claims for aggravated damages were not possible under it.[62] He then went on to consider whether Shell could incur any responsibility under the 1990 Act in respect of pollution caused by 'bunkering', the illicit syphoning of oil from pipelines by third parties. Section 11(5)(b) imposed an obligation on the licensee in respect of its 'neglect ... to protect, maintain or repair any work structure or thing executed under the licence ... .' The word 'protect' could not have been intended to mean that protection was to involve policing or military or paramilitary defence of the pipelines. There had to be neglect on the licensee's part, although:

---

[60]   [2014] EWHC 1973 (TCC).

[61]   Proceedings were also brought against Shell in the Netherlands in respect of pollution in Goi and Oruma. On 30 January 2013 the District Court of the Hague, applying Nigerian law, which was largely based on English law, held that the parent company was not liable and that in four cases involving spills in 2004 and 2005 Shell's Nigerian subsidiary was not liable in respect of spills due to 'bunkering' as it had taken reasonable steps to prevent this. It was, however, found liable in respect of spills caused by bunkering at a disused well in 2006 and 2007 because it could easily have prevented this sabotage by installing a concrete plug before 2006, something it did not do until 2010, once legal proceedings had begun. The decision has been appealed and the first session in the appeal has been scheduled for 12 March 2015. Further details of the Dutch litigation including English language versions of the judgments of 30 January 2013 are available at <https://milieudefensie.nl/english/shell/courtcase/documents> (accessed 7 April 2015).

[62]   The claim settled in January 2015 for £55 million.

It is conceivable however that neglect by the licencee in the protection of the pipeline (as defined above) which can be proved to be the enabling cause of preventable damage to the pipeline by people illegally engaged in bunkering which causes spillage could give rise to a liability.[63]

There are two situations in which the courts will not apply a foreign law, notwithstanding that this is indicated by the application of the analysis undertaken under section 11 and section 12. First, section 14(3)(a) provides that a foreign law will not applied if to do so would involve a 'conflict with principles of public policy'. The application of the law of another jurisdiction, such as India, that made it easier to disregard the separate corporate personalities of parent and subsidiary companies might well be regarded as involving such a conflict, in that it might have the effect of discouraging multinational corporations from having a presence in England. Lord Hoffmann in his dissenting judgment in *Connolly v. RTZ* was clearly unhappy with the prospect of a multinational company being amenable to suit in England by reason of its activities anywhere in the world, merely by reason of the presence of its parent company in the jurisdiction.[64] Similar arguments of public policy were articulated by the Lord Chancellor's Department in September 1998 when it wrote to senior lawyers to propose reversing the decision by legislation, reasoning that 'because multinational companies based in England would be exposed to actions that would more properly be conducted abroad, they may as a result be more reluctant to have a presence in England'.[65] Conversely, section 14(3)(a) may lead to the disapplication of the law of the foreign jurisdiction where it provides an immunity to the defendant from civil liability in respect of the events forming the basis of the claim. The foreign State might, for example, have granted an immunity to human rights violators or may have passed legislation such as purporting to exempt the defendant from liability for an environmental tort.[66]

Secondly, s. 14(3)(b) provides that nothing in Part III of the Act shall affect 'any rules of evidence, pleading or practice' or authorise 'questions of procedure in any proceedings to be determined otherwise than in

---

[63]   *Bodo*, note 60 above, [93].

[64]   *Connolly*, note 40 above, 876.

[65]   H. Ward, 'Foreign Direct Liability: Exploring The Issues', paper given to workshop held at the Royal Institute of International Affairs in London on 7 and 8 December 2000. <www.chathamhouse.org.uk/pdf/briefing_papers/governing_multinationals.pdf> (accessed 8 April 2007).

[66]   An instance of such legislation is the OK Tedi Mine Continuation (Ninth Supplemental) Act 2001 of Papua New Guinea.

accordance with the law of the forum'. The House of Lords in *Harding v. Wealands*[67] held that this provision retains the existing common law rules whereby the law relating to the quantification of damages in tort claims is regarded as procedural, and subject to the law of the forum.

Tort proceedings now fall under Regulation (EC) No 864/2007 on the law applicable to non-contractual obligations (Rome II). The Regulation applies only to events giving rise to damage which occurred on, or after, 11 January 2009. Article 3 provides for the universal application of any law specified by the Regulation, whether or not it is the law of a Member State. The scheme of the Regulation is similar to that contained in the 1995 Act. The general rule is to be found in Article 4.1, as follows:

> Unless otherwise provided for in this Regulation, the law applicable to a non-contractual obligation arising out of a tort/delict shall be the law of the country in which the damage occurs irrespective of the country in which the event giving rise to the damage occurred and irrespective of the country or countries in which the indirect consequences of that event occur.

Accordingly, the applicable law in transnational tort claims against English companies will not be English law, but the law of the foreign jurisdiction in which the damage occurred. Where the claimant and the defendant both have their habitual residence in the same country at the time the damage occurs, Article 4.2 then applies the law of that country. An 'escape route' from these rules is provided in Article 4.3 which provides:

> Where it is clear from all the circumstances of the case that the tort/delict is manifestly more closely connected with a country other than that indicated in paragraphs 1 or 2, the law of that other country shall apply.

A manifestly closer connection with another country might be based in particular on a pre-existing relationship between the parties, such as a contract that is closely connected with the tort/delict in question. Where a claim is made in respect of environmental damage, Article 7 provides for the application of Article 4.1 but gives the claimant the option of basing the claim on the law of the country in which the event giving rise to the damage occurred.

Article 15 provides that;

> The law applicable to non-contractual obligations under this Regulation shall govern ... in particular (a) the basis and extent of liability, including the

---

[67]   [2006] UKHL 32; [2006] 3 WLR 83.

determination of persons who may be held liable for acts performed by them; ... . (g) liability for the acts of another person ... .

Accordingly, claims against a parent corporation in tort, whether directly, vicariously through a finding of agency on the part of the subsidiary, or through a piercing of the corporate veil of the subsidiary, would come within the scope of the Regulation and be determined by the law of the State specified in Article 4. Article 15(c) provides that questions of damages are covered by the applicable law under the Regulation. This reverses the previous position under English law in *Harding v. Wealands* where such issues were dealt with under the law of the forum.

Article 16 preserves the application of the mandatory rules of the law of the forum. Article 26 preserves the application of the public policy of the forum.

4. FUNDING

The initial claims brought by Leigh Day, such as *Connelly* and *Lubbe* were funded by legal aid but this source of funding dried up shortly afterwards. Subsequent litigation was funded on a 'no win, no fee' basis, with recovery being made out of costs payable by the defendant. Richard Meeran of Leigh Day has shown how the effect of the costs changes introduced by LASPO in April 2013 will have a significant negative impact on this funding model for claims against TNCs before the UK courts, notwithstanding the UK government's previous endorsement of the UN Guiding Principles.[68] First, success fees will no longer be recoverable from the losing party and will be deducted from the claimant's recoverable damages. In personal injury cases, the success fee that the lawyer may charge must not exceed 25 per cent of the damages, excluding damages for future care and loss. Secondly, costs should generally not exceed the amount recovered. Where legal costs recoverable from a TNC exceed the amount of recovery the successful claimants' lawyers will recover only a proportion of their costs. Thirdly, 'after the event' insurance policies taken out by the claimants will no longer be recoverable from a losing defendant. This insurance is taken out after the actionable event has occurred and covers the defendant's cost in the event that the defendant loses the case, and may also cover the claimant's costs.

---

[68] *Human Rights Obligations of Business Beyond the Corporate Responsibility to Respect?* S. Deva & D. Bilchitz (eds), Cambridge University Press (2013), 396–8.

The premium is generally not paid by claimants but is recovered from losing defendants. With personal injury claims qualified one way costs shifting (QOCS) has been introduced whereby an unsuccessful defendant will be liable to pay a claimant's costs but an unsuccessful claimant will not be liable to pay the defendant's costs.

7. Customary international law as a cause of action outside the US

Under the ATS, the violation of certain *jus cogens* norms of international criminal law to which private persons are subject, has been held to create a civil cause of action. This chapter will consider whether this cause of action is a peculiarly US phenomenon which looks doomed to extinction after *Kiobel* or whether such a cause of action would subsist in other jurisdictions.

1. CUSTOMARY INTERNATIONAL LAW AS A CAUSE OF ACTION UNDER UK LAW

The critical question is whether violations of customary international law (CIL) generate a distinct cause of action under UK law. The answer to this question depends upon how the UK courts have dealt with the relationship between international law and domestic law. There are two doctrines on this issue. The first is the doctrine of incorporation under which the rules of international law are incorporated into UK law automatically and are considered to be part of UK law unless they are in conflict with an Act of Parliament. The second is the doctrine of transformation under which the rules of international law are not to be considered as part of UK law except insofar as they have been already adopted and made part of our law by the decisions of the judges, or by Act of Parliament, or long-established custom.

In criminal proceedings the theory of transformation has been applied. In *Pinochet (No 3)* the House of Lords were faced with Spain's request to extradite Pinochet to face criminal charges relating to charges involving torture that had occurred while he was President of Chile.[1] For this to happen, the charges against him in Spain also had to constitute criminal acts in the UK. Torture committed outside the UK became criminal only

---

[1]   *R v. Bow Street Metropolitan Stipendiary Magistrate and others, ex parte Pinochet Ugarte (No 3)*, [1999] 2 WLR 827; [2000] 1 AC 147.

when section 134 of the Criminal Justice Act 1988 brought into force the provisions of the UN Convention against Torture which established universal criminal jurisdiction for torture.[2] This came into force on 29 September 1989, and therefore Pinochet could be extradited only in relation to charges of torture that had taken place between that date and the end of his presidency in 1990.[3] In a subsequent decision, the House of Lords has held in *R v. Jones (Margaret)*[4] that international law does not create new criminal offences and therefore the defendants could not advance a defence in criminal proceedings that their conduct had been directed at preventing an international crime. Historically, the courts may have recognised breaches of international law, such as piracy, violations of safe conduct and the rights of ambassadors, as creating domestic crimes.[5] However, since *R v. Knuller*[6] the courts had refused to create any new criminal offences. That was entirely a matter for Parliament. The fact that conduct had achieved the level of a crime under international law did not mean that the same conduct would be a crime under domestic law. However, their Lordships stressed that they were making no finding as regards the potential role of CIL in civil proceedings.

In contrast, in civil proceedings since the decision of the Court of Appeal in *Trendtex Trading Corp v. Central Bank of Nigeria* the theory of incorporation has held sway.[7] The issue was whether to recognise the development in international law which removed immunity from suit for a government department in respect of ordinary commercial transactions, as distinct from acts of a governmental nature. The Court of Appeal held that the defendant bank was not an emanation, arm, alter ego or

---

[2] Lord Millett, however, was of the view that the conduct alleged had become criminal before that date when it had become a criminal offence under CIL.

[3] The 1984 Convention impliedly removed the immunity enjoyed by former Heads of State and accordingly Pinochet lost his immunity from criminal proceedings once the UK and Chile had ratified the Convention. However, Pinochet retained his immunity as Head of State in respect of torture committed before that date, even though it could be said that torture had already become a crime under international law before that date.

[4] [2006] UKHL 16; [2007] 1 AC 136.

[5] Previously, in *Hutchinson v. Newbury Magistrates Court*, (2000) ILR 499, the Divisional Court had held that, although 'waging aggressive war' was a crime under international law, it could not be relied to provide a defence to domestic criminal proceedings due to uncertainty as to how the incorporation of international law would work in the domestic system.

[6] [1973] AC 435.

[7] [1977] QB 529.

department of the State of Nigeria and was therefore not entitled to immunity from suit. Lord Denning and Shaw LJ then went on to consider the position in the event that the bank had been regarded as part of the government of Nigeria. What was the effect of the development in international law that had removed sovereign immunity in respect of commercial transactions by government entities?[8] Lord Denning and Shaw LJ took the view that the doctrine of incorporation applied, in which case the bank would have been unable to rely on sovereign immunity in relation to commercial transactions.[9]

However, to incorporate CIL into domestic law is not a straightforward matter. In *Maclaine Watson v. Dept of Trade and Industry*,[10] which arose out of the collapse of the Tin Council, one of the issues before the Court of Appeal was whether there was a rule of international law that Member States participating in an international organisation, in this case the International Tin Council, could be sued in respect of liabilities incurred by such organisations. Nourse LJ was of the view that there was a rule of international law to this effect which would simply be transposed into national law. Nourse LJ dealt with the argument that the rule of international law existed only on the international plane as follows:

> Above all, there being no clear and definite consensus amongst the sources which we may consult, we ought to welcome an opportunity of supplementing them with reason and justice. Is it not both reasonable and just, and also proper, to impute to the members an intention that they should meet the bill for any amounts outstanding on the I.T.C.'s tin and loan contracts?[11]

Nourse LJ concluded that it was just and proper for the members of the ITC to incur joint and several liability in national courts in respect of undischarged liabilities of the ITC.

However, Kerr LJ was of the view that, even if there were such a rule under international law, the rule did not extend to the municipal plane so as to allow the members of the organisation to be sued in national courts.

---

[8] These developments were evidenced by decisions in Belgium, Holland, West Germany, and, most authoritatively, by the US Supreme Court's decision in *Alfred Dunhill of London Inc v. Republic of Cuba*, 425 US 682 (1976).

[9] This issue is analysed in detail in the 'Report on Civil Actions in the English Courts for Serious Human Rights Violations Abroad' by the International Law Association Human Rights Committee (2001) EHLR 129. However, the discussion on *forum non conveniens* predates the decision in *Owusu v. Jackson*, Case C-281/02, [2005] ECR I-1383.

[10] [1989] Ch 72 (CA).

[11] Ibid., 220.

Thus, it may well be that if an international association were to default upon an obligation to a state or association of states or to another international organisation, then the regime of secondary liability on the part of its members would apply as a matter of international law. But it does not by any means follow that any similar acceptance of obligations by the members can be assumed within the framework of municipal systems of law.[12]

To transpose this liability to the national sphere 'would be tantamount to legislating on the plane of international law; an impossible concept, unfortunately'.[13] This analysis might urge caution in finding that the norm of CIL as to universal criminal jurisdiction, which relates to the criminal jurisdiction of States and International Tribunals, can be translated so as to have horizontal effect in giving rise to a civil right of private parties to claim compensation from other private parties whose conduct constitutes such an international crime.

There have since been two cases in which the claimants based their claims not only on conventional intentional torts, but also on a violation of the international prohibition against torture. The first was *Al Adsani v. Government of Kuwait*[14] in which the Court of Appeal held that section 1 of the State Immunity Act 1978[15] precluded a civil suit being brought against a foreign State for breach of this norm, notwithstanding the fact that torture is recognised as a *jus cogens* norm of CIL,[16] and that the 1984 UN Convention against Torture and Other Cruel, Inhuman and Degrading Punishment, expressly grants universal criminal jurisdiction against torturers. The decision was subsequently upheld by a majority decision of the European Court of Human Rights.[17]

The second was *Jones v. Government of Saudi Arabia*.[18] An attempt was made to argue that an exception to the principles set out in the 1978 Act existed when a civil claim in respect of torture was brought both

---

[12] Ibid., 184–5.

[13] The issue was not reconsidered when the case came before the House of Lords where the decision was based on an analysis of treaty rights rather than the application of CIL.

[14] (1995) 100 ILR 465; The Times 29 March 1996

[15] 'A State is immune from the jurisdiction of the courts of the United Kingdom except as provided in the following provisions of this Part.' This immunity also applies to suits against employees or officers of a foreign State: *Propend Finance Pty v. Sing*, (1997) 111 ILR 611 (CA).

[16] This is a rule of CIL that has received sufficiently widespread acceptance as to be binding even on those States that do not accept it.

[17] *Al Adsani v. UK*, (2002) 34 EHRR 11.

[18] [2004] EWCA Civ 1394; [2005] QB 699; [2006] UKHL 26; [2006] 2 WLR 1424.

against the Kingdom of Saudi Arabia and against an individual State official, Colonel Aziz. Initially, the claimants had been denied leave to serve proceedings out of the jurisdiction of Colonel Aziz because the Kingdom of Saudi Arabia was entitled to claim immunity on his behalf. The Court of Appeal held that a State's immunity was *ratione personae*, and accordingly the claim against the Kingdom of Saudi Arabia should be dismissed under section 1 of the 1978 Act. However, the immunity of an official was *ratione materiae* only, and torture could not be treated as the exercise of a State function so as to attract immunity *ratione materiae* in either criminal or civil proceedings against individuals. The question of whether a claim for systematic torture should be allowed to proceed required the court to consider and balance all relevant factors, including the considerations underlying State immunity, jurisdiction and the availability of an alternative forum, at one and the same time.

However, the House of Lords overruled the decision, on the grounds that the 1984 UN Convention against Torture provides no exception to the principle of sovereign immunity in relation to civil proceedings. Although the 1984 Convention established universal criminal jurisdiction in respect of torture,[19] this did not translate into universal civil jurisdiction[20] and accordingly sovereign immunity could still be invoked in respect of civil claims against individuals who had committed torture. The Convention dealt with civil proceedings in Article 14.1 but this only required a State to grant a civil remedy in respect of torture committed within its jurisdiction. As to the fact that the prohibition on torture was a *jus cogens* norm, Lord Hoffmann approved the following observations of Hazel Fox in *The Law of State Immunity* (2002), 525:

> State immunity is a procedural rule going to the jurisdiction of a national court. It does not go to substantive law; it does not contradict a prohibition contained in a jus cogens norm but merely diverts any breach of it to a

---

[19]   Their Lordships noted that the decision in *Pinochet (No 3)* created an exception to sovereign immunity only in relation to criminal proceedings.

[20]   The reference to 'universal civil jurisdiction' is a reference to mandatory universal civil jurisdiction which would require State parties to UNCAT to allow a civil remedy in respect of torture committed in the jurisdiction of any State party, in the same way that UNCAT mandates State parties to bring criminal proceedings in respect of torture wherever it is committed. The mandatory nature of States' obligations under UNCAT in respect of criminal proceedings must then require a waiver of sovereign immunity.

different method of settlement. Arguably, then, there is no substantive content in the procedural plea of state immunity upon which a *jus cogens* mandate can bite.[21]

The sources of international law did not show that 'the prohibition on torture has generated an ancillary procedural rule which, by way of exception to state immunity, entitles or perhaps requires states to assume civil jurisdiction over other states in cases in which torture is alleged'.[22]

Their Lordships, though, made no comment on whether a violation of the international prohibition on torture gave rise to a cause of action separate from that arising under domestic tort law. The basis of the decision is that the norm of CIL relating to sovereign immunity had not been displaced by the 1984 Convention and gives no guidance as to whether or not the doctrine of incorporation applies in respect of civil proceedings. It would, therefore, seem that there is still some scope for making a claim on the basis of a breach of a violation of a norm of CIL. The decisions in *Al Adsani* and *Jones* rule out any civil claims against a State or its officials where the State claims immunity, but have no effect on claims against private parties.[23] Corporations who collude in international crimes committed by officials of foreign States are unlikely to be

---

[21] Paragraph [44].

[22] Paragraph [45]. Their Lordships' decision on sovereign immunity was upheld by the ECtHR in *Case of Jones and Others v. United Kingdom*, Applications nos. 34356/06 and 40528/06) Judgment 14 January 2014.

[23] Nor do the decisions on immunity exclude the public policy exception to the Act of State doctrine. In *Belhaj v. Strawi*, [2014] EWCA Civ 1394; [2014] WLR(D) 459], the Master of the Rolls Lord Lloyd Jones stated:

The abhorrent nature of torture and its condemnation by the community of nations is apparent from the participation of states in the UN Convention against Torture (to which all of the States concerned with the exception of Malaysia are parties) and the International Covenant on Civil and Political Rights (to which Libya, Thailand, the United States and the United Kingdom are parties) and from the recognition in customary international law of its prohibition as a rule of *jus cogens*, a peremptory norm from which no derogation is permitted. While it is impermissible to draw consequences as to the jurisdictional competence of national courts from the *jus cogens* status of the prohibition on torture (see, for example, *Jones v. Saudi Arabia*, per Lord Bingham at [22] and following, per Lord Hoffmann at [42] and following; *Arrest Warrant of 11 April 2000 (Democratic Republic of Congo v. Belgium)*, ICJ Rep. (2006) 6 at [58], [60], [78]), it is appropriate to take account of the strength of this condemnation when considering the application of a rule of public policy [116].

regarded as agents and the foreign State in question will, therefore, be unable to claim sovereign immunity on their behalf.

Given these developments in ordinary domestic tort law, why should a claimant consider pleading an additional cause of action based on a violation of CIL? In *Al Adsani* and *Jones* the reason was to forestall a plea of sovereign immunity being asserted by the impleaded State on behalf of itself and, in the latter case, on behalf of a State official. In both cases that argument failed. With actions against corporate defendants there is no question of such a plea being asserted.

There is one respect in which a cause of action based on reliance on CIL may yield a substantive advantage over a straightforward tort claim; and that is in respect of aiding and abetting. The relevant law under Article 4.1 of the Rome II Regulation[24] will be that of the country in which the damage occurs. If this is a Commonwealth country its law on the liability of secondary parties in tort is likely to be the same as English law, under which there is no civil claim against one who aids and abets a tort. A claim against a secondary party has to be on the basis that they are a joint tortfeasor. A party who knowingly facilitates a wrong committed by another will not be jointly liable.[25] However, with aiding and abetting an international crime it is arguable that the *mens rea* is one of knowing assistance rather than intentional assistance. Accordingly an action against a company, or a company official, that knowingly gave assistance to State authorities that committed an international crime would result in damages whereas an action based on domestic tort would succeed only if the company had procured the wrongful act or acted in furtherance of a common design or been party to a conspiracy with the State authorities.

If UK law recognises claims based on a violation of a norm of CIL the question will then arise as to how such claims fall to be dealt with under

---

[24] Regulation (EC) No 864/2007 of the European Parliament and of the Council of 11 July 2007 on the law applicable to non-contractual obligations (Rome II).

[25] Mere facilitation of the commission of a tort by another does not make the defendant a joint tortfeasor and there is no tort of 'knowing assistance' nor any direct counterpart of the criminal law concept of aiding and abetting: the defendant must either procure the wrongful act or act in furtherance of a common design or be party to a conspiracy.

W. V. H. Rogers, *Winfield and Jolowicz On Tort*, 21.2 (18th ed. 2010). 'At common law, the fact that a person has facilitated the doing of a tortious act by another is not in itself sufficient to make him liable in tort. This is so even where the facilitation is done knowingly.' (Beatson LJ); ibid., 41; *Fish & Fish Ltd v. Sea Shepherd UK (The Steve Irwin)*, [2013] EWCA Civ 544; [2013] 3 All ER 867, [41].

the Rome II Regulation. The basic rule relating to the proper law of torts is to be found in Article 4.1:

> the law applicable to a non-contractual obligation arising out of a tort/delict shall be the law of the country in which the damage occurs irrespective of the country in which the event giving rise to the damage occurred and irrespective of the country or countries in which the indirect consequences of that event occur.

On facts like those in *Unocal* this would mandate the application of the law of the State in which the forced labour had occurred. A claim based on a violation of international law would raise the question of whether international law was incorporated into the domestic civil law of the country in question. If the answer were 'no', the Rome II Regulation contains two provisions which permit a derogation from the rule in Article 4. First, Article 16, which provides:

> Nothing in this Regulation shall restrict the application of the provisions of the law of the forum in a situation where they are mandatory irrespective of the law otherwise applicable to the non-contractual obligation.

For this to apply the court would have to classify the imposition of civil liability for violations of CIL as a mandatory law of the forum.[26] It might be objected that international law permits but does not require national courts to make available such a remedy. Secondly, Article 26, which provides:

---

[26] In [1999] ECR I-8453 (C-369/96) *Arblade* the ECJ defined 'public order' legislation as:

> national provisions compliance with which has been deemed to be so crucial for the protection of the political, social or economic order in the Member State concerned as to require compliance therewith by all persons present on the national territory of that Member State and all legal relationships within that State.

Recital 32 of the Regulation cites 'the application of a provision of the law designated by this Regulation which would have the effect of causing non-compensatory exemplary or punitive damages of an excessive nature to be awarded' as an example of circumstances that could be regarded as being contrary to the public policy (*ordre public*) of the forum.

The application of a provision of the law of any country specified by this Regulation may be refused only if such application is manifestly incompatible with the public policy (ordre public) of the forum.[27]

Again, the court would have to conclude that the application of Article 4 would be contrary to the public policy of the forum whose domestic legal order had incorporated the norms of CIL.

2. CUSTOMARY INTERNATIONAL LAW IN OTHER JURISDICTIONS

A. Ireland

In 1995 in *The Toledo* a claim against the Irish State was made in respect of a violation of international law obligation on a State to admit vessels in distress to a place of refuge within its domestic waters.[28] Barr J held that where there is a long-standing generally accepted practice or custom in international law, then, subject to established limitations thereon, it is part of Irish domestic law, provided that it is not in conflict with the Constitution or an enactment of the legislature or a rule of the common law.[29] Article 29, section 3 of the Constitution provided: 'Ireland accepts the generally recognised principles of international law as its rule of conduct in its relations with other States. This has been held to refer only

---

[27] *Kuwait Airways Corp v. Iraqi Airways (Nos 4 and 5)*, [2002] UKHL 19; [2002] 2 AC 886 is an example of where the English courts have refused to apply a particular foreign law on such a basis under the common law conflicts rules.

[28] (1995) 3 IR 406, 422–7, 431–4. A claim was brought by a shipowner against the Irish State in respect of a violation of the norm of CIL, being the *prima facie* right of vessels in distress to have access to a place of refuge in the nearest maritime State in which such facilities were available. On the facts, the claim was unsuccessful because the right of access was not absolute and was modified by countervailing considerations such as the risk of oil pollution or of the vessel's sinking or hindering navigation should it be admitted into Irish waters.

[29] Per Davitt P, *In re o Laighleis*, [1960] IR 93,103, referring to the dictum in *West Rand Central Gold Mining Company v. R*, [1905] 2 KB 391:

> Apart from any provision of the Constitution, the position would appear to be that the rules of international law are not part of the domestic law, except in so far as they have been made so by legislation, judicial decision, or established usage. To that extent its rules may be applied by the courts so long as they are not in conflict with an enactment of the legislature or a rule of the common law.

to relations between States and confers no rights on individuals.[30] However, the absorption of CIL into Irish domestic law was not contrary to Article 29, section 3.

> The plaintiff is not seeking redress against the State in international law, but in domestic law on the premise that the prima facie right of a foreign ship in serious distress to the benefit of a port or anchorage of refuge in an adjacent state has in time evolved into Irish domestic law from customary international law.

Nor was it contrary to Article 15, section 2, sub-section 1 of the Constitution which provides: 'The sole and exclusive power of making laws for the State is hereby vested in the Oireachtas: no other legislative authority has power to make laws for the State.' It did not inhibit the evolution of CIL into Irish domestic law but related to the 'making' of laws for the State which, it provides, is a power exclusively reserved to the Oireachtas. Customary law is not made in this sense, but evolved from a practice or course of conduct which in time has become widely accepted.[31]

B. Canada

In Canada rules of CIL pass into domestic law by adoption, in the absence of conflicting legislation.[32] This was the view expressed by Le

---

[30] *Summers Jennings v. Furlong*, [1966] IR 183, 186, 190.

[31] If this interpretation of art 15, s 2 were wrong, the international custom in maritime law whereby a ship in serious distress is entitled to a safe refuge is so long established as to be deemed to have been absorbed into Irish domestic law before the enactment of the Constitution in 1937 in which case art 15, s 2 has no bearing on its validity.

[32] The Court of Appeal for Ontario cited the doctrine of adoption in *Bouzari v. Islamic Republic of Iran*, (2004), 71 OR (3d) 675, stating at para 65 that 'customary rules of international law are directly incorporated into Canadian domestic law unless explicitly ousted by contrary legislation' (leave to appeal refused, [2005] 1 SCR vi). See also *Mack v. Canada (Attorney General)*, (2002), 60 OR (3d) 737 (CA), at para 32 (leave to appeal refused, [2003] 1 SCR xiii). In other decisions, however, the court has not applied or discussed the doctrine of adoption of CIL when it had the opportunity to do so: see, for example, *Gouvernement de la République démocratique du Congo v. Venne*, [1971] SCR 997; *Reference re Newfoundland Continental Shelf*, [1984] 1 SCR 86; *Reference re Secession of Quebec*, [1998] 2 SCR 217; *Suresh v. Canada (Minister of Citizenship and Immigration)*, [2002] 1 SCR 3; 2002 SCC 1. However, no Canadian decision had explicitly rejected the application of the doctrine.

Bel J in *R v. Hape* which involved the application of the Canadian Charter to the activities of the Canadian police who were conducting a money-laundering investigation in the Turks and Caicos.[33] The Charter was held to have no extra-territorial effect. The relevant rule of CIL was that of non-intervention and respect for the territorial sovereignty of foreign States, as held by the ICJ in the *Case concerning Military and Paramilitary Activities In and Against Nicaragua (Nicaragua v. United States of America)*.[34] That indicated that the Charter would have no extra-territorial effect and the same result would flow from the principle that statutes are presumed to be in conformity with international law.

In 2002 a torture claim was brought against Iran in 2002 in *Bouzari v. Islamic Republic of Iran*[35] but foundered on the rocks of sovereign immunity. In 2009 in *Bil'in (Village Council) v. Green Park International Ltd*,[36] a claim was brought in Canada against a corporation, alleging complicity in war crimes and crimes against humanity in the occupied territories in Israel. It was alleged that by transferring part of its civilian population to territory it occupies in the West Bank, Israel was violating international law as well as Canadian and Québec laws and that by constructing and selling condominiums exclusively to Israeli civilians, the corporate defendants were assisting Israel in the perpetration of war crimes contrary to the provisions of the Fourth Geneva Convention.[37] Under the law of Canada these provisions formed part of CIL, but not under the law of Israel, the alternative forum. The Superior Court of Québec dismissed the proceedings on grounds of *forum non conveniens*,

---

[33] [2007] SCC 26; [2007] 1 SCR 292 paras [35]–[39]. The issue was whether evidence obtained as a result of searches in the Turks and Caicos, in violation of the Charter, could be admitted in criminal proceedings in Canada. Bastarache J came to the same conclusion but held that the Charter did apply to the search and seizures conducted in the Turks and Caicos Islands but that Hape had not established a breach of s. 8 of the Charter.

[34] [1986] ICJ Rep 14, 106.

[35] [2002] OJ No. 1624; [2004] OJ No. 2800 Docket No. C38295.

[36] 2009 QCCS 4151.

[37] In violation of art 49(6) of the *Fourth Geneva Convention* dated August 12, 1949, s 3(1), Sch V Protocol 1, Part 1, art. 1(1) and Sch V Protocol 1, Part V, s 11, art 85(4)(a) of the Geneva Conventions Act, RS 1985, c. G-3, arts 8(2)(b)(viii) and 25(c) of the Rome Statute of the International Criminal Court dated July 17, 1998, s 6(1)(c), (3) and (4) of the Canadian Crimes against Humanity and War Crimes Act SC 2000, c. 24, ss 6 and 8 of the Charter of Human Rights and Freedoms, RSQ, c. C-12 and art 1457 of the Civil Code of Québec.

finding that the High Court of Jerusalem was the logical forum and the authority in a better position to decide the case.[38]

Adjudication by the High Court of Jerusalem on the basis of the laws that apply in the West Bank would not be manifestly inconsistent with public order as understood in international relations. The existence of some substantive difference between the domestic law of Israel and the domestic law of Québec did not mean, in and of itself, that the High Court of Jerusalem would not be 'in a better position' to decide the action than the Superior Court. Although the plaintiffs argued that they sought justice in the Québec forum, the action as framed would not lead to a just result. The plaintiffs had failed to implead any of the numerous owners or occupants of the buildings that they sought to have demolished, thereby depriving those persons of the right to be heard, a fundamental tenet of natural justice.[39] Although the plaintiffs had not sued Israel, they were indirectly seeking the essential finding that it was committing a war crime, thereby effectively by-passing Israel's absolute immunity to any judicial proceedings, an immunity which both in Canada[40] and the UK,[41] extended to gross violations of international human rights. Furthermore although the action was civil, it was predicated on a finding that Israel is committing a war crime in violation of public international law, and both the Geneva Conventions Act and Crimes Against Humanity and War Crimes Act prohibited criminal prosecution without the attorney general's authorisation, which the plaintiffs had not obtained.

In *Anvil Mining Ltd. v. Canadian Ass'n Against Impunity* similar proceedings were brought against Anvil Mining by the Canadian Association Against Impunity (CAAI) claiming damages for being an accomplice in war crimes and crimes against humanity. The company operated a copper mine in the Democratic Republic of Congo (DRC) and it was

---

[38]   The decision was subsequently affirmed by the Court of Appeal and the Supreme Court *Bil'in (Village Council) v. Green Park Int'l Inc*, [2010] CA 1455, [2011] 1 SCR vi (Can.) (dismissing application with costs), *available at* http://www.ccij.ca/cases/bilin/. In February 2013 a complaint was filed with the UN Human Rights Committee, claiming that Canada had violated provisions of the International Covenant on Civil and Political Rights by not allowing the case to proceed.

[39]   On this basis, a trial court may refuse to issue the injunctive orders that the plaintiffs are seeking: *Bellavance v. Blais*, [1976] RP 423 (CA).

[40]   *Bouzari v. Islamic Republic of Iran*, (2004) 71 OR (3d) 675 (Ont CA), leave to appeal refused.

[41]   John H. Currie, *Public International Law*, 2nd ed. (Ottawa: University of Ottawa, 2008), 376 and foll.

alleged that it had given assistance to the DRC military during a massacre in 2004 of civilians some 55km distant from Anvil's mine. It was alleged that Anvil had provided rides to the military to the site of the massacre, supplying trucks, drivers, food, and fuel. Anvil operated from Australia but was registered as a corporation in Canada's North West Territories and had a small office in Québec. At first instance the case was allowed to proceed but the decision was overturned by the Court of Appeal who found that the courts in Québec did not have jurisdiction.[42] In particular, section 3148 of the Civil Code of Québec, stated that, to exercise jurisdiction, there must be a 'real and substantial connection to Québec in respect of the claim'. The Court of Appeal found that there was no jurisdiction because Anvil's activity in Québec had no connection whatsoever with the allegations of complicity in international crimes during the operation of its mine in the DRC. The claim could not be brought in Québec under the principle of *forum necessitatis* because the court did not accept that justice could not be obtained in the DRC or Australia. Suit had not been brought in Australia because of the difficulty in finding a lawyer to take the case on there but that was not a sufficiently compelling reason to allow the suit to be brought in Québec.

In 2012 Canada passed the Justice for Victims of Terrorism Act which creates a cause of action in Canada for damage or loss which occurred anywhere in relation to a terrorist act, if (a) the plaintiff is a Canadian citizen or permanent resident; or (b) if the plaintiff is not a Canadian citizen or permanent resident there is a real and substantial connection to Canada. Under the Act a suit in damages may be brought against three categories of entity. The first is 'any person' which includes real or corporeal persons who committed the act or omission that resulted in the loss or damages in a manner related to an act of terrorism. The second is a 'listed entity' which refers to terrorist organisations which have been identified as such by way of an order of the Governor in Council (the Federal executive), pursuant to section 83.05 of the Criminal Code of Canada. The list currently runs to over 40 groups, including Hizbollah and FARC. The third is a foreign State whose immunity has been lifted. The Canadian State Immunity Act has been modified to lift the immunity of a foreign State that has been listed by the Governor in Council as a

---

[42] [2012] CA 117, para 81 (Can Que), available at http://www.canlii.org/fr/qc/qcca/doc/2012/2012qcca117/2012qcca117.html (in French).

sponsor of terrorism. In September 2012 Canada designated Iran and Syria as sponsors of terrorism.

The Act also specifies that property in Canada belonging to a foreign State may be stripped of its immunity to allow for the execution of a judgment pursuant to this statute, and allows for the recognition of a foreign award against a State for reasons which would have justified a similar decision in Canada, as long as the foreign State appears on the Canadian list of State sponsors of terrorism. This is designed to allow the enforcement of US judgments against State sponsors of terrorism.[43] In March 2014 in *Edward Tracy v. The Iranian Ministry of Information and Security*, the Superior Court of Justice in Ontario ordered the attachment of Iranian assets in Canada totalling US\$ 7m to satisfy US judgments against Iran in connection with terrorism.[44]

C. France

In March 2013 in *Association France-Palestine Solidarite 'AFPS' vs Societe Alstom Transport SA* the Versailles Court of Appeal addressed the place of international law in the French domestic legal order and held that there was no norm of CIL under which corporations would be subject to obligations in respect of *jus cogens* norms.[45] In 2007 the case was brought in the Tribunal de Grande Instance de Nanterre against two French companies, Alstom, and Veolia, by two Palestinian NGOs in connection with their involvement in the Jerusalem light rail system. The two French companies had formed an Israeli company, Citypass, which then signed a general concession contract with the State of Israel in connection with the Jerusalem light rail system and also signed a series of separate construction contracts with Citypass. The plaintiffs argued

---

[43] Currently four States are officially designated as sponsors of terrorism and denied foreign State immunity in the US: Cuba, Iran, Syria, and Sudan.

[44] 2014 ONSC 1696 (CanLII). Available at http://www.canlii.org/en/on/onsc/doc/2014/2014onsc1696/2014onsc1696.html <accessed 25 April 2015>. A Canadian claimant, Dr Sherri Wise, had previously been given leave to intervene in the proceedings to ensure that these assets were not all subsumed in enforcing the US judgments.

[45] Available at http://www.google.com/url?sa=t&rct=j&q=&esrc=s&source=web&cd=1&ved=0CB4QFjAA&url=http%3A%2F%2Fwww.intjewishlawyers.org%2Fmain%2Ffiles%2FVersailles%2520Court%2520of%2520Appeals%2520ruling%2520doc%2520English%2520.pdf&ei=a3Q7VZfuOo25aY7PgcAD&usg=AFQjCNHIxaTI0vaN86qhZusv9y-_ILSQmg&sig2=nbGT6a4Kg99MCXGHhe49WQ <accessed 25 April 2015>.

that the general concession contract between Citypass and Israel had an illicit object or purpose in that Israel's motive in the project was the continuance of illegal occupation in the West Bank, in violation of the Hague[46] and Geneva Conventions.[47] They argued that the concession contract and the separate construction contracts should be viewed as a single group of contracts, and that if the concession contract had an illicit object or purpose, that object would automatically be imputed to the construction contracts, and those contracts should be rendered void by the court as being against public policy due to their illicit object or purpose. They also asked the court to order Alstom and Veolia to cease their participation in the project. They also argued that the participation of the defendants in these unlawful contracts necessarily engaged the latter's liability in tort on the grounds of Article 1382 of the French Civil Code and that they had suffered prejudice as a direct result of this misconduct.

The suit was dismissed by the Nanterre Tribunal in 2011 and the dismissal was confirmed by the Versailles Court of Appeal on 23 March 2013. The Court of Appeal held that the treaties relied on by the plaintiffs did not confer rights on private parties. The wording of the two conventions was directed at States and conferred no rights on individuals. If a norm of international law was to allow rights and obligations for private persons in the domestic order to be created, it had to contain sufficiently clear elements concerning the individuals that may benefit therefrom for this purpose. However, individuals were not the subject of the Fourth Geneva Convention, which deals only with groups: 'the protected persons' or 'the population'. Secondly, did the conventions impose obligations on non-State entities? Again, the answer was 'no'. The defending companies were legal persons under private law, and were not signatories to the conventions invoked, nor the recipients of the obligations contained therein. In consequence, they were not the subjects of international law, and did not have international personhood, and therefore the various international norms invoked by the plaintiffs could not be invoked against them. The court also rejected the argument that there was a customary rule enshrining the 'general liability of trans-national companies for breaches of Human Rights'. even if the relevant law of occupation provisions could be shown to constitute *jus cogens*.

---

[46] Articles 23g and 46(2) of the Hague Convention of October 18, 1907 and arts 4.1 and 4.3 of the Hague Convention of 1954 with regard to the Protection of Cultural Property in the Event of Armed Conflict

[47] Articles 49 and 53 of the Fourth Geneva Convention of August 12 1949.

The court held that such a norm could not be evidenced by the US cases under the ATS as they involved the application of domestic law or involved a criminal aspect. Nor were the examples from French decisions, such as the prosecution of Total for its involvement in kidnapping and false imprisonment in Burma, relevant as they too related to criminal matters.

8. Voluntary codes and the UN Guiding Principles

Paralleling, and perhaps not unconnected with, the development of home State litigation the last 15 years have seen the corporate embrace of the corporate social responsibility agenda, with corporations adopting human rights policies and triple bottom line reporting policies. A series of voluntary initiatives have emerged for corporations to sign up to, particularly in the problematic extractive sector. This so-called 'soft law' approach has an obvious appeal to corporations as it entails no legal commitment. This is TNCs doing it for themselves. In 2011 this voluntary approach culminated with the endorsement in June 2011 of John Ruggie's 'Guiding Principles on Business and Human Rights: Implementing the United Nations 'Protect, Respect and Remedy' Framework' by the UN Human Rights.

1. VOLUNTARY CODES

A. The Global Compact

On 31 January 1999 in a speech in Davos, Secretary-General Kofi Annan launched a call for business leaders to combine with the UN to initiate a global compact whereby business would embrace, support and enact a set of core values in the areas of human rights, labour standards, and environmental practices. The Global Compact, a global CSR initiative based on voluntary business membership, was officially launched in a meeting in New York in July 2000. Its initial membership comprised businesses plus representatives from UN agencies, NGOs and trade unions. The Global Compact initially contained nine principles, which became ten in 2004. To join the Global Compact a company must indicate its continuing support for these principles and its intention to implement them. Participating companies are expected to report actions taken in support of the principles and publish their report publicly on the Global Compact website. The Global Compact currently has over 12,000 corporate participants and other stakeholders from over 145 countries, making it the largest voluntary corporate responsibility initiative in the world.

The UN Global Compact currently sets out ten principles, under four headings, which companies are asked to embrace, support and enact, within their sphere of influence.[1] The first heading concerns human rights. Principle 1 states that 'Businesses should support and respect the protection of internationally proclaimed human rights' and Principle 2 states that they should make sure they are not complicit in human rights abuses. For this purpose the Global Compact identifies three levels of complicity:

- direct complicity – when a company provides goods or services that it knows will be used to carry out the abuse;
- beneficial complicity – when a company benefits from human rights abuses even if it did not positively assist or cause them;
- silent complicity which is least likely to result in legal liability – when the company is silent or inactive in the face of systematic or continuous human rights abuse.

The second heading concerns labour rights. Principle 3 provides that businesses should uphold the freedom of association and the effective recognition of the right to collective bargaining. Principle 4 provides for the elimination of all forms of forced and compulsory labour. Principle 5 provides for the effective abolition of child labour. Principle 6 provides for the elimination of discrimination in respect of employment and occupation. The third heading is that of the environment. Principle 7 requires businesses to support a precautionary approach to environmental challenges. Principle 8 requires businesses to undertake initiatives to promote greater environmental responsibility. Principle 9 requires them to encourage the development and diffusion of environmentally friendly technologies. The final heading is that of anti-corruption with Principle 10 providing that businesses should work against corruption in all its forms, including extortion and bribery.

There is a complaints mechanism for drawing the attention of the Global Compact to companies that appear to be committing 'systemic or

---

[1] The principles derive from: the UN Guiding Principles on Business and Human Rights by John Ruggie; the Universal Declaration of Human Rights; the International Labour Organization's Declaration on Fundamental Principles and Rights at Work; the Rio Declaration on Environment and Development; the United Nations Convention Against Corruption.

egregious abuse' of its overall aims and principles. As a last resort, such companies can be removed from the list of participants in the Global Compact, but the chief aim of the complaints mechanism seems to be creating dialogue between the complainer and the target of the complaint with a view to putting pressure on the latter to change its behaviour. The Global Compact website lists companies which are 'non-communicating' and 'inactive' but does not distinguish between companies that have been dropped for actually violating the Global Compact principles and those dropped simply for neglecting to regularly report on how they are implementing these principles. The Global Compact is an undemanding initiative which may encourage corporate members to embody a set of principles in their operations, but does not seem to put pressure on them actually to do so.

B. The Voluntary Principles on Security and Human Rights

Launched in 2000, the Voluntary Principles on Security and Human Rights is a set of guidelines for companies in the extractive sector to reduce the risk of their security arrangements leading to human rights abuses. There are currently nine government participants,[2] 28 corporate participants,[3] and ten NGOs. The Voluntary Principles comprise three sections: risk assessment; interactions between companies and public security, comprising headings on Security Arrangements, Deployment and Conduct, Consultation and Advice, Response to Human Rights Abuses; interactions between companies and private security. The Voluntary Principles make a clear distinction between use of public security and private security as can be seen in the following provisions of the Voluntary Principles. Where private security is involved the Voluntary Principles provides that:

Private security *should* (emphasis added):

(a)   not employ individuals credibly implicated in human rights abuses to provide security services;
(b)   use force only when strictly necessary and to an extent proportional to the threat; and

---

[2]   Australia, Canada, Colombia, Ghana, The Netherlands, Norway, Switzerland, the UK, and the US.
[3]   These include many corporations whose names are familiar from ATS suits: Chevron, Freeport McMoran Copper and Gold, Occidental Petroleum, Rio Tinto, Shell, Talisman Energy.

(c)   not violate the rights of individuals while exercising the right to exercise freedom of association and peaceful assembly, to engage in collective bargaining, or other related rights of Company employees as recognized by the Universal Declaration of Human Rights and the ILO Declaration on Fundamental Principles and Rights at Work.

By contrast, where public security is involved the Voluntary Principles stipulate that companies should use *their influence* to promote these principles. Companies operating in areas of political instability will need to use State security but will then seek to distance themselves from any abuses by State security forces by stating that they have no control over them.

The Voluntary Principles have been adopted by the International Finance Corporation (IFC), a private-sector arm of the World Bank Group which invests in private-sector projects in developing countries, into its Performance Standards on Social and Environmental Sustainability, which companies must satisfy in order to receive financial support.[4] These standards are also applied by the Equator Principles under which 40 banks have agreed to apply in project financings with total capital costs of $10 million or more. Accordingly, the Voluntary Principles are becoming a global benchmark for corporate responsibility for human rights. However, the Voluntary Principles are a voluntary code with no enforcement mechanism. The only possible sanction is expulsion of a corporation, but this must be initiated by other participants and is not open to the victims of security operations. Reports on implementation of the principles are produced by the corporations themselves, are not independently verified, and remain confidential. The Voluntary Principles itself provides a summary of reports but does not identify named companies, as 'all proceedings of the Voluntary Principles process are on a non-attribution and non-quotation basis and no distribution of documents to non-participants is permitted except as required by valid legal

---

[4]   The paragraph on Public Security Personnel Requirements in Performance Standard Four, which covers community health, safety and security, states:

If government security personnel are deployed to provide security services for the client, the client will assess risks arising from such use, communicate its intent that the security personnel act in a manner consistent with [the] paragraph ... above, [which reflects the Voluntary Principles,] and encourage the relevant public authorities to disclose the security arrangements for the client's facilities to the public, subject to overriding security concerns.

process or otherwise required by law'. Effectively, the Voluntary Principles is a self-policing, closed shop. For this reason two NGO participants, Amnesty International and Oxfam America, have left the Voluntary Principles.

A recent report by Rights and Accountability in Development (RAID) 'Principles Without Justice, The Corporate Takeover of Human Rights'[5] highlights this deficiency in the Voluntary Principles by referring to the case of Acacia Mining (formerly African Barrick Gold). This involved the use of lethal force by local police against local people at or close to its North Mara mine in Tanzania, resulting in 16 deaths, 11 injuries, and allegations of rape and sexual assaults by police and security employees of African Barrick Gold. The Canadian company Barrick Gold Corp, which has a majority holding in Acacia Mining, joined the Voluntary Principles after media publicity of police brutality and rapes at its Porgera gold mine in Papua New Guinea. Barrick has used an independent consultancy, Avanzar, to produce confidential human rights impact assessments, but has published very little about the allegations relating to the North Mara mine. Its 2013 Human Rights summary merely confirmed that a human rights assessment was conducted at the mine. Only during the course of discovery in proceedings brought in the UK[6] was access obtained to a key security document, the Memorandum of Understanding (MOU) between Barrick and the Tanzanian police. Barrick's MOU advocates compliance with the Voluntary Principles which require promotion of the observance of the UN Basic Principles on the Use of Force and Firearms, but sets out no consequences should the Tanzanian police breach those standards. Notwithstanding Barrick's adherence to the Voluntary Principles, shootings at or near the mine by Tanzanian police have continued. The report also makes similar findings in relation to a killing by public security forces at Glencore's mining operations in the Democratic Republic of Congo. Responding to public criticism of its failure to ensure respect for human rights at its KCC site, Glencore has stated: 'It should be noted that the deployment of Mine Police officers on site is done so by the State to protect their interests. The Mine Police are not contracted out or subordinated to the mines and hence remain outside of the control of the mining companies.'[7]

---

    [5] http://www.raid-uk.org/sites/default/files/principles-justice-summary.pdf <accessed 17 April 2015>.

    [6] The claim settled in February 2015.

    [7] Glencore Response to Key Findings and Questions, presented by Bread for All, the Swiss Catholic Lenten Fund and RAID, 17 June 2014, available at:

C. The OECD Guidelines for Multinational Enterprises

The OECD Guidelines for Multinational Enterprises (the Guidelines), are recommendations addressed by governments to multinational enterprises, and were originally adopted in 1976 since when they have been subject to several revisions. The current Guidelines were adopted on 25 May 2011 by the governments of all 42 Member countries of the OECD (which includes the UK), as well as Argentina, Brazil, Egypt, Latvia, Lithuania, Morocco, Peru and Romania. Chapter I states that these are joint recommendations by OECD governments, and those of several non-OECD States, to multinational enterprises and provide 'principles and standards of good practice consistent with applicable laws'. However, Chapter I then goes on to state that, 'The Guidelines are recommendations jointly addressed by governments to multinational enterprises' and that 'Observance of the Guidelines by enterprises is voluntary and is not legally enforceable.' The Guidelines contain chapters on disclosure, employment and industrial relations, the environment, information disclosure, combating bribery, consumer interests, science and technology, competition taxation, and in 2011 added a new chapter on human rights based on the UN Guiding Principles on Business and Human Rights.

In 2000 the Guidelines provided for the establishment of National Contact Points (NCP) to which complaints about the operation of a multinational enterprise could be directed. Any interested party can submit a complaint to a NCP in the government where the complaint arose, or where the country is not a member of the OECD, to the NCP in the home State. The NCP can investigate the complaint and at the end of the process will issue statements reporting on the issue, the mediation processes, and can provide recommendations.[8] The OECD's website contains a list of statements or press releases issued by NCPs with regard to specific instances which have arisen in the implementation of the Guidelines until July 2013.[9] The practice of national NCPs varies, with

---

http://www.glencore.com/assets/media/doc/news/2014/201406170700-Response%20to%20BFA,%20RAID%20and%20Fastenopfer,%20June%202014.pdf. <accessed 17 April 2015>.

   [8]   In the UK some 30 per cent of such claims are rejected, 30 per cent result in a settlement or final statement and 40 per cent fall away. The UK NCP is staffed by the Department of Business.

   [9]   http://www.oecd.org/investment/mne/ncpstatements.htm <accessed 23 April 2015>.

the US adopting a rather passive stance on complaints,[10] producing three statements, and the UK adopting a proactive role, producing 29 statements.

There have been several final statements by the UK upholding complaints against UK companies.[11] However, these are not binding rulings and companies are free to disregard them. An example is the complaint filed by Survival International (SI) against Vedanta Resources, a UK mining company, on the grounds that its aluminium refinery and planned bauxite mine on Niyam Dongar Mountain in Orissa, India would violate the rights of the Dongria Kondh tribe to whom the mountain is sacred. It was alleged that neighbouring tribes have been forcibly evicted to make way for the aluminium refinery. The allegations led to the Norwegian government disinvesting in Vedanta. The NCP published a final statement in September 2009 upholding SI's allegations that Vedanta acted in violation of the OECD Guidelines and made recommendations to Vedanta to bring its business practices in line with the OECD Guidelines and requested that both parties provide an update on the implementation

---

[10] Human Rights Watch's statement of 3 November 2010 before the US Bureau of Economic, Energy, and Business Affairs noted that the US NCP often gives one of two grounds for inaction; the existence of parallel legal proceedings, and the lack of investment nexus, stating:

> But this 'nexus' can be narrowly or broadly construed to reach or not reach, for example, abuses by supply chain firms (who are often bound by the multinational's code of conduct), or by firms that rely on loans from overseas banks. The US NCP typically says that the investment nexus is insufficient and refuses to act, while other NCPs are more ready to take up such cases.

http://www.hrw.org/print/news/2010/11/08/us-review-us-national-contact-point-oecd-guidelines-multinational-enterprises <accessed 23 April 2015>.

[11] Two significant findings were made in summer 2008. On 17 July 2008 the NCP upheld a complaint by Rights and Accountability in Development that DAS Air: (i) failed to apply due diligence when transporting minerals from Entebbe and Kigali, which had a reasonable probability of being sourced from the conflict zone in the Democratic Republic of Congo (DRC); and (ii) undertook flights between Entebbe airport and the conflict zone in Eastern DRC. These flights coincided with an illegal occupation of the area by the Ugandan military, during a period when the UN and NGO's recorded human rights abuses. A flight ban between DRC and Entebbe was in place during the applicable period, meaning these flights were in direct contravention of international aviation conventions (the Chicago Convention). On August 28, 2008, the NCP issued a final statement in the complaint brought by Global Witness against Afrimex Ltd in which it found Afrimex in violation of the OECD Guidelines in that it had paid bribes to a rebel group in the DRC and purchased minerals from mines in the DRC that employ child and forced labour.

in three months. In March 2010, UK NCP issued a follow-up statement urging Vedanta to immediately work with the Dongria Kondh people to explore alternatives to resettlement of the affected families and recommended Vedanta include a human rights impact assessment in its project management process and take concrete action to implement any self-regulatory practices it adopts.

D. The Extractive Industries Transparency Initiative (EITI)

The Extractive Industries Transparency Initiative (EITI) is a global Standard to promote open and accountable management of natural resources, first launched in September 2002 by UK Prime Minister Tony Blair at the World Summit on Sustainable Development in Johannesburg. The EITI maintains the EITI Standard which countries implement to ensure full disclosure of taxes and other payments made by oil, gas and mining companies to governments, in an annual EITI Report. The aim is for these reports to enable citizens to see for themselves how much their government is receiving from their country's natural resources. The EITI Standard requires that EITI Reports are comprehensible, actively promoted and contribute to public debate. Any country with extractive industry sectors can adhere to the EITI Standard. Currently, 29 countries are 'compliant countries' and 17, including the UK and the US, are 'candidate countries'.

E. Brands and Supply Chain Codes

Two industrial disasters in the Bangladesh garment industry have highlighted the responsibilities of brands that source their products from factories in Bangladesh. On 24 November 2012, a fire at the Tazreen Fashions factory killed at least 112 workers. When the fire started the factory workers were told to ignore the alarm and keep on working, with a radio being turned to cover up the alarm. By the time workers tried to leave it was impossible to leave by the ground floor where the fire had started and management had locked gates on several of the building's upper floors leading many workers to jump to their deaths to escape the fire.

A few months later, the Rana Plaza building collapse of 24 April 2013 killed 1,100 workers and injured a further 2,500. The previous day cracks had appeared in the walls of the eight-storey building. The industrial police had recommended that the factory owners using the building suspend operations until the safety of the building could be established but the clothing factory owners allegedly ignored these directions and the building was declared safe by engineers working for the owner of the building. Many workers returned to their machines faced with losing a day's pay or dismissal.

The immediate cause of the building's collapse was its poor construction and the fact that it was built purely for retail purposes.[12] However, the 'governance gap' which has made Bangladesh such an attractive source for garment manufacture, is also a major contributory facto to the disasters. Western brands are the principal customers of the Bangladesh garment industry and garments for many household names were being manufactured in the Rana Plaza building and at Tazreen Fashions. The report of the Bangladesh All Party Parliamentary Group of the UK Parliament into the Bangladesh garment industry identified the contribution brands themselves had made to the human rights issues in their supply chain.[13] Most low- to medium-value brands work on a 'fast fashion' model which involves stores hosting nine to 12 annual fashion seasons which demands very short lead times for orders from suppliers. Brands reserve the right to make changes to designs prior to production which can lead to excessive hours being worked and to unauthorised sub-contracting so as to meet contractual deadlines.[14] The report noted:

> For the past 30 years the permissive business environment in Bangladesh has benefitted brands driven by the dictates of the bottom line. The brand that claimed that it had 'no choice' but to source from the country has, just like other brands that source from Bangladesh, profited from a gap in governance and enforcement. Frustrations with the weak compliance culture are genuine and well-founded, but to focus solely on the failings of middle management, owners, and government bodies is to divest brands of their responsibility to incentivise compliant behaviour. Moreover, it shifts attention away from the role that brands play in perpetuating and encouraging poor practice in the supply chain. ...
>
> The brands that create the risk are able to delimit their liability by correctly claiming that the units were sub-contracted on an unauthorised basis. In this

---

[12] The combined load of the 5,000 garment workers and the electrical generators was estimated to be almost six times greater than what the building was intended to bear.

[13] *After Rana Plaza* 13 November 2013, available at http://www.annemain.com/content/anne-launches-appg-report-rana-plaza-collapse <accessed 21 April 2015>.

[14] One instance of this is evidence of Walmart labels being found in the burned-out factory at Tazreen despite the fact that Walmart stated that the factory had been removed from its list of suppliers, a situation attributed to unauthorised sub-contracting by a supplier, Success Apparel.

scenario, where poor purchasing practices incentivise sub-contracting, the risk is safely offloaded to suppliers, deadlines are kept and fast fashion thrives.

Codes of conduct exist but are purely voluntary and brands are under no legal obligation to act on the findings of audits of their suppliers, which are confidential and not subject to any independent verification. Audits are frequently undermined by falsification, with workers being coached as to what to say when interviewed, protective equipment being rented in for the day of the audit, and false records of pay and hours being prepared to show auditors that the suppliers are complying with the code. The report states: 'However, in a highly competitive industry the business case for sustainable sourcing is one that can only afford to be made collectively and if brands are not the only envoys advocating for decent working conditions and higher wages.'

This collective approach has manifested itself in the Accord on Fire and Building Safety in Bangladesh signed by 82 clothing brands and retailers and covering, as of August 2013, approximately 1,500 factories. The Accord is a five-year legally enforceable contract between brands, international trade unions IndustriALL and UNI Global, and Bangladesh trade unions, containing a binding arbitration mechanism. The Accord provides for an independent factory inspection regime with brands supporting upgrading of factories found to need improvement and being called on to sever relationships with those factories that refuse to make the necessary improvements. The Accord's Secretariat must inform workers' organisations and factory participation committees of the risks to workers and the anticipated response from the Accord's partners. Signatories are committed to staying within Bangladesh for the first two years of the Accord. The Accord's Advisory Board assigns roles to government officials, unions and suppliers and reserves positions on the Steering Committee for brands and workers' representatives. In October 2014, Alan Roberts, the executive director of international operations at the Accord on Fire and Building Safety reported that, after initial inspections, safety hazards, from minor to significant, were found at more than 1,100 factories covered by the agreement and over 80,000 safety issues were identified as needing to be resolved. Of the structural inspections under the Accord 17 have resulted in 'critical findings', leading the inspection team to recommend temporary suspension of (parts of) the production in the factories.[15] An alternative scheme was

---

[15] http://www.theguardian.com/sustainable-business/2014/oct/15/bangladesh-accord-factory-hazards-protect-worker-safety-fashion <accessed 22 April 2015>.

launched by US brands, such as GAP and WalMart, the Alliance for Bangladesh Worker Safety. Unlike the Accord, the scheme is not legally binding.

F.   Corporate Reporting Legislation

There have been various initiatives at international and national level to address the governance gap through imposing reporting requirements on companies. An international initiative directed at stemming the flow of 'conflict diamonds' which have been used to fund wars in Sierra Leone and Liberia is The Kimberley Process Certification Scheme which came into effect in January 2003 with 52 State participants. The process requires State participants to pass laws to exclude 'conflict diamonds' from import and export, to trade diamonds only with each other, and to attach Kimberley Process certificates to their exports of rough, or uncut, diamonds. As stated by the US chair of the Kimberley Process at Harare in 2012, ambassador Gillian Milovanovic, its scope is, '… limited to ensuring rough diamonds are free from armed conflict and armed violence; KP certification is not designed to address human rights, financial transparency, economic development, or other important questions though they clearly impact the diamond sector'.[16] Certification has been granted to exports from two companies operating in the Marange diamond fields in Zimbabwe which had been seized by the Zimbabwean army in 2008, and reportedly led to the killing of about 200 miners. This led Global Witness, an official observer to the process at its outset, to leave the scheme in 2011.

At a national level, there have been two US initiatives, and three in the UK. The Dodd-Frank Act Section 1502 was passed by the US Securities and Exchange Commission (SEC) and implemented in August 2012. It requires companies using 'conflict minerals' – gold, tin, tungsten and tantalum – to make efforts to determine if those materials came from the DRC or an adjoining country and, if so, to carry out a 'due diligence' review of their supply chain to determine whether their mineral purchases are funding armed groups in eastern DRC. The due diligence measures must conform to a nationally or internationally recognised due diligence framework, such as the due diligence guidance approved by the Organisation for Economic Co-operation and Development (OECD). If the review shows that conflict minerals have been used, the company must

---

[16]   http://harare.usembassy.gov/kimberley_process_chair_remarks.html <accessed 30 April 2015>.

provide the SEC with a report detailing the measures to exercise due diligence. The measure mandates disclosure but does not prohibit the use of conflict minerals. On 22 April 2015 Amnesty USA issued a report which surveyed the 2014 conflict minerals reports of 100 US companies and found:

> 79 of the 100 companies analyzed failed to meet the minimum requirements of the U.S. conflict minerals law. Most companies in the sample are not doing enough to map out the supply chain of the minerals they purchase. Only 16 percent go beyond their direct suppliers to contact, or attempt to contact, the smelters or refiners that process the minerals. More than half of companies sampled do not even report to senior management when they identify a risk in their supply chain.[17]

The measure has been challenged on the grounds that by forcing companies to label their products on their websites, it violates the Constitution's First Amendment guarantee of freedom of speech. The Court of Appeals for the DC Circuit struck down that part of the rules requiring issuers to describe certain products as having been 'not found to be DRC conflict free', as violating the First Amendment.[18] The DC Circuit Court of Appeals, sitting *en banc*, overruled this part of the decision and on November 18 2014, it agreed to rehear arguments related to the First Amendment questions.[19]

Section 1504 of Dodd-Frank requires the SEC to issue rules mandating resource extraction issuers to disclose payments made to a foreign government or the federal government for the purpose of the commercial development of oil, natural gas, or minerals. In *American Petroleum Institute v. Securities and Exchange Commission* the DC District Court vacated the rules, finding that the SEC wrongly concluded that Section 1504 of Dodd-Frank required reports of resource extraction issuers to be made publicly available.[20] The SEC has decided not to appeal the

---

[17] http://www.amnestyusa.org/news/press-releases/nearly-80-of-surveyed-us-companies-fail-to-meet-requirements-of-conflict-minerals-law   <accessed   29 April 2015>.

[18] *National Association of Manufacturers v. Securities and Exchange Commission*, 748 F 3d 359 (CA DC 2014.)

[19] *National Association of Manufacturers v. Securities and Exchange Commission*, 2014 US App LEXIS 21753 (Nov. 18, 2014).

[20] 953 F Supp 2d 5 (DDC 2013.)

decision but, instead, to work on rules which will meet the court's objections. The SEC has not yet issued a new rule.[21]

Mandatory supply chain reporting was introduced into California in January 2012 with the Transparency in Supply Chains Act 2010. This requires retailers and manufacturing corporations with worldwide annual revenues of $100 million to provide a statement disclosing to what extent the corporation: (1) engages in verification of product supply chains to evaluate and address risks of human trafficking and slavery; (2) conducts audits of suppliers; (3) requires direct supplies to certify that materials incorporated into the product comply with the laws regarding slavery and human trafficking of the countries in which they are doing business; (4) maintains accountability standards and procedures for employees or contractors that fail to meet company standards regarding slavery and human trafficking; and (5) provides employees and management training on slavery and human trafficking.[22]

Recently, the UK has introduced three pieces of legislation on corporate human rights reporting. First, the Companies Act 2006 (Strategic Report and Directors' Report) Regulations 2013 (the 'Strategic Report Regulations') which require all quoted companies to include in their annual strategic report, to the extent necessary for an understanding of the development, performance or position of the company's business, information about social, community and human rights issues and any policies of the company in relation to such issues and the effectiveness of those policies.[23] The strategic report must expressly state if it does not include this information. Second, the Reports on Payments to Governments Regulations 2014 implementing Chapter 10 of the 2013 EU

---

[21]   For a detailed discussion of the two legal challenges see the Congressional Research Service report of 2 April 2015 by Michael V. Seitzinger and Kathleen Ann Ruane, *Conflict Minerals and Resource Extraction: Dodd-Frank, SEC Regulations, and Legal Challenges*. https://www.hsdl.org/?view&did=764181 <accessed 22 April 2015>.

[22]   Brazil and Australia have also introduced similar legislation.

[23]   The Regulations came into effect on 1 October 2013 and apply for financial years ending on or after 30 September 2013. Similar reporting obligations are imposed by Directive 2014/95/EU on disclosure of non-financial and diversity information by certain large undertakings, which will apply to some large companies with more than 500 employees. The Directive entered into force on 6 December 2014. EU Member States have two years to transpose it into national legislation.

Accounting Directive[24] require disclosure of payments made to all governments[25] in respect of extraction activities and apply to the first accounting period commencing on or after 1 January 2015 and cover the payments made within each period, the first report being required to be filed within 11 months of the period end.[26] Third, there is section 54 of the Modern Slavery Act 2015, which received the Royal Assent on 25 March 2015, just prior to the dissolution of Parliament. This requires all commercial organisations with a prescribed total turnover to prepare a 'slavery and human trafficking statement' for each financial year, setting out a statement of the steps which the organisation has taken to ensure slavery and human trafficking is not taking place in any of its supply chains or in any part of its own business or a statement that no such steps have been taken. The obligation to produce such a statement will be imposed on commercial organisations with a total turnover of not less than an amount prescribed by regulations made by the Secretary of State. Consultations are still continuing about the turnover threshold.[27] The Act leaves it to businesses to choose what they disclose. The disclosure statement is meant to be a prominent document accessible from the business's website homepage but there is no central repository to which all statements must be uploaded. The reporting obligation is imposed on companies carrying out all or some of their business in the UK[28] but does not require companies in the UK to report on all the supply chains in their groups overseas, such as those of wholly owned subsidiaries abroad.

---

[24] Directive 2013/34/EU on the annual financial statements, consolidated financial statements and related reports of certain types of undertakings, amending Directive 2006/43/EC of the European Parliament and of the Council and repealing Council Directives 78/660/EEC and 83/349/EEC.

[25] In contrast the EITI only mandates firms to report on payments to the government of their State of incorporation.

[26] Payments below a threshold of £86,000 need not be reported if the payment relates to a single obligation and is not part of a series of related payments. Subsidiaries are exempt from preparing a report if the payments to governments are included in the consolidated report drawn up by a parent undertaking.

[27] In August 2015 the Secretary of State set a threshold of £36 million annual gross worldwide revenues for companies that do any part of their business in the United Kingdom.

[28] 'Commercial organisation' is defined in section 12(a) as 'a body corporate (wherever incorporated) which carries on a business, or part of a business, in any part of the United Kingdom'.

2. UN INITIATIVES: THE ROAD TO THE GUIDING PRINCIPLES

In the UN the first initiative on TNCs was the establishment in 1974 of the Commission on Transnational Corporations, an information and research centre whose principal task was to draft a code of conduct for TNCs plus other international arrangements for banning illicit payments in international commercial transactions and for international standards of accounting and reporting.[29] Negotiations on the Code began in 1977 but were never completed and in 1992 the Commission was wound up. During this period in 1977 the International Labour Organisation (ILO) adopted the Declaration of Principles concerning Multinational Enterprises and Social Policy (MNE Declaration) which offer guidelines on industrial relations issues addressed to enterprise, both multinational and domestic, governments, employers and workers. The MNE Declaration is based on the ILO Conventions and was last updated in 2006.[30]

The next development was an initiative of an expert Sub-Commission on the Promotion and Protection of Human Rights of the United Nations Commission on Human Rights which led to the publication in August 2003 of draft Norms on the Responsibilities of Transnational Corporations and Other Business Enterprises with Regard to Human Rights (the Draft Norms) in August 2003. The Draft Norms broke with the voluntary approach of the Global Compact by recognising that TNCs and other business enterprises owed obligations under international and national law in respect of specified human rights, consumer rights and environmental protection obligations, drawn from existing international human

---

[29] Somewhat ironically the proposal was initiated by the Chilean government of Salvador Allende in 1972. Plans to nationalise Chilean assets of US corporations led to a concerted attempt to drag the country into economic chaos in 1973, a process which culminated with the first '9/11', the military coup that toppled Chile's democratically elected government.

[30] In 1998 at its 86th International Conference, the ILO adopted The Declaration on Fundamental Principles and Rights at Work which stated that all Members of the ILO were to be bound by eight core ILO Conventions by virtue of their membership of the ILO even if they had not ratified them. The Conventions in question are: The Freedom of Association and Protection of the Right to Organise Convention, 1948, No 87; The Right to Organise and Collective Bargaining Convention, 1951, No 98; The Forced Labour Convention, 1930, No 29; The Abolition of Forced Labour Convention, 1957, No 105; The Minimum Age Convention, 1973, No 138; The Worst Forms of Child Labour Convention, 1999, No 182; The Equal Remuneration Convention, 1951, No 100; The Discrimination (Employment and Occupation) Convention, 1958, No 111.

rights, labour and environmental conventions: the right to equal opportunity and non-discriminatory treatment;[31] the right to security of persons;[32] the rights of workers;[33] respect for national sovereignty and human rights;[34] obligations with regard to consumer protection;[35] and obligations with regard to environmental protection.[36] Compliance with the norms by transnational corporations and other businesses enterprises was to be subject to periodic monitoring and verification by the UN, contained compensation provisions whereby the Draft Norms were to be applied by national courts and/or international tribunals, pursuant to national and international law. As well as complying with the Draft Norms, TNCs and 'other business enterprises' were to apply and incorporate the Draft Norms in their contracts or other arrangements and dealings with contractors, subcontractors, suppliers, licensees, distributors, or natural or other legal persons.

3. THE GUIDING PRINCIPLES ON BUSINESS AND HUMAN RIGHTS

Not surprisingly, the Draft Norms were not well received in the corporate community. In April 2004, the inter-governmental Commission on Human Rights, declined to adopt the Draft Norms and referred the question of business and human rights to the Office of the United Nations High Commissioner for Human Rights (OHCHR), asking it to collect submissions from interested parties and compile a report about existing initiatives and standards relating to TNC responsibilities concerning human rights and compare them with the draft norms. In February 2005 the OHCHR issued a report which took no position on the Draft Norms but noted deep disagreements about the human rights responsibilities of

---

[31] Section B.

[32] Section C. Article 3 stipulates:

Transnational corporations and other business enterprises shall not engage in nor benefit from war crimes, crimes against humanity, genocide, torture, forced disappearance, forced or compulsory labour, hostage-taking, extrajudicial, summary or arbitrary executions, other violations of humanitarian law and other international crimes against the human person as defined by international law, in particular human rights and humanitarian law.

[33] Section D

[34] Section E.

[35] Section F.

[36] Section G.

TNCs. On 25 July 2005 the UN Commission on Human Rights passed a resolution recommending that the Secretary General appoint a United Nations Special Representative on Human Rights and Transnational Corporations, with a mandate to determine human rights standards applicable to TNCs, to clarify the roles of States and corporations, to develop a human rights impact assessment methodology and to collect best practices of States and TNCs on the issue. In August 2005 the Secretary-General appointed John Ruggie, who had previously acted as Special Adviser on the Global Compact, as Special Representative.

Ruggie broke with the legalism of the Draft Norms and in June 2008 proposed the 'Protect, Respect, and Remedy' framework on business and human rights to the UN Human Rights Council in June 2008.[37] This consisted of three pillars: the State duty to protect against human rights abuses by third parties, including business; the corporate responsibility to respect human rights; and greater access by victims to effective remedy, both judicial and non-judicial. The Human Rights Council unanimously approved the Framework in 2008 and extended the Special Representative's mandate until 2011 with the task of 'operationalizing' and 'promoting' the Framework. In March 2011, Special Representative Ruggie issued 'Guiding Principles on Business and Human Rights: Implementing the United Nations 'Protect, Respect and Remedy' Framework' which was endorsed by the UN Human Rights Council in June 2011.

A. Pillar One: The State Duty to Protect Human Rights

The first pillar is the State duty to protect human rights. GP 1 states that States *must* protect against human rights abuse within their territory and/or jurisdiction by third parties, including business enterprises. This is an uncontroversial statement of the obvious and is one of only two places in the GP where the word 'must' is used, the other being in GP 25. The obligation is limited to abuses occurring within the territory and/or jurisdiction of the state and requires 'taking appropriate steps to prevent, investigate, punish and redress such abuse through effective policies, legislation, regulations and adjudication'.

GP 2 then provides, 'States should set out clearly the expectation that all business enterprises domiciled in their territory and/or jurisdiction respect human rights throughout their operations.' As with GP 1 what is required of the State is limited by reference to its territory and/or

---

[37] The UNHRC was established in 2006 as the successor to the UN Commission on Human Rights, and is a subsidiary body of the UN General Assembly.

jurisdiction and so would not affect a State's relationship with foreign subsidiaries of parent corporations domiciled within its territory. The Commentary notes that:

> At present States are not generally required under international human rights law to regulate the extraterritorial activities of businesses domiciled in their territory and/or jurisdiction. Nor are they generally prohibited from doing so, provided there is a recognized jurisdictional basis. Within these parameters some human rights treaty bodies recommend that home States take steps to prevent abuse abroad by business enterprises within their jurisdiction.

> There are strong policy reasons for home States to set out clearly the expectation that businesses respect human rights abroad, especially where the State itself is involved in or supports those businesses. The reasons include ensuring predictability for business enterprises by providing coherent and consistent messages, and preserving the State's own reputation.

Section B then sets out the operational principles in relation to general State regulatory and policy functions. GP 3 deals with the obligations of States in meeting their duty to protect, as set out in GP 1, in two ways. First, in relation to enforcement of laws, States should: '(a) Enforce laws that are aimed at, or have the effect of, requiring business enterprises to respect human rights, and periodically to assess the adequacy of such laws and address any gaps;' The Commentary notes that:

> The failure to enforce existing laws that directly or indirectly regulate business respect for human rights is often a significant legal gap in State practice. Such laws might range from non-discrimination and labour laws to environmental, property, privacy and anti-bribery laws.

States should also: '(b) Ensure that other laws and policies governing the creation and ongoing operation of business enterprises, such as corporate law, do not constrain but enable business respect for human rights;' The Commentary notes:

> It is equally important for States to review whether these laws provide the necessary coverage in light of evolving circumstances and whether, together with relevant policies, they provide an environment conducive to business respect for human rights. For example, greater clarity in some areas of law and policy, such as those governing access to land, including entitlements in relation to ownership or use of land, is often necessary to protect both rights-holders and business enterprises.

Second, States should give guidance to business enterprises on how to respect human rights throughout their operations[38] as well as encouraging, and where appropriate, requiring them to communicate how they address their human rights impacts.[39] Examples of the former might be the European Commission's sector specific guidance to corporations on the application of the Guiding Principles,[40] while an example of the latter would be domestic legislation requiring business enterprises to report on human rights issues, of the sort introduced in the UK by amending the Companies Act 2006 so as to require larger UK companies to report on their human rights impacts, with effect from October 2013.

GP 4 provides that additional steps are required of States where there is a State-business nexus, such as where business enterprises are owned or controlled by the State, or where State agencies, such as export credit agencies and official investment insurance or guarantee agencies, provide substantial support and services to business enterprises. Where appropriate, this may call for the State to require human rights due diligence. This reflects the international law responsibility of States as set out in Article 8 of the ILC's Draft Articles on the Responsibility of States for Internationally Wrongful Acts. The Commentary points out that such enterprises are also subject to the corporate responsibility to respect human right in Pillar Two.

The responsibilities of States in relation to their relations with business enterprises is further addressed in the next two provisions. GP 5 provides:

> States should exercise adequate oversight in order to meet their international human rights obligations when they contract with, or legislate for, business enterprises to provide services that may impact upon the enjoyment of human rights.

GP 6 provides: 'States should promote respect for human rights by business enterprises with which they conduct commercial transactions.'

---

[38] Paragraph (c).

[39] Paragraph (d).

[40] Guides have been provided for three sectors: Information and communication technologies, oil and gas, employment and recruitment agencies. http://eeas.europa.eu/delegations/un_geneva/documents/eu_statments/human_right/2013-1203_forum_buz_hr-panel-i.pdf p3. <accessed 7 March 2015> The guides are downloadable at <http://www.ihrb.org/publications/reports/ec-sector-guides/>. <accessed 7 March 2015> There is also a guide for small and medium-sized enterprises ec.europa.eu/enterprise/policies/sustainable-business/files/csr-sme/human-rights-sme-guide-final_en.pdf. <accessed 7 March 2015>

GP 7 then addresses what States should do to support business respect for human rights in conflict-affected areas. In such areas the risk of human rights abuses is increased as the host State may be unable to discharge its obligations to protect human rights because it lacks effective control over its territory. The role of the home State in this situation is to give advice and assistance to business enterprises operating in such areas to avoid their becoming involved with such abuses. Where a business enterprise is so involved and refused to co-operate in addressing its involvement in human rights abuses, the home State should deny it access to public support and services. Home States should also ensure the effectiveness of their current policies, legislation, regulations and enforcement measures in addressing these risks. The Commentary provides:

> To achieve greater policy coherence and assist business enterprises adequately in such situations, home States should foster closer cooperation among their development assistance agencies, foreign and trade ministries, and export finance institutions in their capitals and within their embassies, as well as between these agencies and host Government actors; develop early-warning indicators to alert Government agencies and business enterprises to problems; and attach appropriate consequences to any failure by enterprises to cooperate in these contexts, including by denying or withdrawing existing public support or services, or where that is not possible, denying their future provision.

GP 8 requires States to ensure awareness and observance of their human rights obligations among all State institutions that shape business practices. This includes provision of relevant information, training and support. GP 9 deals with State practice in concluding international investment agreements, such as bilateral and multi-lateral investment treaties.[41] These have the potential to constrain States from fully implementing new human rights legislation, as can be seen with South Africa's experience with its Black Economic Empowerment policy which has led to it progressively terminating its bilateral investment agreements to avoid investor-State arbitration proceedings claiming compensation for economic expropriation.[42] GP 9 provides: 'States should maintain adequate domestic policy space to meet their human rights obligations

---

[41] Such as NAFTA and the proposed TTIP agreement between the US and the EU.

[42] Such a claim was brought in 2007 by investors from Luxembourg and Italy, arguing that South Africa's Mining and Petroleum Resources Development Act (MPRDA) contained provisions that expropriated their mineral rights.

when pursuing business-related policy objectives with other States or business enterprises, for instance through investment treaties or contracts.' Pillar One concludes with GP 10 which provides that States should take the human rights agenda into multilateral institutions of which they are members, such as the WTO, when dealing with business related issues. States should:

(a) Seek to ensure that those institutions neither restrain the ability of their member States to meet their duty to protect nor hinder business enterprises from respecting human rights;

(b) Encourage those institutions, within their respective mandates and capacities, to promote business respect for human rights and, where requested, to help States meet their duty to protect against human rights abuse by business enterprises, including through technical assistance, capacity-building and awareness-raising;

(c) Draw on these Guiding Principles to promote shared understanding and advance international cooperation in the management of business and human rights challenges.

The Commentary notes that:

> States retain their international human rights law obligations when they participate in such institutions. Collective action through multilateral institutions can help States level the playing field with regard to business respect for human rights, but it should do so by raising the performance of laggards.

B. Pillar Two: The Corporate Responsibility to Respect Human Rights

The second pillar of the Guiding Principles is the corporate responsibility to respect human rights. Throughout the word 'should' is used to avoid any impression that the Guiding Principles are intended to impose legal obligations on corporations. The Guiding Principles refer throughout to 'business enterprises' but do not define the term, unlike the OECD Guidelines on Multinational Enterprises. In a multi-layered group structure, each separate company would constitute a separated 'business enterprise' which 'should' comply with the foundational and operational principles set out in Pillar II. Nothing is said about how these principles

http://hsfnotes.com/arbitration/2013/08/21/south-africa-terminates-its-bilateral-investment-treaty-with-spain-second-bit-terminated-as-part-of-south-africas-planned-review-of-its-investment-treaties/ <accessed 7 March 2015>

apply to parent companies in respect of the activities of their subsidiaries. The issue of separate corporate personality is relocated to Pillar III 'Access to Remedy' where it is likely to surface in GP 26 which provides that:

> States should take appropriate steps to ensure the effectiveness of domestic judicial mechanisms when addressing business-related human rights abuses, including considering ways to reduce legal, practical and other relevant barriers that could lead to a denial of access to remedy.

Pillar II distinguishes between where a business enterprise 'causes or contributes to an adverse impact' or whether it is involved 'solely because the impact is directly linked to its operations, products or services by a business relationship'.[43] The first situation would apply to each company in a corporate structure. Where a parent company is actively involved in the operations of the subsidiary that causes an adverse human rights impact then it could be said to have 'caused or contributed' to that impact, in the same way in which under national laws the parent corporation may incur a direct liability in tort.[44] The second would cover a linkage with another business enterprise, such as a subsidiary company with whom the parent has no direct involvement, or a company with whom it is contractually linked in a supply chain. It is only in the first situation where a business enterprise causes or contributes to adverse impacts that GP 22 on remediation kicks in which provides that in such circumstances the enterprise should 'provide for or cooperate in their remediation through legitimate processes'.

The second pillar starts with section A, 'Foundational Principles'. The substance of the 'human rights' which business enterprises 'should respect' is left deliberately open ended. Ruggie departed from the specific listing of human rights that characterised the draft norms on the grounds that business enterprises should respect all human rights. 'Human rights' are broadly defined in GP 12 as referring to '[a]t a minimum, as those expressed in the International Bill of Human Rights[45] and the principles

---

[43] GP 19.

[44] In the US this would be through a finding that the subsidiary had acted as the parent's agent, and in the UK it would be through a finding that the parent's involvement created a duty of care to those affected by the subsidiary's activities, of the sort found in *Chandler v. Cape Industries*.

[45] This consists of the Universal Declaration of Human Rights and the main instruments through which it has been codified: the International Covenant on Civil and Political Rights and the International Covenant on Economic, Social and Cultural Rights.

concerning fundamental rights set out in the International Labour Organization's Declaration on Fundamental Principles and Rights at Work'.

GP 11 states the basic principle of the second pillar, 'Business enterprises should respect human rights. This means that they should avoid infringing on the human rights of others and should address adverse human rights impacts with which they are involved.' Two elements are involved. The first is avoiding the infringement of the human rights of others – 'do no harm'. The commentary to the Guiding Principles states that this responsibility is:

> a global standard of expected conduct for all business enterprises wherever they operate. It exists independently of States' abilities and/or willingness to fulfil their own human rights obligations, and does not diminish those obligations. And it exists over and above compliance with national laws and regulations protecting human rights.

This is confirmed in GP 13(a) which requires business enterprises to, '[a]void causing or contributing to adverse human rights impacts *through their own activities*', and address such impacts when they occur (emphasis added). The second is addressing adverse human rights with which the business enterprise is involved. The Commentary states that this requires taking 'adequate measures for their prevention, mitigation and, where appropriate, remediation'.[46] This is confirmed in GP 13(b) which requires business enterprises to '[S]cek to prevent or mitigate adverse human rights impacts that are directly linked to their operations, products or services *by their business relationships*, even if they have not contributed to those impacts (emphasis added).'[47]

GP 14 makes it clear that the responsibility to respect human rights is universal and applies to 'all enterprises regardless of their size, sector, operational context, ownership and structure'. This is subject to the caveat that 'the scale and complexity of the means through which enterprises meet that responsibility may vary according to these factors and with the severity of the enterprise's adverse human rights impacts'. The Commentary elaborates:

---

[46] This will be subject to the limitations in GP 22.

[47] Further guidance on how business enterprises should 'seek to prevent or mitigate' such adverse human rights impacts is to be found in GP 19.

Severity of impacts will be judged by their scale, scope and irremediable character. The means through which a business enterprise meets its responsibility to respect human rights may also vary depending on whether, and the extent to which, it conducts business through a corporate group or individually.[48]

GP 15 then requires business enterprise to put in place policies and processes appropriate to their size and circumstances, to meet these human rights responsibilities. First, there should be 'a policy commitment to meet their responsibility to respect human rights'. Second, there should be 'A human rights due-diligence process to identify, prevent, mitigate and account for how they address their impacts on human rights.' Third, there should be 'Processes to enable the remediation of any adverse human rights impacts they cause or to which they contribute.' Again, it is worth stressing that the remediation aspect applies only to adverse human rights impacts caused or contributed to by the business enterprise and does not apply to adverse impacts caused by business relationships directly linked to their operations.

These policies and processes are more specifically fleshed out in section B 'Operational principles'. GP 16 requires business enterprises to adopt a statement of policy on their commitment to their responsibility to respect human rights. The policy must: be approved at the most senior level of the business enterprise; be informed by relevant internal and/or external expertise; stipulate the enterprise's human rights expectations of personnel, business partners and other parties directly linked to its operations, products or services; be publicly available and communicated internally and externally to all personnel, business partners and other relevant parties; be reflected in operational policies and procedures necessary to embed it throughout the business enterprise.

The next step is a proactive obligation to undertake human rights due diligence. GP 17 provides that this process includes assessing actual and potential human rights impacts as well as 'integrating and acting upon the findings, tracking responses, and communicating how impacts are addressed'. The due diligence process extends to adverse impacts that may be directly linked to the business enterprise's operations, products or services by its business relationships, thereby imposing some responsibility to undertake due diligence as regards the operations of subsidiary companies and contractually related enterprises in a supply chain.

---

[48] There is a hint here of the issue of separate corporate personality which is not otherwise addressed in the second Pillar.

GP 18 follows on from this with outlining a process for identification of any actual or potential adverse human rights impacts with which the business enterprise may be involved. The process should: '(a) Draw on internal and/or independent external human rights expertise; (b) Involve meaningful consultation with potentially affected groups and other relevant stakeholders, as appropriate to the size of the business enterprise and the nature and context of the operation.' The Commentary stresses the need for periodic assessments at regular intervals and not just prior to a proposed business activity. Consultation with stakeholders should be done directly '[i]n a manner that takes into account language and other potential barriers to effective engagement'.

Having conducted the impact assessments mandated in GP 18, GP 19 then requires the business enterprise to integrate their finding across relevant internal functions and processes, and to take appropriate action. Effective integration requires that:

> (i) Responsibility for addressing such impacts is assigned to the appropriate level and function within the business enterprise; (ii) Internal decision-making, budget allocations and oversight processes enable effective responses to such impacts.

The Commentary points out that integration can only be effective if the business enterprise's human rights policy commitment has been embedded into all relevant business functions.

What constitutes 'appropriate action' will depend on whether the adverse impact is caused or contributed to by the business enterprise. If that is the case the Commentary specifies that actual impacts should be the subject of remediation under GP 22 and where there are potential impacts the business enterprise should take the necessary steps to cease or prevent the impact. Where the business enterprise is involved because the adverse impact is directly linked to its operations by a business relationship, then its appropriate action will depend on the extent of its leverage in addressing the adverse impact. The Commentary amplifies the issue of leverage as follows:

> Among the factors that will enter into the determination of the appropriate action in such situations are the enterprise's leverage over the entity concerned, how crucial the relationship is to the enterprise, the severity of the abuse, and whether terminating the relationship with the entity itself would have adverse human rights consequences. The more complex the situation and its implications for human rights, the stronger is the case for the enterprise to

draw on independent expert advice in deciding how to respond. If the business enterprise has leverage to prevent or mitigate the adverse impact, it should exercise it.

If that business relationship is crucial to the business enterprise, in that it provides a product or service that is essential to the enterprise's business, and for which no reasonable alternative source exists, the Commentary requires the severity of the adverse impact to be addressed:

> the more severe the abuse, the more quickly the enterprise will need to see change before it takes a decision on whether it should end the relationship. In any case, for as long as the abuse continues and the enterprise remains in the relationship, it should be able to demonstrate its own ongoing efforts to mitigate the impact and be prepared to accept any consequences – reputational, financial or legal – of the continuing connection.

GP 20 provides the next element in the operational process in the second pillar, tracking the effectiveness of the business enterprise's response to adverse human rights impacts. This should: '(a) Be based on appropriate qualitative and quantitative indicators; (b) Draw on feedback from both internal and external sources, including affected stakeholders.' The Commentary requires tracking to be integrated into relevant internal reporting processes and that particular efforts be made 'to track the effectiveness of their responses to impacts on individuals from groups or populations that may be at heightened risk of vulnerability or marginalization'.

GP 21 deals with transparency and requires business enterprises to be prepared to communicate externally how they address their human rights impacts. Where their operations pose risks of severe impacts they should report formally on how they address them. It provides:

In all instances, communications should:

(a) Be of a form and frequency that reflect an enterprise's human rights impacts and that are accessible to its intended audiences;
(b) Provide information that is sufficient to evaluate the adequacy of an enterprise's response to the particular human rights impact involved;
(c) In turn not pose risks to affected stakeholders, personnel or to legitimate requirements of commercial confidentiality.

GP 22 deals with remediation through legitimate processes, but only where business enterprises identify that they have caused or contributed to adverse impacts. 'Legitimate processes' may include operational-level grievance mechanisms on which further guidance is provided in the third pillar in particular GP 31 which sets out the core criteria for such mechanisms. GP 23 deals with the role of law and business enterprises in relation to human rights impacts. It provides:

In all contexts, business enterprises should:

(a) Comply with all applicable laws and respect internationally recognize human rights, wherever they operate;
(b) Seek ways to honour the principles of internationally recognized human rights when faced with conflicting requirements;
(c) Treat the risk of causing or contributing to gross human rights abuses as a legal compliance issue wherever they operate.

Although the Guiding Principles do not seek to impose any new legal obligations on business enterprises, this provision reminds business enterprises of the existing legal risks of causing or contributing to adverse human rights. The Commentary states:

> Business enterprises should treat this risk as a legal compliance issue, given the expanding web of potential corporate legal liability arising from extra-territorial civil claims, and from the incorporation of the provisions of the Rome Statute of the International Criminal Court in jurisdictions that provide for corporate criminal responsibility. In addition, corporate directors, officers and employees may be subject to individual liability for acts that amount to gross human rights abuses.

This is a clear nod to civil suits in the US under the ATS and potential criminal liability for violations of international criminal law in jurisdictions such as Australia. There is an implied link here with State obligations under the third pillar, 'Access to remedy', because if there is no effective legal sanction against business enterprises for causing, or contributing to, adverse human rights impacts, there is no need to treat this as a legal compliance issue, and signing up to the GP has purely reputational consequences.

The second pillar concludes with GP 24 which deals with prioritisation of addressing actual and potential adverse human rights impacts. Priority should be given to those that are 'most severe or where delayed response would make them irremediable'. The Commentary expands as follows:

> In the absence of specific legal guidance, if prioritization is necessary business enterprises should begin with those human rights impacts that would be most severe, recognizing that a delayed response may affect remediability. Severity is not an absolute concept in this context, but is relative to the other human rights impacts the business enterprise has identified.

C. Pillar Three: Access to Remedy

The third pillar sets out the responsibility of States to provide access to remedy through State-based judicial mechanisms, State-based non-judicial mechanisms, and to facilitate access to non-State-based grievance mechanisms. The foundational principle is set out in GP 25 which complements the obligation on States set out in GP 1 in relation to human rights abuses that occur within their territory or jurisdiction. GP 25 stipulates that where such abuses occur States 'must' take appropriate steps to ensure that those affected have access to effective remedy, 'through judicial, administrative, legislative, or other appropriate means'. The Commentary gives examples of State-based grievance mechanisms which include:

> the courts (for both criminal and civil actions), labour tribunals, National Human Rights Institutions, National Contact Points under the Guidelines for Multinational Enterprises of the Organization for Economic Cooperation and Development, many ombudsperson offices, and Government-run complaints offices.

The Commentary then amplifies what is meant by 'remedies' in the third pillar.

> The remedies provided by the grievance mechanisms discussed in this section may take a range of substantive forms the aim of which, generally speaking, will be to counteract or make good any human rights harms that have occurred. Remedy may include apologies, restitution, rehabilitation, financial or non-financial compensation and punitive sanctions (whether criminal or administrative, such as fines), as well as the prevention of harm through, for example, injunctions or guarantees of non-repetition. Procedures for the provision of remedy should be impartial, protected from corruption and free from political or other attempts to influence the outcome.

Part B then sets out the operational principles of the 'Access to remedy' pillar. GP 26 deals with State-based judicial mechanisms and provides:

> States should take appropriate steps to ensure the effectiveness of domestic judicial mechanisms when addressing business-related human rights abuses, including considering ways to reduce legal, practical and other relevant barriers that could lead to a denial of access to remedy.

This provision is potentially very important in that it acts as a prompt to States to consider existing legal obstacles to obtaining remedy due to the governance gap considered in this book. It applies generally to 'business-related human rights abuses' without territorial limitation, as is the case with GP 25. The Commentary identifies various existing legal barriers that can prevent access to remedy for business-related human rights abuse.

- The way in which legal responsibility is attributed among members of a corporate group under domestic criminal and civil laws facilitates the avoidance of appropriate accountability;
- Where claimants face a denial of justice in a host State and cannot access home State courts regardless of the merits of the claim;
- Where certain groups, such as indigenous peoples and migrants, are excluded from the same level of legal protection of their human rights that applies to the wider population.

Practical and procedural barriers to accessing judicial remedy can arise where, for example:

- The costs of bringing claims go beyond being an appropriate deterrent to unmeritorious cases and/or cannot be reduced to reasonable levels through government support, 'market-based' mechanisms (such as litigation insurance and legal fee structures), or other means;
- Claimants experience difficulty in securing legal representation, due to a lack of resources or of other incentives for lawyers to advise claimants in this area;
- There are inadequate options for aggregating claims or enabling representative proceedings (such as class actions and other collective action procedures), and this prevents effective remedy for individual claimants;
- State prosecutors lack adequate resources, expertise and support to meet the State's own obligations to investigate individual and business involvement in human rights related crimes.

GP 27 moves on to State-based, non-judicial grievance mechanisms and provides: 'States should provide effective and appropriate non-judicial grievance mechanisms, alongside judicial mechanisms, as part of a comprehensive State-based system for the remedy of business-related human rights abuse.' The Commentary identifies how gaps in the provision of remedy could be filled in this way:

> [b]y expanding the mandates of existing non-judicial mechanisms and/or by adding new mechanisms. These may be mediation-based, adjudicative or follow other culturally-appropriate and rights-compatible processes – or involve some combination of these – depending on the issues concerned, any public interest involved, and the potential needs of the parties.

The role of States with regard to non-State-based grievance mechanisms is one of considering facilitation of access and GP 28 provides: 'States should *consider* ways to facilitate access to effective non-State-based grievance mechanisms dealing with business-related human rights harms (emphasis added).'

The role of business enterprises' operational grievance mechanisms, which was raised in GP 22 on remediation, is reiterated in GP 29 which provides: 'To make it possible for grievances to be addressed early and remediated directly, business enterprises should establish or participate in effective operational-level grievance mechanisms for individuals and communities who may be adversely impacted.' The Commentary identifies two key functions of such mechanisms:

- First, they support the identification of adverse human rights impacts as a part of an enterprise's on-going human rights due diligence. They do so by providing a channel for those directly impacted by the enterprise's operations to raise concerns when they believe they are being or will be adversely impacted. By analyzing trends and patterns in complaints, business enterprises can also identify systemic problems and adapt their practices accordingly;
- Second, these mechanisms make it possible for grievances, once identified, to be addressed and for adverse impacts to be remediated early and directly by the business enterprise, thereby preventing harms from compounding and grievances from escalating.

GP 30 then deals with grievance mechanisms in the context of codes of conduct, performance standards and global framework agreements between trade unions and transnational corporations, and provides: 'Industry, multi-stakeholder and other collaborative initiatives that are based on respect for human rights-related standards should ensure that effective grievance mechanisms are available.' Seven criteria for effective non-judicial-grievance mechanisms are then set out in GP 31. They apply to any State-based or non-State-based, adjudicative or dialogue-based mechanism and provide that the mechanism should be: legitimate; accessible; predictable; equitable; transparent; rights-compatible; and a source of continuous learning. In addition operational-level mechanisms that business enterprises help administer should be: 'Based on engagement and dialogue: consulting the stakeholder groups for whose use they are intended on their design and performance, and focusing on dialogue as the means to address and resolve grievances.'

The focus of the Guiding Principles is very much on voluntarism, which is what has led to their adoption by the UN in 2011 and by their positive reception in the business world. However, the Guiding Principles may be regarded as an unsatisfactory response to the issue of the governance gap. First, there is a lack of clarity as to what human rights corporations should respect. The basic answer is 'all of them'. However, as Sullivan and Hanchez point out, saying they should respect every HR instrument gives no meaningful guidance to corporations.

> Our concern is that by discussing the 'corporate responsibility to respect' mostly in terms of an elusive and relative obligation of 'due diligence' rather than in terms of substance and outcomes (i.e. that human rights be respected as the fundamental social and legal norms that they are), the effect is to suggest that the responsibility of corporations with regard to human rights is more one to 'manage' than one to 'respect'. This is not merely a matter of semantics and, in fact, has serious practical consequences in terms of corporate accountability. As we have explained above, accountability for performance requires that there be clarity around expectations and responsibilities, which can easily be translated into a 'compliance/non-compliance' assessment framework. The self-standing 'due diligence' requirement in the Ruggie framework, coupled with a vague reference to the general body of international human rights law, does not provide the level of specificity that we think is required.[49]

Second, the role of legal access to remedy, an important catalyst in encouraging corporations to subscribe voluntary codes, has played a somewhat subdued role in the Guiding Principles and has been almost completely overlooked in the National Action Plans that have been produced so far. The Guiding Principles create no new legal obligations for corporations but do recognise the importance of existing legal obligations in GP 23 where the Commentary identifies a legal compliance issue arising out of the risks of enterprises becoming complicit in gross human rights abuses by others, such as security forces. The preferred solution to this risk is the adoption of human rights policies and the development of non-legal grievance mechanisms. The attraction of soft law as a protection against hard law, explains the decisions of US corporations to sign up to the Global Compact and the Voluntary Principles, despite their initial misgivings. In 'Private Empire' Steve Coll comments on the experience of ExxonMobil, a US corporation involved in a long-running suit arising out of human rights abuses by Indonesian security personnel at its operations in Aceh in the early 2000s.

---

[49] The UN Guiding Principles On Business And Human Rights – Foundations And Implementation, Radu Mares, (ed.), Leiden, Martinus Nijhoff, 2012, 230.

Although it was not foolproof, the Voluntary Principles would shield Exxon-Mobil from human rights cases like *Doe* in the future by helping the corporation to argue to a jury or judge that it had taken all the steps it reasonably could to protect civilians in its areas of operations. This might be self-interested, but the compact had been constructed to appeal to such corporate instincts. The practical effect would be to bring ExxonMobil more closely into line with the corporate responsibility practices of other large multinationals – to socialise Exxon in an era of global norms increasingly influenced by civil society.[50]

Third, with corporate adherence to non-binding norms the only sanction in the event of non-compliance is reputational. The Guiding Principles leave it up to businesses as to what policy they adopt and just what they publish. The encouragement of non-legal grievance mechanisms may also oust legal claims through waivers and confidentiality agreements, as seen in the claims against Barrick Gold arising out of rapes and beatings over a period of years by security personnel at its gold mine at Porgera in Papua New Guinea, operated by the Porgera Joint Venture (PJV) of which Barrick was a member.[51] The Canadian NCP accepted the complaint, and Barrick agreed to negotiate. By the time of the first mediation meeting in November 2012, Barrick had put in place a remediation framework for victims of rapes by PJV employees, but not for those raped by members of police who were housed, fed and supported by PJV on PJV property. The settlement contained waivers which required the claimant to agree:

> [t]hat she will not pursue or participate in any legal action against PJV, PRFA [Porgera Remediation Framework Association Inc.] or Barrick in or outside of PNG. PRFA and Barrick will be able to rely on the agreement as a bar to any legal proceedings which may be brought by the claimant in breach of the agreement.

This implies that the victims would be barred from participating in criminal proceedings against the company, or giving evidence in claims brought by other victims who did not accept the settlement, or to pursue other civil claims against Barrick unrelated to the settlement agreement. In July 2013 the Office of High Commissioner for Human Rights' reported on the Barrick's grievance mechanism, and considered the position of waivers under the Guiding Principles, stating:

---

[50]   Allen Lane, 2012, 405.
[51]   http://www.raid-uk.org/content/barrick-gold-papua-new-guinea   <accessed 30 April 2015>.

Nonetheless, and as there is no prohibition per se on legal waivers in current international standards and practice, situations may arise where business enterprises wish to ensure that, for reasons of predictability and finality, a legal waiver be required from claimants at the end of a remediation process. In such instances, the legal waiver should be as narrowly construed as possible, and preserve the right of claimants to seek judicial recourse for any criminal claims.[52]

Barrick subsequently amended the waivers so that rape victims accepting a settlement from it agreed only not to pursue civil claims in respect of the same complaint. In April 2015 11 victims accepted an improved settlement offer from Barrick.[53]

Although the commentary to art. 31 of the GPs states that adjudication under non-legal grievance mechanisms should be provided by a legitimate, independent third-party mechanism, this, like almost everything else in the Guiding Principles is a recommendation only, and is not mandatory, and the Guiding Principles make no provision for establishing any independent third-party monitoring body. Both business and their home States would have been strongly opposed to any such body, as was the case with the Draft Norms on TNCs. This means that corporations may end up investigating themselves, as evidenced by a RAID's report into the activities of two TNCs operating in Africa, Acacia Mining, and Glencore which states:

An initial and obvious criticism is the total lack of independence and credibility in a process whereby a company investigates itself, determines its own culpability (or exoneration) and then decides what redress (if any) is needed. A second criticism is that such private investigations are invariably kept confidential, depriving victims and the wider public of any powers of scrutiny or sense of accountability.[54]

---

[52] *Re: Allegations Regarding the Porgera Joint Venture Remedy Framework,* 8 www.ohchr.org/Documents/Issues/Business/LetterPorgera.pdf <accessed 30 April 2015>.

[53] http://www.smh.com.au/world/200-girls-and-women-raped-now-11-of-them-win-better-compensation-from-the-worlds-biggest-gold-miner-20150403-1m7ibq.html <accessed 27 April 2015>.

[54] *Principles Without Justice. The Corporate Takeover of Human Rights* http://www.raid-uk.org/sites/default/files/principles-justice-summary.pdf <accessed 17th April 2015>.

4. IMPLEMENTING THE GUIDING PRINCIPLES

After the adoption of the Guiding Principles, the UN Working Group on business and human rights (UNWG), the body mandated to promote the effective and comprehensive dissemination and implementation of the Guiding Principles, called upon States to consider the adoption of National Action Plans (NAPs) in its first report to the Human Rights Council in 2012.[55] In the EU the European Commission in 2011 and the Council of the European Union in 2012 invited all Member States to develop national plans for implementing the Guiding Principles.

First off the blocks was the UK which on 4 September 2013 published its national implementation plan for the UN Guiding Principles, Good Business. Implementing the UN Guiding Principles on Business and Human Rights.[56] It listed seven actions already taken to implement the Guiding Principles, including: negotiating and agreeing the OECD 2012 Common Approaches, including a requirement for Export Credit Agencies (ECAs) to take into account not only potential environmental impacts but also social impacts, which is defined to include 'relevant adverse project-related human rights impacts'; playing a leading role in developing the International Code of Conduct for Private Security Service Providers (ICOC) which sets out companies' commitments to standards of behaviour, particularly on human rights, and will be independently audited; providing financial support for the Global Compact and for promoting the UN Guiding Principles. It also lists 11 prospective actions, including: beginning the certification of private security companies in the UK based on the agreed UK standard for land-based companies, by working with the UK Accreditation Service (UKAS) to take forward the certification process. With Pillar 3, 'access to remedy' the focus is entirely on non-legal forms of remediation.[57]

---

[55]   In December 2014 the UNWG published its Guidance on National Action Plans on Business and Human Rights. http://business-humanrights.org/en/un-working-group-releases-guidance-on-natl-action-plans <accessed 16 April 2015>.

[56]   Cm 8695, available at https://www.gov.uk/government/publications/bhr-action-plan <accessed 15 April 2015>.

[57]   In Chapter 4 of the NAP, 17–18, the UK government states that it will:

(ii)   task UK Trade and Investment (UKTI) teams in the markets where they operate to advise UK companies on establishing or participating in grievance mechanisms for those potentially affected by their activities and to collaborate with local authorities in situations where further State action is warranted to provide an effective remedy;

There is no mention of any steps taken to improve access to legal remedy. Indeed, the changes to the costs system introduced five months earlier in April 2013 when the Legal Aid, Sentencing and Punishment of Offenders Act 2012 came into force, will make it more difficult for firms to take on human rights cases against UK TNCs in their home State.

NAPs have since been adopted by the Netherlands in December 2013, Denmark in March 2014, Finland in April 2014, and Lithuania in February 2015.[58] As is the case with the UK's NAP, none of these NAPs have much to say about access to legal remedy.[59] The Danish NAP contains a brief reference to the possibilities of civil law measures against companies committing gross human rights violations abroad and the Dutch NAP contains a brief reference to the issue of corporate personality. The Lithuanian NAP is more positive referring to improved access to legal aid, and the availability of class actions in civil claims as from 1 January 2015.

With companies the rate of adoption has to date been quite small. A 2013 study for the European Commission assessed 200 randomly selected large European companies and found that only 3 per cent made

---

(iii) encourage companies to extend their domestic UK practice of providing effective grievance mechanisms to their overseas operations, adapting them where necessary according to local circumstances and consulting interested parties. This also applies to dispute arbitration/mediation mechanisms through their sector of activity or collective industry organisations.

[58] NAPs are currently being developed by Azerbaijan, Belgium, Brazil, Colombia, France, Germany, Greece, Italy, Ireland, Jordan, Latvia, Mauritius, Mexico, Morocco, Mozambique, Myanmar, Norway, Poland, Slovenia, the US. http://business-humanrights.org/en/un-guiding-principles/implementation-tools-examples/implementation-by-governments/by-type-of-initiative/national-action-plans <accessed 16 April 2015>.

[59] For an analysis of the first three NAPs, see Damiano De Felice and Andreas Graff, 'The Potential of National Action Plans to Implement Human Rights Norms: An Early Assessment with Respect to the UN Guiding Principles on Business and Human Rights.' 7(1) *J Human Rights Practice* (2015): 40–71 first published online January 5, 2015. They conclude at p. 65:

As far as content is concerned, none of the three governments that have already released their NAP (Denmark, the Netherlands and the UK) recognizes the normative validity of the UN Guiding Principles as the authoritative interpretation of the state duty to protect. The documents focus too heavily on preventive measures, and are largely silent on how to improve access to remedy. With the partial exception of the Dutch NAP, they avoid legally binding mechanisms, thus ignoring the 'smart mix' of voluntary and mandatory instruments which characterizes the UN Guiding Principles.

reference to the Guiding Principles.[60] Even fewer companies are prepared to publicise their human rights impact assessments. Nestle was the first large company to do so in 2013 with its 'Taking the Human Rights Walk' document.[61] It has been followed by Stora Enso on 5 February 2015.[62] In February 2015 a detailed reporting framework for companies was published, 'The UN Guiding Principles Reporting Framework', developed through the Human Rights Reporting and Assurance Frameworks Initiative (RAFI).

Despite the international consensus behind the Guiding Principles in 2011, the call for a legally binding instrument has been resurrected in two resolutions on human rights and business adopted by the UN Human Rights Council in June 2014. The first was a resolution of 23 June drafted by Norway and supported by 22 countries from all regions, which includes a request that the UN Working Group prepare a report considering, among other things, the benefits and limitations of legally binding instruments.[63] The second was a resolution of 24 June drafted by Ecuador and South Africa, supported by 22 countries, which proposed the establishment of an intergovernmental working group with a mandate to elaborate an international legally binding instrument on human rights and transnational corporations.[64] The resolution excludes 'local businesses registered in terms of relevant domestic law'. On 26 June, the UN

---

[60] The study showed that 68 per cent referred to 'corporate social responsibility' or an equivalent term, 40 per cent referred to at least one internationally recognised CSR instrument, 33 per cent referred to the UN Global Compact, OECD Guidelines or ISO 26000, and 2 per cent to the ILO MNE Declaration. *European Commission, An Analysis of Policy References made by large EU Companies to Internationally Recognised CSR Guidelines and Principles March 2013*, 6. available at: http://ec.europa.eu/enterprise/policies/sustainable-business/files/csr/csr-guide-princ-2013_en.pdf <accessed 27 April 2015>.

[61] www.nestle.com/asset-library/documents/.../nestle-hria-white-paper.pdf <accessed 27 April 2015>.

[62] Available at http://www.storaenso.com/about/news/stora-enso-launches-group-wide-human-rights-assessment-results-together-with-the-danish-institute-for-human-rights <accessed 27 April 2015>.

[63] UN Doc A/HRC/26/L.1

[64] UN Doc A/HRC/26/L.22/Rev.1

Human Rights Council adopted Ecuador and South Africa's resolution.[65] On 27 June, the Council adopted by consensus Norway's resolution.[66]

5. FROM 'SOFT LAW' TO 'HARD LAW'

The measures we have examined in this chapter are soft law instruments which entail no legal commitments in companies adhering to them. However, in some circumstances, companies may find that 'soft' law has turned 'hard'. This may happen when courts determine the scope of a parent company's primary duty of care in respect of its subsidiary's overseas activities. The courts might be persuaded to find a duty of care arising out of an assumption of responsibility[67] through a company's public statement that it has signed up to a voluntary code of conduct available, such as the Global Compact or the UN Guiding Principles. Some support for such an approach may be derived from the *BATCO* case in 1979 when the fact that a parent company had explicitly stated that its policies were informed by the Guidelines was one of the factors considered by a Dutch court in granting an injunction to prevent the

---

[65]   20 countries voted in favour (Algeria, Benin, Burkina Faso, China, Congo, Côte d'Ivoire, Cuba, Ethiopia, India, Indonesia, Kazakhstan, Kenya, Morocco, Namibia, Pakistan, Philippines, Russia, South Africa, Venezuela, Vietnam), 14 voted against (Austria, Czech Republic, Estonia, France, Germany, Ireland, Italy, Japan, Montenegro, South Korea, Romania, Macedonia, UK, USA), with 13 abstentions (Argentina, Botswana, Brazil, Chile, Costa Rica, Gabon, Kuwait, Maldives, Mexico, Peru, Saudi Arabia, Sierra Leone, UAE).

[66]   Ruggie has commented on the resolutions in *Quo Vadis? Unsolicited Advice to Business and Human Rights Treaty Sponsors* 9 September 2014, available at http://lcbackerblog.blogspot.co.uk/2014/09/john-ruggie-on-frame work-for-new.html <accessed 16 April 2015>. He observes:

> If Ecuador and its supporters hold fast to their current positions then their effort can lead to only one of two possible outcomes. Either the negotiations drag on for a decade or more and follow the path of the 1970s code of conduct negotiations; or they manage to persuade enough developing countries to adopt such a treaty text, but which home countries of most transnational corporations do not ratify and, therefore, are not bound by. Either outcome would represent another dead end, delivering nothing to individuals and communities adversely affected by corporate conduct.

[67]   Concerns about exposure to liability were one of the reasons for late adherence to the Global Compact by US companies and by US brands' refusal to join the legally binding Accord on Fire and Building Safety in Bangladesh.

parent from closing its Amsterdam factory.[68] Support can also be derived from *Choc v. Hudbay*[69] where evidence of public representations by Hudbay concerning its relationship with local communities and its commitment to respecting human rights, which would have led to expectations on the part of the plaintiffs, formed part of the material which led to Carole. J. Brown J holding that the claim against the parent company should not be struck out as there was evidence that it owed a direct duty of care to the plaintiffs.

In contrast, in France in *Association France-Palestine Solidarite 'AFPS' vs Societe Alstom Transport SA*[70] it was held that there could be no claim that of a wrongdoing in breach of international law on the grounds of failure to abide by their codes of ethics and by the Global Compact to which the defendant companies adhered. The Global Compact expresses values that the companies wish to see their personnel apply during the course of their work for the company, and contained only recommendations and rules of conduct. It did not create any obligations or commitments to the benefit of the parties who may wish to see them observed. Similarly in the US in *Doe v. Walmart* the existence of a code of conduct in a contract with a foreign supplier was held not to give rise to a liability in contract or in tort to employees of the supplier.[71]

Corporate statements about adopting ethical policies have also formed the basis of claims brought by consumers in the US in so-called 'greenwash' claims. In *Kasky v. Nike, Inc* the suit claimed that Nike had made representations about labour conditions in its suppliers' factories that manufactured its trainers, constituting unfair and deceptive practices under California's Unfair Competition Law and False Advertising Law. Nike claimed that the lawsuit was barred by the US Constitution's First Amendment guarantee of free speech. The California Supreme Court held that Nike's statements were commercial speech which is entitled to less constitutional protection than non-commercial speech. The US Supreme Court then agreed to hear the case but in 2003 it decided it had granted *certiorari* improperly and dismissed the case.[72] The case was

---

[68] BATCO, Amsterdam Commerce Chamber of the Court of Amsterdam Court of Appeals 21 June 1979, (NJ 1980, 71). The parent company had failed to consult with employees before closing the factory, contrary to recommendations contained in the 1976 version of the Guidelines.

[69] 2013 Carswell Ont 10514.

[70] Decision of the Versailles Court of Appeal on 23 March 2013.

[71] 572 F 3d 677 (9th Cir 2009).

[72] *Kasky v. Nike*, 27 Cal 4th 939 (2002), *cert. granted*, 123 S Ct 817, *and cert. dismissed*, 539 US 654 (2003), 123 S Ct 2254 (2003).

subsequently settled with Nike agreeing to pay $1.5 million, in investments to strengthen workplace monitoring and factory worker programmes. A second Californian claim was made in *Laderer v. Dole Food Co. Inc* No. 12-09715[73] where Dole was sued by a consumer who claimed that the corporation had misrepresented its practices in its banana plantations in Guatemala and that he would not have purchased the company's bananas or 'paid as much for them', had he known that its 'production methods contaminate water supplies, destroy wetlands, cause flooding, destroy the crops of local communities, and/or cause illnesses in children'. The complaint cited company materials indicating its 'unwavering commitment' to 'environmental responsibility and social accountability' claiming alleged violation of two Californian consumer fraud laws[74] and added two common law claims of fraud by concealment, and unjust enrichment. In January 2013 Dole, without admitting liability, settled the case by agreeing to help deliver a water filter project in local communities in Guatemala.

---

[73] No 12-09715 Class Action Complaint filed 13 November 2012 (US Dist Ct, CD Cal Los Angeles).

[74] Consumer Legal Remedies Act (Cal Civ Code s 1750 et. seq) and The California Unfair Competition Law (Cal Bus & Prof Code s 17200 et seq).

9. Conclusion

An important element of the third pillar of the Guiding Principles, 'Access to Remedy', is access to legal remedies. Yet substantial obstacles still remain in accessing legal remedies for legitimate cases involving business-related human rights abuse such as: the doctrine of separate corporate personality which enables the use of corporate group structures to facilitate the avoidance of accountability; the dismissal of home country suits on grounds of *forum non conveniens* and other grounds of abstention; the difficulties in enforcing host State judgments following such dismissals; the costs of litigation and claimants' difficulties in securing adequate legal representation; the lack of resources for host State prosecutors to investigate and initiate criminal proceedings relating to allegations of individual and corporate human rights abuses.[1]

Since the publication of the Guiding Principles in 2011 the position with regard to access to remedy has actually deteriorated, and the contribution made by home State legal proceedings against TNCs has been almost completely overlooked in the NAPs that have been produced to date. This regression has been most pronounced in the US, although the change to the costs regime introduced in the UK in April 2013 will have an adverse impact on such cases in the UK. After the high water mark of ATS claims in 2009, with the high profile settlement of the *Wiwa* claim, we have seen first the assault on corporate liability under the ATS in *Kiobel I* in 2010, followed by the emasculation of the ATS by the Supreme Court in *Kiobel II* in 2013. Not only did the decision kill off 'foreign cubed' claims, which would have been killed off anyway by the subsequent decision on personal jurisdiction in *Baumann*, it also looks likely to have killed off most 'foreign squared' cases brought against US defendants. Any hope that the Supreme Court might clarify its requirement that the claims must 'touch and concern' the US have been dashed

---

[1] A detailed list of recommendations to address deficiencies in access to remedy in the US, Canada and the EU is to be found in a report submitted in December 2013 *The Third Pillar. Access to Judicial Remedies for Human Rights Violations by Transnational Business* Skinner, McCorquodale, De Schutter, Lambe. *humanrightsinbusiness.eu/portfolio/the-third-pillar/* <*accessed 23 February 2015*>.

with its decision on 20 April 2015 not to grant *certiorari* on this question in *Chiquita*. There remain a series of claims where leave to amend has been given to allow pleadings to allege that relevant conduct of the defendant took place in the US, but given the pleading rules in *Iqbal*, it is unlikely that the plaintiffs will be able to obtain evidence as to what was going on at home in the US parent corporation without discovery.

There are signs of cross-infection from *Kiobel's* distaste for entertaining claims arising outside the US, in recent dismissals of state law tort claims, such as those recently dismissed on comity grounds in *Mujica v. Airscan* with comity.[2] It may well be that there will be a migration of human rights claims to state courts but even there the foreign affairs pre-emption doctrine, widely interpreted by the district court in *Mujica v. Occidental Petroleum Corp*,[3] may see the suit bounced back into the federal courts where it can then be dismissed for political question or comity – an inherent problem with cases involving complicity in violations committed by state actors.

However, home States do have an interest in hearing cases about what their corporations get up to overseas. These considerations were articulated at length by Judge Doggett in *Dow Chemicals v. Castro Alfaro*,[4] a claim against the US manufacturer of DBCP injuries in respect of injuries said to have been sustained by workers in using the chemical on a Standard Fruits' banana plantation in Costa Rica, in a finding that *forum non conveniens* did not form part of the law of Texas:

> The banana plantation workers allegedly injured by DBCP were employed by an American company on American-owned land and grew Dole bananas for export solely to American tables. The chemical allegedly rendering the workers sterile was researched, formulated, tested, manufactured, labeled and shipped by an American company in the United States to another American company. The decision to manufacture DBCP for distribution and use in the third world was made by these two American companies in their corporate offices in the United States. Yet now Shell and Dow argue that the one part of this equation that should not be American is the legal consequences of their

---

[2]   771 F 3d 580, 605 (9th Cir 2014). Judge Bybee:

While Kiobel and its progeny specifically address the interpretation of a statute – the ATS – and not the prudential international comity doctrine, the guiding principle of those cases applies equally in the context of adjudicatory comity: the weaker the nexus between the challenged conduct and US territory or US parties, the weaker the justification for adjudicating the matter in US courts and applying US federal or state law.

[3]   381 F Supp 2d 1164 (CD Cal 2005).
[4]   786 SW 2d 674 (S Ct Tex 1990).

actions.... In the absence of meaningful tort liability in the United States for their actions, some multinational corporations will continue to operate without adequate regard for the human and environmental costs of their actions. This result cannot be allowed to repeat itself for decades to come.[5]

Similarly in *Doe v. Exxon Corporation*[6] Judge Oberdorfer, finding that US law governed the State law tort claims arising out of alleged complicity in human rights abuses in Indonesia, stated: 'Ultimately, the United States, the leader of the free world, has an overarching, vital interest in the safety, prosperity, and consequences of the behavior of its citizens, particularly its super-corporations conducting business in one or more foreign countries.' These views, however, are in the minority. The prevailing judicial consensus in the US is that claims arising outside the jurisdiction should be heard in the courts of the State in which the claims arose.

What will this mean for the development of civil liability for violation of a norm of customary international law? Early on in the post-*Filartiga* renewal of the ATS, Judge Bork commented in *Tel-Oren v. Libyan Arab Republic*:

> Courts ought not to serve as debating clubs for professors willing to argue over what is or what is not an accepted violation of the law of nations. Yet this appears to be the clear result if we allow plaintiffs the opportunity to proceed under § 1350. Plaintiffs would troop to court marshalling their "experts" behind them. Defendants would quickly organize their own platoons of authorities. The typical judge or jury would be swamped in citations to various distinguished journals of international legal studies, but would be left with little more than a numbing sense of how varied is the world of public international 'law.'[7]

To some extent this is exactly what has happened with the subsequent development of ATS suits. If you want to know what constitutes customary international law, study the ATS cases over the last 33 years. However, what this US jurisprudence has revealed is that there are a limited number of norms of customary international law that touch and concern non-State actors, which are derived from international criminal law. These prohibitions on the conduct of non-State actors may then form the basis of a civil cause of action in a domestic court in a State that

---

[5] Ibid., 686.

[6] *Doe v. Exxon Corp (Plaintiffs' Motion to Amend Complaint)*, not reported in F Supp 2d, 2 March 2006, WL 516744 (DDC).

[7] 726 F 2d 774, 823 (DC Cir 1984).

incorporates customary international law into its domestic legal order. This then forms the basis for a potential universal civil liability for breaches of those norms of customary international law that touch and concern the conduct of non-State actors. The resulting substantive law should, in theory, be the same in any nation.[8] The possibility, therefore, remains for customary international law to have a horizontal effect on civil liability in jurisdictions other than the US, where the Supreme Court's decision in *Kiobel* as to the territorial limits of the ATS is likely to curtail the viability of such suits in future.

If foreign courts are to develop such a universal civil liability, they will have to grapple with all the issues as to the shape of international criminal law that have occupied the US federal courts in ATS cases over the last decade. In particular, they will have to determine whether international law authorises States to impose civil liability on corporations that commit international crimes, either as principals or as aiders and abetters.

In determining this issue, a domestic court could go one of two ways. It could determine that customary international law provides the prohibitive norms and it is then left to each State to determine how to apply them within its domestic legal order. Domestic law would then determine the issue of corporate liability. This is the approach taken by Judge Leval in *Kiobel*[9] and by Judge Possner in *Flomo*.[10] Alternatively, it could adopt the view expressed by the majority of the Second Circuit in *Kiobel* – that corporations cannot incur civil liability for violations of customary international law that constitute international crimes, because only natural persons can be prosecuted for international crimes.[11]

It is quite likely that if other jurisdictions were to admit actions based on violations of international criminal law, this theoretical uniformity would soon split, with different jurisdictions giving different decisions as to whether corporations could be liable and also as to the *mens rea* for

---

[8]   *In re South African Apartheid Litigation v. Barclays National Bank Ltd* 617 F Supp 2d 228, 256 (SDNY 2009), Judge Schiendlin: 'Ideally, the outcome of an ATCA case should not differ from the result that would be reached under analogous jurisdictional provisions in foreign nations such as Belgium, Canada, or Spain.'

[9]   *Kiobel v. Royal Dutch Petroleum Co,* 621 F 3d 11, 173–6 (2d Cir 2010).

[10]   *Flomo v. Firestone Natural Rubber Co, LLC,* 643 F.3d 1013, 1019–20 (7th Cir 2011).

[11]   This approach would still leave open the possibility that individual corporate officials could incur civil liability for conduct constituting an international crime.

aiding and abetting. Corporate liability also raises problems of attribution – which corporate officials do we look to when determining issues of whether 'knowing assistance' or 'purposive assistance'? International criminal law can give us no answer to this question, as from Nuremberg to the International Criminal Court, corporations have never been susceptible to proceedings before international criminal tribunals. To answer this question we would either have to look to some domestic law, such as the *lex fori* or the *lex loci delicti* or the *lex loci societatis*. This would lead to different outcomes on liability depending on the rules of corporate attribution in the jurisdiction in which the action was brought. It remains to be seen whether lawyers outside the US will pick up the baton of pleading claims on this basis, or whether the horizontal effect of the law of nations will prove to be a purely US phenomenon that ended with *Kiobel*.

However, the existence of a cause of action based on violation of norms of customary international law is not critical to legal access to remedy. ATS-type claims for human rights abuses can be brought as common or garden tort claims, and have been brought on this basis in the US, the UK and in Canada. The main obstacles to legal remedy are threefold: the inability or unwillingness of host States to accommodate civil claims or criminal proceedings against TNCs operating in their jurisdiction; the doctrine of separate corporate personality which allows parent corporations to insulate themselves from liabilities arising out of the activities of their subsidiaries; the existence of grounds of abstention that result in the dismissal of home State suits on grounds such as *forum non conveniens*, and act of State – a problem particularly acute with suits in the US. All these factors need to be addressed by home and host States, something clearly recognised in GP 26 and its commentary, and reiterated in the UN Working Group's Guidance published in December 2014. Under the heading of 'potential measures' we find:

- Ensuring that parent companies can be held legally accountable for adverse human rights impacts by other members of the enterprise under their control;
- Ensuring that host State courts have the competency to adjudicate cases related to business and human rights;
- Ensuring that the civil liability regime allows for tort suits based on the domicile and/or listing of the business enterprise in the home State;
- Ensuring access to home State courts where claimants of legitimate cases face a denial of justice in a host State;

- Ensuring that victims have an adequate remedy available before a court can dismiss a case under a doctrine of *forum non conveniens*.[12]

This is where work needs to be done by home and host States, and unfortunately the NAPs produced to date show that this is not happening. The Commentary to GP 3 states: 'States should not assume that businesses invariably prefer, or benefit from, State inaction, and they should consider a smart mix of measures – national and international, mandatory and voluntary – to foster business respect for human rights.' However, the mix offered up by States in NAPs so far, by overlooking legal access to remedy, is far from smart. Corporate human rights policies and non-legal grievance mechanisms on their own will not be enough to close the governance gap.

---

[12]   Pp. 30–31. Available at http://www.ohchr.org/EN/Issues/Business/Pages/NationalActionPlans.aspx <accessed 21 April 2015>.

Index